'This is a vital and timely resource on personal tutoring in higher education, offering practical strategies to enhance student belonging, well-being, and success. Rooted in evidence-informed practice and enriched with new content on inclusive pedagogy, coaching, and emotional labour (and more), the book equips both new and experienced staff with the tools they need. In short, the book is a toolkit, an inspiration, and a challenge for what personal tutoring is – and what it could, and should, be.'

Professor Peter Felten, *Center for Engaged Learning, Elon University (US); Co-author of* Connections Are Everything: A Student's Guide to Relationship Rich Education *(John Hopkins University Press, 2023)*

'I welcome this updated edition of *Effective Personal Tutoring and Academic Advising in Higher Education*. With mounting pressures on personal tutors to offer ever more professional student support—while juggling diverse demands—this book provides relevant scholarship, practical strategies, and space for thoughtful reflection at one's own pace. It is a timely, indispensable resource for anyone seeking to offer the highest standards of academic and pastoral support and guidance.'

Professor Harriet Dunbar-Morris PFHEA, *NTF, Pro Vice-Chancellor (Academic) and Provost, The University of Buckingham*

'This second edition is academically outstanding, delivers fundamental contemporary content, and inspires transformational tutoring practices. The new edition makes a strong evidential case for the positioning, purposes and pedagogies of tutoring in the current higher education landscape, challenging and enhancing existing notions of what tutors do, how, and why. Activities throughout model what great tutoring does: making the learning relevant to the individual reader, and providing high-quality professional development. This new edition should be required reading for everyone currently involved in tutoring in higher education: tutors, tutoring leads, managers and university executive leaders.'

Dr Melanie Pope, *Senior Lecturer in Learning and Teaching, Arden University, UK*

'Effective Personal Tutoring and Academic Advising in Higher Education is a publication written by practitioners for practitioners. This guide helps new, mid-career, and novice-level professionals gain insights into the tutoring and advising field in the UK and abroad. This text is ideal for training and development activities for individuals and/or teams of tutors and advisors, as it offers case studies, critical thinking activities, and reflective exercises necessary for anyone looking to grow in the field. It covers the topics affecting our current student populations and prepares us to be change agents for student success. It covers universal themes that help us in our work to assist in transforming global citizens on our campuses throughout their student life cycles.'

Gavin Farber, *Coordinator for Undergraduate Advising, School of Business, The College of New Jersey, USA, NACADA Board of Directors (2023–2026)*

'The first edition of this book was my go-to recommendation for anyone, tutors, student support staff, senior leaders, looking to deepen their understanding of tutoring and advising. However, with significant changes happening across the sector, institutions are now scrutinising their tutoring and advising practices more closely than ever. I'm pleased to say that this new and improved edition fits seamlessly into that evolving conversation.

'It serves as an ideal reference companion for anyone involved in tutoring. Like the previous edition, it includes helpful summaries, critical thinking exercises, and strikes the perfect balance between informality and professionalism, making it both accessible and engaging.

'That said, this edition also introduces several valuable additions, including discussions on emotional labour, widening participation, updated references and statistics, professional identity, and key concepts such as effective student interactions, engagement, and relationships. It also covers a fascinating chapter on the pedagogy of personal tutoring.

'As the sector increasingly recognises the vital role of tutoring and advising, I expect this book to become even more widely used and for very good reason.'

Professor Andrew Fisher, *University Senior Tutor, PFHEA Recognised Leader in Advising UKAT, NTF, University of Nottingham*

Effective Personal Tutoring and Academic Advising in Higher Education

This is a comprehensive guide for higher education (HE) professionals engaged in student support, advising or personal tutoring roles. It covers a range of key topics relating to tutoring in the HE landscape including definitions, pedagogy, coaching, core values and skills, boundaries, monitoring students, undertaking group and individual tutorials and the need to measure impact.

A scholarly and practical text, it brings together relevant academic literature to inform personal tutoring practice and contextualise the role within HE policy. This second edition has been thoroughly updated, and explores topical and timely content with new chapters that examine the pedagogy of personal tutoring, key concepts surrounding effective student interactions, and inclusive personal tutoring. Further emphasis is placed on student engagement and motivation as well as how to effectively share responsibility and manage expectations. Reflective exercises are provided throughout the text to encourage critical thinking about this key role and support tutors' own professional development.

Packed with actionable steps, this is a vital toolkit for higher education professionals at any stage of their career, and offers a wealth of expert guidance, resources and checklists to help develop meaningful and impactful connections with students throughout their learning journey.

Dave Lochtie is the Operations Manager for the Ann Craft Trust, a leading authority in safeguarding adults, University of Nottingham. He is Co-chair of the Association for Peer Learning and Support which promotes best practice in student-led learning.

Emily McIntosh is Chief Student Officer at Harper Adams University (HAU) where she has executive responsibility for the holistic student journey and student experience.

Andrew Stork is a University Teacher and Programme Director for the Postgraduate Certificate in Medical Education at the University of Sheffield. He delivers personal tutoring and staff development and has presented at national and international conferences, including as an invited keynote speaker.

Ben W. Walker is a Senior Lecturer in Educational Development at Oxford Brookes University, where he leads on academic advising, supports colleagues to gain fellowship of Advance HE and is an active educational researcher.

Nienke Alberts is a Higher Education researcher, specialising in student support and educational inequalities. She led on the Personal Tutoring Project at the University of Bristol, investigating staff and student experiences of personal tutoring. Nienke has worked as a lecturer in Anthropology at various universities.

Alison Raby is a Senior Lecturer, Senior Tutor and Programme Leader at the University of Lincoln, in addition to being co-Project Manager of the University's partnership with Guizhou University in China.

Higher Education Series

Books in the series:

Effective Personal Tutoring in Higher Education
By Dave Lochtie, Emily McIntosh, Andrew Stork and Ben W. Walker

The Higher Education Personal Tutor's and Advisor's Companion Translating Theory into Practice to Improve Student Success
Edited by Dave Lochtie, Andrew Stork and Ben W. Walker

Effective Personal Tutoring and Academic Advising in Higher Education
By Dave Lochtie, Emily McIntosh, Andrew Stork, Ben W. Walker, Nienke Alberts and Alison Raby

Find out more about this series at www.routledge.com/Higher-Education/book-series/CRITHE.

Effective Personal Tutoring and Academic Advising

IN HIGHER EDUCATION

Second Edition

Dave Lochtie, Emily McIntosh, Andrew Stork,
Ben W. Walker, Nienke Alberts and Alison Raby

Taylor & Francis Group

LONDON AND NEW YORK

Text design by Greensplash
Cover design by Out of House Ltd.

Second edition published 2026
by Routledge
4 Park Square, Milton Park, Abingdon, Oxon OX14 4RN

and by Routledge
605 Third Avenue, New York, NY 10158

Routledge is an imprint of the Taylor & Francis Group, an informa business

© 2026 Dave Lochtie, Emily McIntosh, Andrew Stork, Ben W. Walker, Nienke Alberts and Alison Raby

The right of Dave Lochtie, Emily McIntosh, Andrew Stork, Ben W. Walker, Nienke Alberts and Alison Raby to be identified as authors of this work has been asserted in accordance with sections 77 and 78 of the Copyright, Designs and Patents Act 1988.

All rights reserved. No part of this book may be reprinted or reproduced or utilised in any form or by any electronic, mechanical, or other means, now known or hereafter invented, including photocopying and recording, or in any information storage or retrieval system, without permission in writing from the publishers.

For Product Safety Concerns and Information please contact our EU representative GPSR@taylorandfrancis.com. Taylor & Francis Verlag GmbH, Kaufingerstraße 24, 80331 München, Germany.

Trademark notice: Product or corporate names may be trademarks or registered trademarks, and are used only for identification and explanation without intent to infringe.

First published in 2018 by Critical Publishing Ltd.

British Library Cataloguing-in-Publication Data
A catalogue record for this book is available from the British Library

ISBN: 978-1-041-05527-3 (hbk)
ISBN: 978-1-916-92505-2 (pbk)
ISBN: 978-1-041-05526-6 (ebk)

DOI: 10.4324/9781041055266

Typeset in ITC Franklin Gothic Std
by KnowledgeWorks Global Ltd.

To Hannah, Willow, Violet, May and Marceline for their inspiration.
DL

To Klo – thanks for teaching me so much.
EM

To Lorna.
AS

To Petra, Sisi and Carly.
BW

To Rachel, Kelly, Sam & Melissa, for all your support
NA

To Anna, Sarah, Agnieszka, Antoni, Naomi, Myeisha, Lee, Sheila & Tony.
AR

Contents

Meet the authors — xii

Authors' websites — xv

Acknowledgements — xvi

A note on terminology — xvii

Foreword by Michelle Morgan and Liz Thomas — xviii

Introduction — 1

1. What is a personal tutor? — 9
2. The pedagogy of personal tutoring — 28
3. Core values and skills of the personal tutor — 44
4. Setting boundaries — 63
5. Key activities: Identifying and supporting student populations — 82
6. Key activities: Effectively supporting all stages of the student lifecycle — 112
7. Key concepts for effective personal tutoring — 142
8. Reflective practice and professional development — 154
9. Measuring impact — 177
10. What next? — 197

References — 217

Index — 238

Meet the authors

Dave Lochtie

I am a Senior Fellow of Advance HE, qualified teacher and coach, Operations Manager for the Ann Craft Trust (a leading authority in safeguarding adults at the University of Nottingham), Co-chair of the Association for Peer Learning and Support and co-author of Effective Personal Tutoring in HE and The Personal Tutor's and Advisor's Companion. I have worked in student services leadership roles at the Open University, University of Derby and University of New Orleans, as well as serving as a Director, Trustee and Governor of the University of Roehampton and Bournemouth University Students' Union.

Emily McIntosh

I am Chief Student Officer at Harper Adams University (HAU) where I have executive responsibility for the student experience. I have held a variety of leadership roles in learning, teaching and the student experience in several UK universities. I am a Principal Fellow of the Higher Education Academy (PFHEA, 2017) and a National Teaching Fellow (NTF, 2021), between 2016 and 2020 I was part of the UKAT executive committee, as Vice-Chair Research and Chair of the UKAT Research Committee. I am an Executive Member & Trustee of the Heads of Educational Development (HEDG) group and an Independent Board Member of Trafford & Stockport College Group (TSCG) where I am Chair of the HE Curriculum and Quality Committee. I have published widely on a variety of topics from academic advising, personal tutoring and peer learning to integrated practice.

Meet the authors • **xiii**

Andrew Stork

I am an academic and Programme Director in postgraduate medical education in the School of Medicine and Population Health at the University of Sheffield. I am co-author of three highly regarded texts on personal tutoring and academic advising, a Senior Fellow of Advance HE have delivered keynote conference presentations on the subject, and I am a personal tutor. I have experience in a wide range of educational sectors and contexts, and have taught and led postgraduate education programmes across a range of sectors. Previously, I was cross-institutional quality lead for personal tutoring and student experience, and have held a wide variety of curriculum leadership, quality, learning & teaching enhancement and staff development positions. I believe in and advocate a holistic approach to students and their education, which can transform lives.

Ben W. Walker

I am a Senior Lecturer in Educational Development within the Oxford Centre for Academic Enhancement and Development at Oxford Brookes University, where I lead the Advance HE Fellowship experiential scheme, deliver staff development and undertake educational research projects. Previously holding positions at the University of Lincoln, Manchester Metropolitan University and the University of Derby, I have supported a wide range of trainee teachers and existing practitioners. I have been programme leader of Postgraduate Certificate In Higher Education programmes and been an invited keynote speaker at national and international conferences. As co-author of books and journal articles on personal tutoring, I am at the forefront of professional development and research in this field and am committed to developing it further.

Nienke Alberts

I am a Higher Education researcher with an interest in personal tutoring, student support and educational inequality. I am an Honorary Senior Research Associate at the University of Bristol, where I led a six-year research project on personal tutoring, investigating various aspects of personal tutoring, including personal tutoring models, and the experiences of staff and students. I have worked on research projects with the Sutton Trust and AccessHE investigating social mobility through education, and I have advised universities on impact evaluation of widening participation activities. I have worked as a lecturer in Anthropology and as a personal tutor at University College London, the University of Bristol, the University of Roehampton and the University of East London.

Alison Raby

I am a Senior Lecturer, Senior Tutor and Programme Leader at the University of Lincoln, in addition to being co-Project Manager of the university's partnership with Guizhou University in China. Prior to this, I worked with international students at Nottingham Trent International College, after leaving Poland, where I taught EFL and ran an English school. I have a master's degree in Applied Linguistics and have completed a PhD on An Exploration of the Relationships between Chinese Students and their Personal Tutors: an IPA Study. I have published book chapters and journal articles on personal tutoring, and am currently part of UKAT's leadership team.

Authors' websites

To find out more about the authors' work, visit their websites:

Dave Lochtie: www.davelochtie.com

Emily McIntosh: https://www.thirdspaceperspectives.com/

Andrew Stork: www.andrewstork.co.uk

Ben W. Walker: www.walker-heconsultancy.co.uk

Nienke Alberts: orcid.org/0000-0002-3712-2816

Alison Raby: https://www.arwrites.net/

Acknowledgements

We would like to thank:

- our families, for getting us through when it was difficult, being patient in our absence and for their unwavering support.
- Liz Thomas for providing the foreword, for the body of work we have referenced throughout and for permission to use Figure 1.5 *Features of effective practice.*

A note on terminology

In some universities, the same activity and role of individual support is referred to using different terms, for example 'personal academic tutor', 'academic mentor' and 'progress tutor'. Since 'academic advising' is common to many - half of the institutions, who contributed case studies to our 2022 book use it – the term is used alongside 'personal tutoring' in the title of this book. Its content uses the term 'personal tutor' unless directly quoting or it is relevant to use an alternative.

The term Postgraduate Certificate in Learning and Teaching in Higher Education is used in this text as an umbrella term referring to postgraduate-level qualifications related to learning and teaching. This is done with an awareness of the variety of titles used for similar programmes across the sector such as Postgraduate Certificate in Academic Practice, Postgraduate Certificate in Teaching in Higher Education and Academic Professional Apprenticeship.

Foreword

Michelle Morgan and Liz Thomas

The role of the personal tutor in higher education has never been more important than it is now. As students juggle ever-increasing employment burdens, with their academic workloads and other commitments, personal tutors offer information, guidance and support. While the personal tutoring role can encompass many different approaches, including one-to-one and group sessions, and traditional meetings, proactive sessions and coaching-informed activities, the potential contribution to the student experience is broadly similar. Personal tutors help students engage in their learning, connect to their higher education community and support – and make them feel like they belong to their course, department and university. Personal tutors are critical in supporting the retention, progression and success of our students, especially with increasing diversity among home and international students.

But the importance and value of this role are often not recognised by higher education providers or by students. For example, there is little or no recognition or reward in annual personal development reviews or when considering staff promotions. Personal tutors can also be undervalued by students who do not understand the role, nor see the value of it, and many fail to make the most use of such a valuable resource. There is also limited support and development for the personal tutoring role, and it is (often implicitly) assumed that anyone can do it.

With so much turbulence, change and increasing demands on academic staff time as well as challenges for students, this book provides strategic guidance and advice on the role and responsibilities of the personal tutor. The structure of the book takes you through a journey beginning by understanding what the role entails, and it provides multiple lenses through which to look at the role to develop understanding and expertise. The text makes explicit the roles and activities of personal tutors that are so often hidden and done implicitly. The contents are well grounded in the literature, which improves credibility and confidence, while being practically oriented. This new edition has additional new chapters with valuable advice on: effective student interactions, engagement and relationships and the pedagogy of personal tutoring. The new content also includes guidance on widening participation, campus-, commuter- and remote learning students and inclusive personal tutoring.

The book is aimed at developing individual personal tutors – to benefit themselves, their students and institutions. The text can be used as part of new lecturer and personal tutor training programmes, or enjoyed by individuals looking to improve their practice, irrespective of whether they are new staff or staff who want to reinvigorate and update their personal tutoring practice. The authors have succeeded again in providing a well-evidenced and informed book that is 100% practical and useful to colleagues across the higher education sector.

Dr Michelle Morgan, Dean of Students at the University of East London; Independent HE Consultant

Professor Liz Thomas, Research Centre Leader, Centre for Research on Education and Social Justice, University of York; Independent HE Consultant

Introduction

Personal tutoring in higher education

Personal tutoring in UK higher education (HE) has reached a pivotal moment. The role of the personal tutor is as important as ever: increases in student loneliness and mental ill health, which were seen before the Covid-19 pandemic and the cost-of-living crisis, and have accelerated since, have emphasised how the way universities are run affects the well-being of their students. Creating a sense of belonging, feelings of mattering and connectedness for students from all backgrounds is now more important than ever, as in recent years there has been greater acknowledgement of the structural inequalities in HE, such as the degree awarding gap for racially minoritised students. Personal tutoring is a key way to deliver connection, individual relationships and tailored, individual support and learning to increase a sense of belonging and mattering (Gravett and Winstone, 2022; Hallam, 2023) as well as increase equity and inclusion (Gabi et al, 2024; Gabi et al, 2025). Student support is becoming increasingly important to delivering teaching in HE (Lochtie et al, 2022), and increases in market competition are encouraging universities to focus on how they deliver support to students (Woods, 2023).

At the same time, increasing student numbers has led to pressures on personal tutors (McFarlane, 2016), and the diversification of the student body has meant the support needs of students have also broadened (Stephen et al, 2008; McFarlane, 2016; OfS, 2022a), at a time when academic staff already face high workloads and many competing demands on their time (UCU, 2022). Yet, personal tutoring remains an area that is under-resourced in UK HE. The current funding model for HE is causing increasing financial pressures across the sector. As a result, universities have focused on continued growth, particularly by focusing on international students; yet wider changes, such as Brexit, and government decisions, such as changes to student visas, have made global recruitment volatile. As a result, the UK HE sector is in financial crisis (Kastelic, 2024; Office for Students, 2024b; Adams, 2025), and HE providers are having to take 'bold and transformative action' to ensure their financial sustainability (OfS, 2024a). Therefore, many

DOI: 10.4324/9781041055266-1

universities are reviewing the way they support students, including personal tutor systems (Grey et al, 2024).

As the scale and complexity of the needs of students have risen, along with an increase in the recognition that academics need support in their roles as personal tutors, and a push to achieve more consistency in the student experience, there has been a move towards professionalisation of the skills of personal tutors. This is seen, for example, by the introduction of a professional recognition scheme for personal tutors and academic advisors in 2019 by the UK Advising and Tutoring Association (UKAT) (UKAT, 2023). UKAT promotes the practice and scholarship of personal tutoring and academic advising. UKAT's Professional Framework for Academic Advising and Personal Tutoring is discussed in Chapter 3 (core values and skills), Chapter 6 (key activities) and Chapter 8 (reflective practice and professional development). This increasing professionalisation is also seen in the trend in professional, primary role personal tutors across the sector (Maxwell and Briggs, 2024; WonkHE, 2024b; Jones et al, 2025). Nevertheless, due to the current financial crisis in the HE sector, many institutions are not able to make such investments in personal tutoring.

Despite these pressures, increases in student numbers along with rising mental health issues among students make it more important than ever to preserve the quality of the day-to-day interactions that universities have with their students. The way in which academic and professional support staff work in partnership with students to shape the curriculum, the academic community and the university environment are vital to managing student expectations, nurturing student ownership of learning, and their sense of belonging. Meaningful relationships and human interactions are fundamental to the core values of UK HE, that is to champion lifelong learning, to advocate learning for learning's sake and to support students from a variety of backgrounds to achieve autonomy, to pursue their dreams and to realise their potential. This book is written in the spirit of staff–student partnership and collaboration; it is intended for a broad audience and introduces practical strategies for working with students, and with other colleagues, to improve the quality of these interactions and to encourage students to think critically, to solve problems and to try out new things.

What is new in this edition?

We have made several changes and additions in this new edition. In Chapter 1, we have expanded on the three models of personal tutoring (Earwaker, 1992) to include two additional, recent models. Chapter 2 is a completely new chapter created around the pedagogy of personal tutoring, which we believe explains the relationship with other related pedagogies and forms a coherent model for future scholarship and research. Chapter 4 now includes content around emotional labour when considering boundaries. New content has been added to Chapter 5 to include widening participation and inclusive personal tutoring, both important topics for UK HE. In addition to the student populations already mentioned in this chapter, we include campus-, commuter- and remote learning students, the latter of which have seen an increase since the Covid-19 pandemic. Chapter 7 on key concepts is a new chapter, looking at managing expectations, effective relationship building, student engagement and motivation, and how these concepts can lead to student success. There is new content in Chapter 8 around training, developing a professional identity and supporting personal tutors. Chapter 9 on measuring impact now outlines how to use a Theory of Change and various study designs to measure the impact of personal tutoring. New ideas have been added to Chapter 10 under existing topic areas, and the whole book has undergone a refresh in terms of current policies, practice and up-to-date literature.

Why is personal tutoring so important?

In the context of rising levels of loneliness among students, where nearly one in four students feel lonely 'most' or 'all' of the time (Neves and Brown, 2022), personal tutoring is a key opportunity for institutions to focus on relationships and foster meaningful connections between students and academic staff as well as their peers. Such meaningful relationships help students feel that they matter and that university is a place they belong (Gravett and Winstone, 2022). There is an increasing body of evidence showing that there are clear benefits to having a personal tutor and that the tutor–tutee relationship is one of the most important relationships students have with staff (Gravett and Winstone, 2022). Having a good relationship with a personal tutor improves the student experience (Braine and Parnell, 2011; McFarlane, 2016; Yale, 2019), buffers against some of the challenges students experience (Ross et al, 2014) and increases the sense of belonging at university (Thomas, 2012; Gravett and Winstone, 2022), which in turn improves retention (Karp et al, 2021), progression (Braine and Parnell, 2011; Karp et al, 2021) and attainment (Karp et al, 2021). Personal tutoring also has the potential to help break barriers (Gabi et al, 2025), improve equity and help address the degree awarding gap for racially minoritised students (Alves, 2019; Gabi et al, 2024), and is an important way in which institutions can deliver the individual, tailored support that is so important to student continuation and success.

Despite these clear benefits, personal tutoring remains an area that is chronically undervalued and under-resourced and the purpose of personal tutoring is often still not clearly articulated to students and staff. This has separated tutoring from other teaching and learning activities such as the delivery of lectures and seminars, and personal tutoring is 'bolted on' instead of being a central part of pedagogical practice, leading to low student engagement. It also means that the supporting infrastructure and systems are often under-resourced, and it is not viewed with parity of esteem compared to other academic functions such as teaching and research, meaning personal tutoring tasks can be time-consuming and require emotional labour that feels challenging to provide. It can be an area that is undervalued (Walker, 2022), meaning that personal tutoring is not prioritised in workloads and individuals are not recognised for their work as personal tutors.

Regardless of this lack of coherence and clarity, you, as a personal tutor, can play a key role in helping a student to develop their learning and identity, whether you do personal tutoring as part of an academic role or are a professional primary role advisor. By drawing on our experience of working with varied cohorts of students and staff, the book will cover the tools and skills you will need to become an effective personal tutor.

A brief history of personal tutoring

Personal tutoring in UK HE is certainly not a new phenomenon. Rather, in the HE sector's quest to restore its value base and improve the personalisation of student learning, tutoring is experiencing a renewed focus, even renewed vigour, despite the current issues within HE. The models to articulate this delivery can differ quite substantially, as can the definitions and naming conventions associated with tutoring (Walker, 2018), and this is covered in significant detail in Chapters 1 and 3. For the purposes of this book, the term 'personal tutoring', discussed in more detail in Chapter 1, encompasses all activities where academic or professional staff work in partnership with students to provide one-to-one support, advice and guidance of either an academic or pastoral nature. The broad definition of the term, as adopted here, is designed to ensure that the guidance provided in this book is applied widely and flexibly.

Tutoring, in one form or another, has always been present in the delivery of HE. In 1852, Cardinal Henry Newman, a clergyman and Oxford academic, gave a series of lectures reflecting on the purpose of the university, which were later published in his book *The Idea of the University*. For Newman, the university's 'soul' can be best measured in the mark it leaves on its students, with his notion of the 'ideal university' described as a place which is residential, where teaching is prized above research, where a community of students, as learners, engage in the pursuit of a broad, liberal education and where students simply 'flourish' (Newman, 2014, p 68). While Newman brought personalised, even individualised, learning to the forefront of university consciousness in the mid-1800s, models of tutoring in fact go back further than this.

The tutorial method of teaching, that is, one where students learn in small groups of two or three, can be traced back to the eleventh century when the universities of Oxford and Cambridge established their collegiate systems. In the fifteenth century, the role of the tutor was described in more detail; it was made clear that older academics were given responsibility for the conduct and instruction of their younger colleagues (Moore, 1968; Palfreyman, 2008). In this regard, early models of tutoring were clearly pastoral as well as academic. The University of Oxford's highly regarded tutorial system, as it is conceived of today, with its significant emphasis on the dialectic of the individual, was established by Professor Benjamin Jowett several decades after the time when Newman was writing, in 1882 (Markham, 1967). These tutorials embraced the Socratic Method, where students were engaged in discussion and supported to learn and to think for themselves. Thus, the earliest models of tutoring were designed to foster independence of thought, harnessing the key skills of critical thinking and problem-solving. These student-centred pedagogies, with tutorials at the heart of the system, are still highly valued today. Nevertheless, just over a century later in the 1960s when universities were expanding considerably, the tutorial method was once again under the spotlight with critics arguing that it was outdated, inefficient and unfit for purpose. While the tutorial method, as originally conceived, is still a hallmark of an Oxbridge education today, it has evolved considerably and been adapted significantly in other universities, both modern and old, in order to suit different institutional missions, curricula and values. The concept of tutoring, as originally conceived, is therefore less coherent today. As universities are expanding, fewer resources have been dedicated to personal tutoring, it has become less structured and, in some institutions, is somewhat separated from the mainstream delivery of the curriculum. In the quest for efficiency, and with increasing massification and diversification of the student body, the models and fundamental practices of tutoring require further examination. Current organisational and structural models of student support are discussed in detail in Chapter 1.

Who this book is for

You may have picked up this book because you are a new academic in HE or delivering HE in a further education setting. It could be that you are an experienced academic or specialised, professional personal tutor within one of these sectors. Or, you may work within HE but be employed purely within student support or student services. Equally, you could be a manager within HE who oversees student support, the student experience or curriculum delivery. Indeed, you will find that some of the content of this book is more relevant to those in leadership roles than it is to individual personal tutors (for example, Chapter 9 on measuring impact). However, it is also beneficial for personal tutors to have an understanding of the issues covered in this chapter. More widely, you may be employed in one of the many different student-facing roles, such as Graduate Teaching Assistant (GTA) or within a student support coordinator or liaison role. It is important to state that whichever one of these describes you best – and there will be other related roles that come under a slightly different description from those mentioned – this book is relevant to you. As you will see from the next section, the book has been written with the new academic foremost in our minds; however, it is not exclusive to this audience. Student support, which is at the core of the book, is delivered in many ways and through a variety of roles so, indeed, anyone who works with students in any capacity will find this book useful in the day-to-day context of carrying out their role.

Your first activity

» *In terms of your personal tutor or support role, think about your level of knowledge and how effective you feel you are. On a scale of one to ten, with one being very little knowledge and very limited effectiveness and ten being extensive knowledge with highly effective practice, where are you on the scale? Keep this number in mind because we will be revisiting it at the end of the book.*

The purpose of this book

The life of an academic – and particularly a new academic – can seem like a whirlwind. The pace of life in HE is fast and roles in teaching and learning change rapidly. Academic staff are increasingly asked to perform more duties and carry out additional responsibilities. Typical activities include teaching, creating resources, student support, marking assessments, designing the curriculum, taking on leadership and administrative roles as well as undertaking research and, often, additional qualifications and continuing professional development (CPD) opportunities. Working with students directly remains one of the most rewarding, and challenging, parts of the role.

We often hear from academics that there is little training or support for personal tutors, and many are not clear about the role and remit of the personal tutor. This book aims to address both those issues. Based on the latest research, this book discusses good practice in tutoring and will help you to develop your own approach. Given that this is an underdeveloped area in HE, is increasingly important for new and experienced academic tutors.

The book will act as a 'toolkit' for you by providing the tools to achieve effectiveness in personal tutoring and coaching to meet student needs. In turn, these key elements will have a positive impact on key performance indicators, the strategic ambitions of your university and the measurement of core metrics such as continuation, completion and graduate outcomes. These will inform the ongoing development of your academic role, whether you are a new or an experienced member of staff.

It is important to emphasise that the book should not only be viewed as relevant to your personal tutor role. Since personal tutoring values and skills are fundamental to student-centred pedagogy, the book is intended to inform your whole practice and locate tutoring as central to, rather than separate from, the mainstream delivery of the curriculum regardless of academic discipline. The book covers these aspects comprehensively and provides an invaluable resource in what is currently an under-resourced area of practice.

How does this book link to your role?

If you are a new academic, the link between the book's content and your PG Cert HE qualification is clear when you consider that personal tutoring, coaching and student-centred pedagogy are areas that are implicit within your qualification. Moreover, it will contextualise this content into real-world educational situations that you will come across in various teaching and learning contexts or in your day-to-day encounters with students. If you are a new or experienced academic, it will provide an in-depth overview of the role of personal tutoring, coaching and supporting students. If you are a leader within the area of personal tutoring, it will provide information on how you can support staff, enable opportunities for their professional development within your institution, and measure and evidence the impact of personal tutoring in your department or institution. Alternatively, you may be a primary role personal tutor/advisor, or an Educational Developer who trains personal tutors, in which case, the book will be a valuable resource and toolkit for you.

Of course, hopefully you can see that principles to be covered are not restricted to academics but also are invaluable to those in other student-facing roles, for example dedicated support staff (such as student support advisors) and, as such, are transferable. As we mentioned at the outset, the skills are delivered in many ways and sometimes through different roles – indeed, by anyone who works with students in any capacity.

Chapter summaries

Chapter 1 sets the scene for the whole book by answering the question 'what is a personal tutor'? It does this, firstly, by defining the term and looking at the relationship between personal tutoring and coaching. Different theoretical models are used to further understand the role, as well as how it fits into organisational structures.

Chapter 2 provides valuable information around understanding the strong relationship between teaching and personal tutoring. It explores the pedagogy of personal tutoring and the impact of advising theory on this. Coaching and mentoring approaches are examined as part of personal tutoring pedagogy, and the importance of relational pedagogy and co-creation with students is emphasised. This chapter differs from the others in that it is mainly theoretical and does not include the self-assessment, but provides relevant and up-to-date information for both researchers and practitioners in the field of personal tutoring.

In the first part of Chapter 3, we outline and explore the core values of the personal tutor through examples of these in action. We discuss the core skills in the second part of the chapter, differentiating these from the core values by clarifying that values motivate you to undertake actions, whereas core skills enable you to perform those actions. The importance of setting boundaries between you and students, and between students themselves, and how you can go about doing this, are explored in Chapter 4. Chapters 5 and 6 are lengthier chapters which comprehensively cover the toolkit you need to provide effective support to students. We have named these 'key activities' since, by putting these tools into action, you will be covering all aspects of a student's experience. Firstly, we define the overall aims of using these tools: ensuring each student gets the most out of their course by improving student engagement, progression, learning gain and success. We have divided the key activities into identifying and supporting student populations (Chapter 5) and effectively supporting all stages of the student lifecycle (Chapter 6). Here, the topics include the tracking and monitoring of students; characteristics of at risk students; inclusive personal tutoring; working with students who have additional support needs; safeguarding; using learning analytics; transition and progression; one-to-one tutorials (we refer to these as 'one-to-ones' throughout); group tutorial planning; and a tutoring curriculum.

In Chapters 7 to 9, we build on the toolkit to develop your higher-level support skills through managing expectations, effective relationship building and student engagement and motivation (Chapter 7); reflective practice and professional development (Chapter 8) and measuring impact (Chapter 9). Finally, in Chapter 10, we look at the 'bigger picture'. This allows you to explore and prioritise your own professional development activities as well as to consider the development activities of the institution you work within and how you could influence positive change within your organisation.

About the book and how to use it

We hope the experience of reading the book will be engaging and rewarding, with the additional opportunity to dip in and out of content to suit your needs since each chapter can be read and used in isolation. Therefore, it can be used as a reference book or read in sequence as a whole.

Chapter content includes aims, case studies and examples which are linked to critical thinking activities. All examples are fictional but rooted in our experience. You should review the example dialogues presented in the book by aligning them to your own experiences and clarifying whether you would have acted in a similar or slightly different way. It might be helpful to do this with a mentor or colleague and discuss your views. Examples are transferable to different institutions, making this book vital for anyone working with students in a learning capacity.

At the end of each chapter there is a chapter summary and critical reflections which pose some key questions for you to answer in note or essay form and prompt you to critically analyse your practice.

In addition, at the end of each chapter (from Chapter 3 onwards), there is an individual and institutional self-assessment system which allows you to score your own performance and that of your educational institution on the key theme of each chapter. The rating will be measured against minimum standard, beginner, intermediate, advanced and expert levels, all accompanied with a star rating, enabling you to reach a cumulative score and level at the end of the book.

1 What is a personal tutor?

Chapter aims

This chapter helps you to:

- understand the role of personal tutoring within the modern academic profession;
- define the personal tutor;
- explore the useful relationship between personal tutoring and coaching;
- consider different coaching and support models and how to apply these to different situations;
- understand how personal tutoring can form an important part of a holistic model of student support;
- understand and evaluate different organisational and structural models of student support;
- explore how organisational and structural models of student support are applied at institutional level and reflect upon personal tutoring at your own institution.

The role of personal tutoring within the modern academic profession

The academic profession is complex. Over the past decades, the number of students entering HE has steadily grown. With efforts to increase participation rates of home students and universities targeting recruitment of international students, universities have an increasingly diverse intake of students (Bolton, 2024). As more international students and students from 'non-traditional' backgrounds enter HE, supporting student transition into and progress across HE has become central to student success.

Successful transition and progress involves the management of expectations and the overcoming of certain challenges. Kift (2009) has called for a holistic transition pedagogy which transcends the silos of individual university department support (this is discussed in more detail in Chapters 2 and 5). In this book, we argue that personal tutors are key to managing these transitions. Often, they are the 'face' of the university for students: an important first point of contact who can help 'buffer' against some of the challenges that first-year students typically face, as well as contribute towards a sense of belonging (Zepke and Leach, 2010; Thomas and Jones, 2017; Yale, 2019; Drew, 2023).

This larger and more diverse population of students (identified in Chapter 5) requires higher levels of support (OfS, 2022a) as well as more structured support. Therefore, the traditional systems for supporting students are increasingly inappropriate. It has been suggested that the expansion and diversification of HE may render the informal relationships between staff and students less reliable and potentially inequitable (Myers, 2008) and more traditional forms of engagement may have become 'inappropriate for a new generation of diverse student experiences' (Thomas and Jones, 2017, p 3). For example, universities increasingly provide specialist support (Sheldon et al, 2021) in response to the growing number of students with mental health issues (Sheldon et al, 2021; Sanders, 2023).

The Covid-19 pandemic forced academics and students into new ways of working, rapidly adopting technology for teaching, learning and student support. Post-pandemic, universities increasingly have a blended approach to teaching and learning, necessitating academics to develop new skills, particularly in terms of working with digital technology. The cost-of-living crisis has had a significant impact on students, affecting their health and well-being further (Dabrowski et al, 2025).

The role of the academic is therefore constantly changing in response to the massification and diversification of HE, as well as the impact of the Covid-19 pandemic and cost-of-living crisis. At the same time, the culture within HE is changing. The increase in the tuition fee cap has changed the relationship between the university and its students, and the language and terminology used to describe that relationship (McIntosh and Cross, 2017). Students are increasingly seen as both partners and consumers (Symonds, 2020; Gupta et al, 2023). Further, there is an ongoing debate about universities' statutory duty of care and responsibility for students. As a result, there have been some inevitable and fundamental changes in the student–tutor relationship (Morgan, 2012a; Thomas et al, 2015).

At the start of the book, we outlined the clear benefits for students of having a meaningful relationship with their personal tutor. Despite these benefits, with academic workloads increasing, it can be challenging for tutors to maintain such relationships with their tutees and to provide individual, personalised support. Many academics are asked to juggle 'lecturing, assessing, researching and administrative commitments' (Ghenghesh, 2017, pp 1–2) alongside their role in supporting students. Yet, post-pandemic, the focus has remained on student well-being, engagement and having a sense of belonging, and the relationships between students and their personal tutor are as important as ever (Felten and Lambert, 2020; Lochtie et al, 2022). If the time spent on these vital activities is not, or at least not sufficiently, acknowledged and allocated within staff workloads, they may neglect to carry out this duty, be forced to work additional hours beyond their contract or perform the duties at the expense of their research and own well-being (Walker, 2020; Augustus et al, 2023). This delicate balance of academic activities is covered in more detail in Chapter 4.

Tutors require accurate and timely information about their students in order to understand how to support them. Across the sector, the use of dashboard systems (Chapter 5) is now common, and the use of engagement data allows personal tutors to give students data-driven advice and support, and flag students who are at risk (Gutiérrez et al, 2020). These dashboards present engagement data to tutors, often in a visual format, and offer insights into how a student is engaging with the university by gathering data from other university systems and holding them in one place. It must be noted that different dashboards report on different types of engagement data, and this may include attendance, library engagement or activity on the virtual learning environment (VLE). Alongside this engagement data, learning analytics use algorithms to predict student success, which has the potential to assist tutors by identifying disengaged students as well as students with significant potential. While dashboards are useful, the data provided offer 'flags' and snapshots for tutors which must be explored with the student in person. This is covered in greater detail in Chapter 5.

Definitions of the personal tutor

Although the majority of academics in the UK undertake the personal tutor role, there is no agreed-upon singular definition of the role (Mynott, 2016; Grey and Osborne, 2020). A single, succinct, one-sentence definition of a personal tutor may be too 'reductionary' (Wootton, 2007, p 157) and inflexible. Nevertheless, the lack of an agreed-upon definition of personal tutoring and a shared understanding of the role and responsibilities of the personal tutor is problematic, creating some indistinguishable boundaries which must be acknowledged and examined (Wootton, 2006; Mynott, 2016; Yale, 2019), as they are in Chapter 4.

Based on the working definitions of Thomas (2006), Stork and Walker (2015) and Walker (2018), cross-referenced and combined with a range of other complementary literature on broader student support, we define the personal tutor as follows: a personal tutor is typically, though not always, an academic member of staff who supports a number of students (often referred to as tutees) on a range of academic and pastoral issues; they usually draw on a variety of insights and expertise, signposting and referring to other academic and professional colleagues, where appropriate, to provide consistent and robust advice and guidance.

As mentioned later on in this chapter, the tutoring model in which tutors work has a significant impact on how this works in practice. This definition of a personal tutor, therefore, represents an ideal which may or may not be reflected in the reality of your institution. There is also a wide variety of advisor and counsellor roles who may perform aspects of the tutor role and for whom this book is also intended.

UKAT (2023) also defines personal tutoring in their Professional Framework for Advising and Tutoring (2023). They describe personal tutoring as:

> support[ing] students to achieve their academic and personal aspirations. A purposeful personal relationship with their personal tutor/advisor enables students to become autonomous, confident learners and engaged members of society. This ongoing and collaborative relationship creates an authentic connection between students, their advisor, and their institution, supporting them through their course and beyond.
>
> (UKAT, 2023, p 2)

Below, we provide an overview of the typical activities and responsibilities of personal tutors in UK HE, as identified in the literature. It is recommended you consider these in relation to your own role and organisation.

- **Academic feedback and development** with support for study skills and other learning development activities to maximise learning and decision-making on optional units (Yale, 2019; Grey and Osborne, 2020; Walker, 2020).

- **Well-being support** by advising, informing, suggesting and providing insight to meet students' pastoral needs (Gubby and McNab, 2013; Small, 2013; Augustus et al, 2023).

- **Signposting to further information and support** with a broad knowledge of university professional services and the support that they provide (Gubby and McNab, 2013; Small, 2013; Yale, 2019; Walker, 2020). This is covered in Chapter 4.

- **Embodiment and representative of the university** assisting students to navigate systems/processes and normalise features of the learning experience (Small, 2013; Yale, 2019).

- **Giving information about HE processes, procedures and expectations** during induction to support effective transition (Braine and Parnell, 2011; Calcagno et al, 2017; Grey and Osborne, 2020; Walker, 2020).

- **Engendering a sense of mattering and belonging** in all years, with the foundations of this in the transition and induction experience, with personal tutors as the key first points of contact (Flett et al, 2019; Yale, 2019; Grey and Osborne, 2020; Lochtie et al, 2022).

- **Goal/target setting and monitoring of achievements** evidenced by data and conversations with students (Calcagno et al, 2017; Ghenghesh, 2017; Grey and Osborne, 2020; Walker, 2020).

- **Solution-focused coaching** to unlock a student's potential and support their academic success as an independent learner (Gurbutt and Gurbutt, 2015; Thomas et al, 2015; Ralston and Hoffshire, 2017; de Witt, 2022; Seraj and Leggett, 2023).

- **Personal development and employability** such as personal development planning and identification of skills. This includes advising on placements, further study or careers and writing references for tutees (Assender and Leadbeater, 2022; Ayton and Walling, 2022; Dunbar-Morris, 2022).

Personal tutoring and coaching: definitions and history of the terms

Viewing the 'stock' dictionary definitions of the terms and their derivation (source and original meanings) aids understanding. The definitions and derivations from *The Concise Oxford English Dictionary* and the online etymology dictionary are given in Table 1.1.

Table 1.1 Personal and tutor: dictionary definition and history

Term	Definition	History
Personal	*Adjective* 1. one's own; individual; private	Late fourteenth century Middle English via Old French (twelfth century) from Latin *personalis* – 'as person'
Tutor	*Noun* a private teacher, esp. one in general charge of a person's education *Verb* 1. act as a tutor to 2. work as a tutor 3. restrain, discipline (The Concise Oxford English Dictionary, 1995)	Late fourteenth century From Latin *tutor* – 'Guardian, Watcher' (noun) or *tutor* (verb) – 'to watch over'

As you can see, the modern word 'tutor' is rooted within the academy. However, the original Latin meaning of 'guardian, watcher' and its verb form 'watch over' is certainly relevant to personal tutoring principles. Also, by putting the two together, with the adjective 'personal' modifying the noun 'tutor', we have a sense of a practice tailored to the individual.

Although there is an association with a particular field (sport), the term coach (Table 1.2), both as a noun and a verb, contains meanings with immediate relevance: instructor, trainer, train, teach, give hints to. Its history gives us the highly relatable sense of 'carrying through'. A very pertinent image is provided with the meaning broadening from the literal physical carrying of 'stagecoach' to the metaphorical sense of carrying a student through an exam. In our context, the 'carrying through' is widened to include many aspects of the learning process such as the programme of study and barriers to learning, to name but two.

Table 1.2 Coach: dictionary definition and history

Term	Definition	History
Coach	*Noun* 1. an instructor or trainer in sport 2. a private tutor *Verb* 1. train or teach (a pupil, sports team, etc.) as a coach 2. give hints to; prime with facts (The Concise Oxford English Dictionary, 1995)	From the French *coche* (sixteenth century) as in *stagecoach*. Used in the athletic sense from 1861. Used as *instructor/trainer* from circa 1830 as a result of Oxford University slang for a tutor as one who 'carries a student through an exam'. (Online Etymology Dictionary, nd, online)

The relationship between personal tutoring and coaching

It is possible to see the common ground and also the subtle distinctions between personal tutoring and coaching. More often than not, definitions try to harness all of the component parts into what is usually quite a clunky and awkward sentence or series of sentences. With this in mind, Table 1.3 provides our interpretation of the two elements divided into approach, core focus and context, along with how it helps students. The jagged line illustrates the close relationship between the two.

Table 1.3 Relationship between personal tutoring and coaching

	Personal tutoring	**Coaching**
Approach	Can be prescriptive/directive (you take more of a lead and offer advice and guidance) or non-directive/developmental (encouraging the student to take more of the lead and reflect back the content they bring), focusing on stretching (intellectual/academic need) or nurturing (emotional need).	Can be directive or non-directive. Generally focuses on stretching (usually intellectual/academic need, but can be related to an emotional need if required).
Core focus	Following an educational/learning agenda. Develop longer-term trusting relationship.	Affect an immediate improvement in skills, approach or knowledge. Usually within short time frames.
Context	More relationship-based between the personal tutor and student than a functional process.	More of a functional process, in other words designed to be immediately practical and useful.
How it helps students	Helps students acquire new skills and knowledge, nurturing emotional well-being through regular communication, either through group tutorials and/or one-to-ones.	Helps to improve student performance and skills through one-to-one coaching conversations.

Personal tutoring focuses on developing a trusting, longer-term relationship with a student through listening and regular communication. It can take the form of being prescriptive or developmental, focusing on working with individual students over a significant period of time to help them acquire new skills and improve their confidence (Lancer and Eatough, 2018) and approach to learning. It can assist in addressing common concerns such as time management, stress and social relationships (Lancer and Eatough, 2018), developing focus, motivation and skills in independent learning and reflection, as well as making students aware of the support available through student support services.

Coaching skills and actions lend themselves more towards regular one-to-one conversations with students either within a class or while having an arranged one-to-one meeting, in order to influence a more immediate improvement in performance and the development of skills.

To avoid confusing personal tutoring and coaching, we need to view them as related to each other but not the same. A coach is not a personal tutor. However, tutoring may include elements of coaching when formulating personal learning goals or personal development planning with students (Gurbutt and Gurbutt, 2015). Personal tutoring is relationship-based, while coaching is a development activity that can be used as part of that relationship to develop specific personal or professional competencies (Thomas, 2012; Gurbutt and Gurbutt, 2015; de Witt, 2022). Training personal tutors to use a coaching approach would enhance the experience of students because it allows students to address common concerns and develop their confidence (Lancer and Eatough, 2018). Chapter 2 looks in more detail at how to use a coaching approach in personal tutoring.

Critical thinking activity 1

1. How well do the definitions of personal tutoring and coaching fit with your own experience, whether that is through 'doing', being on the receiving end or from observing these activities in practice?

2. From your own experience, how would you define personal tutoring and coaching? Make a note of your definitions so that you can see whether your definitions change as you read through the rest of the book.

As a new academic, an awareness of these definitions is a good starting point in terms of understanding personal tutoring. However, it is important to explore the tutoring and coaching roles further and situate them, as defined, into relatable contexts.

CASE STUDY

Rachel's story

Rachel is a new academic working in her first role at a post-1992 institution. She has been assigned 30 third-year business students as her tutees.

Week 4

One of the topics Rachel should cover with her tutees in their final year is employability skills, including the writing of a CV and researching employers or routes to further study. Rachel has contacted the team in the Career Service and they have agreed to collaborate on the delivery of a session to her tutees. As part of this session students develop their personal development plans, which Rachel is planning to review in this term's one-to-one meetings. Rachel is also keeping track of her tutees' progress, attendance and engagement via the university's dashboard system, and flags up any concerns she has to the senior tutor.

Week 6

Six weeks into the term, one of Rachel's tutees, George, emails to ask if he can come and see her. During the meeting, George confides in her that he is finding he cannot keep up with all of the expectations of the course and he feels he is falling behind. It is obvious that he feels anxious and is particularly concerned about the amount of work required for the final year project. Rachel allows George to express his concerns and uses exploratory questions to find out whether he is actually behind with his work and the reasons behind this. As the conversation develops, it becomes clear to Rachel that George is not actually too far behind but that his confidence has been knocked by some recent assessments in which he did worse than expected. Rachel steers the conversation towards George's strengths and enables him to explore the potential actions he could take to regain his confidence and get back on track. They agree some small next steps for George to take and decide to review the outcomes of his actions towards the end of term.

Week 8
At the end of her second month, Rachel is due to hold her termly one-to-one meetings with her tutees. She explores with each student how they are feeling and encourages them to discuss the issues they are facing both inside and outside of their course. Rachel asks questions and challenges the students to think about and express their issues more deeply than they might normally do, providing encouragement and guidance if needed. Her main aim is to give the students a chance to look at themselves more closely, reflecting on their progress and exploring new ideas to help build their confidence. She encourages the students to take the initiative – any actions resulting from the meeting that contribute to their learning and progress remain their responsibility. She helps them to think about potential outcomes in more detail and how long they think it would take for them to make progress. Rachel has discovered that tutees tend to behave differently in a one-to-one setting than they do in a lecture or seminar. She has found working with her tutees on this basis a rewarding and welcome change from normal lecture delivery.

Critical thinking activity 2

» *Having read through this case study of interactions between a tutor and tutee, and drawing on your own knowledge and experience, decide which aspect of the role is being described in each instance – personal tutoring or coaching. Then compare your answers with those offered in the discussion below.*

Discussion

Week 4: more personal tutoring than coaching; Rachel worked on monitoring and developing the tutees' academic performance and their employability skills.

Week 6: more coaching than personal tutoring; through questioning and discussion, Rachel helps George to explore the reasons behind his drop in confidence and academic performance and helps him to set his own actions and the dates to review.

Week 8: personal tutoring (however, there are strong elements of a coaching approach); Rachel starts to develop a long-term trusting relationship with the students individually through regular communication to develop their emotional well-being as well as develop new knowledge and skills.

Further ways to understand the personal tutor role

It is important to unpick the role of the personal tutor and recognise the different types of help and support you can give to your students. To do this, it is useful to look at the diagram (Figure 1.1) developed by Clutterbuck (1985, cited in Gravells and Wallace, 2007) which should start to provide greater clarity. The diagram was designed to explore the role of the mentor in further education, but it is also a useful one to apply to the role and functions of the personal tutor.

Figure 1.1 Some ways in which mentors give support
(Gravells and Wallace, 2007)

As a lecturer, a large part of your time is devoted to helping students, but the help you provide can take many guises. Figure 1.2 gives an overview of typical personal tutoring examples related to Clutterbuck's 1985 model.

COACH (directive and challenging)

The directive actions you take with students are where you actively attempt to help your students to achieve a desired outcome and the challenging aspect is where you develop an intellectual need, for example to develop an improvement in a skill or in the student's approach to a problem.

For example, the coaching role could be where Rachel is observing a student's presentation, providing feedback and advice as to how they may improve it and setting targets for the next time they present. It is worth nothing at this point that teaching, training and assessment (assessment for learning and assessment of learning) also appear within this section.

CARE TAKER (directive and supporting)

The supporting aspect of the model relates to helping a student address an emotional need.
Therefore, the care taking part of Rachel's role might be where she takes a student to student support services to make a referral such as for a meeting with a trained counsellor or an assessment for additional support.

Best practice and the boundaries in doing so are explored in Chapter 4.

FACILITATOR (non-directive and challenging)

The non-directive approach is helping a student in response to a need that has arisen through a discussion or observation of a student's circumstances.

The facilitator role could be where Rachel passes on names of colleagues within the institution who can offer possible career pathway advice or passing on contacts within local businesses who might be able to provide the student with work experience opportunities.

COUNSELLOR (non-directive and supporting)

The counsellor aspect of helping students usually relates to actively listening to them.

An example of this is where a student may approach Rachel to discuss that they are suffering from course-related stress. They may want to tell her how this is making them feel and discuss whether what they are doing about it is the right course of action. Rachel may ask questions to help the student understand the situation more fully. More directive actions may happen at the end of this conversation to seek further support for stress management.

Figure 1.2 Personal tutoring examples related to Clutterbuck's 'Some ways in which mentors give support' model
(cited in Gravells and Wallace, 2007)

As you can see, as a personal tutor, you may be called upon to show an abundance of skills and perform a variety of roles within one lecture or seminar, group tutorial or one-to-one conversation.

Klasen and Clutterbuck (2002, cited in Gravells and Wallace, 2007) developed a more detailed model (see Figure 1.3) which allows us to consider styles of helping students in more detail. This diagram was also designed to explore the role of the mentor in further education, but again, it is useful to apply it to the role and functions of the personal tutor in HE.

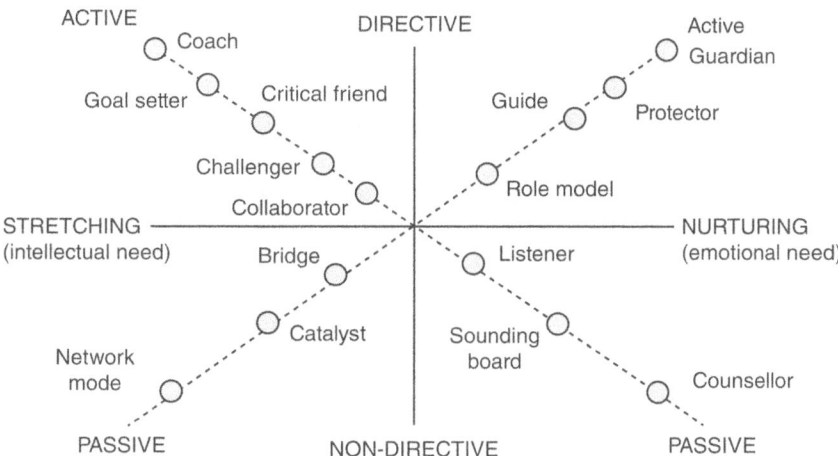

Figure 1.3 *Various styles of helping*
(Gravells and Wallace, 2007)

Critical thinking activity 3

Take a detailed look at Figure 1.3: Klasen and Clutterbuck's (2002) model as adapted by Gravells and Wallace (2007).

1. Pick the two styles you feel you relate to the most in your current position and note down specific examples of when you have had to, or might have to, exhibit these styles of helping.

2. Using the examples you provided for question 1, list the qualities and attributes you:

    a. feel you displayed well which benefitted the student and the situation;

    b. feel you did less well, and you would like more opportunity to develop.

3. Note down specific next steps that you will take to start to improve the qualities and attributes you identified as requiring further development. Ensure you make your next steps specific, measurable, actionable, relevant and time-bound (SMART). They may be simple, small actions, for example, talking to someone experienced who you have seen do these things well, practising them again with the same or a different set of students, or asking someone to observe you and provide feedback.

It is likely that you will use all of the different styles of helping included in Klasen and Clutterbuck's model within your teaching and personal tutoring career. As a lecturer and personal tutor, both within and outside of class, you will switch between being directive and challenging (stretching) in one situation to being non-directive and supportive (nurturing) in the next. As your skills, knowledge and experience develop through practice and reflection, choosing the approach you take with students will become more intuitive, and you will make the transition from being 'consciously incompetent' to 'unconsciously competent'. However, you will not always get it right. The unpredictability of students' needs will always present new challenges. Nevertheless, this is part of the enjoyment of teaching and personal tutoring.

Student support: organisational models

Why is it important to know about models?

As will be demonstrated in the upcoming chapters, becoming an effective personal tutor means thinking critically about your role and its relationship to other roles in the institution as well as the HE sector. This affects the level of influence you may have. In order to do this, you will need clarity over your place in the institution, along with knowledge of the organisational structure and the model of tutoring that it employs. This knowledge will help you to see how your activities and objectives link to other roles within the institution, which will help you with personal development and promotional opportunities. As shown in the final chapter, thinking about how you 'integrate vertically' – in other words, how your objectives meet the objectives of different layers ascending through your organisation – means employing critical thinking skills to be most effective in your role and to see beyond this immediate role. This is central to your career development.

How were the models established and how have they evolved?

In 1992, Earwaker first outlined various approaches to student support – the pastoral, professional and curricular models – which have become the baseline of much of the subsequent literature on personal tutoring (Walker, 2018; Grey and Osborne, 2020; Lochtie et al, 2022). Clearly, HE has changed significantly since Earwaker proposed these models, including approaches to teaching and learning and structures within institutions. The move to a more professional, 'service' approach to student support that Earwaker (1992) identified is now commonplace in universities, and personal tutoring has become part of a wider, holistic approach to student academic and well-being support. Generally, personal tutoring models now fall within five categories. Most of the literature focuses on personal tutoring models for undergraduate students, although increasingly postgraduate models are considered too (e.g. Bosch and Jacobi, 2025). In Table 1.4, we expand on the work of Earwaker (1992) and outline these five categories of personal tutoring models, the rationale for them and challenges associated with them.

What is a personal tutor? • 21

Table 1.4 Established student support models

	Pastoral	Professional tutors	Curriculum	Professional mentors	Team tutoring
Description	Long established in practice and research as the default model of support. Rooted in Oxbridge sixteenth-century practices of being *in loco parentis*. In modern versions of this model, tutors refer or signpost students to student support services.	Trained, professional tutors, often 'third space professionals', for whom personal tutoring is their primary role. Tutors are often based within departments or schools, but may also be part of a central team. This model of professional 'academic advisors' is well-established in the US and is becoming increasingly common in the UK.	Structured group tutorials are embedded within or aligned with the formal curriculum. Can be part of a credit-bearing unit to maximise impact. Focus on the development of skills in all students. This model is becoming more common in the UK.	Tutoring is done by an external professional, for example working in the NHS. The professional mentor may work with the student in addition to a tutor in their school or department. The focus of tutorials is on personal development and professionalism. This model is common in the Health Sciences and subjects with strong links to industry, such as Engineering. Students may use e-portfolios as part of their programme to reflect on and evidence their development.	Tutoring is done by a team of academics within the students' school or department. Students do not have a named tutor, but they can book in with a particular tutor. Tutors may specialise in certain areas of support.

Table 1.4 (Cont.)

	Pastoral	Professional tutors	Curriculum	Professional mentors	Team tutoring
Rationale	Aims to support beyond academic issues, a need well established in the literature. Helps foster a personal relationship between students and an academic, which is highly valued.	Trained, professional staff are well-equipped to support students, and they follow a professional code of practice that meets external standards. Can reduce academic workload and allow greater research focus. Can reduce inconsistency in provision and can be easier to monitor.	Support is embedded into the academic experience, which is most effective. Developmental rather than remedial and linked to learning outcomes as part of an effective transition. Helps to foster a sense of belonging and engagement. Can reduce inconsistency in provision. Effective tutoring with time constraints. Students are more aware of the personal tutor role and more likely to take up opportunities to meet.	Students learn about professional development from a professional in their field.	Can be cost-effective for large cohorts of students. Academics who choose to be tutors are highly motivated and engaged. Frees up time for other academics.

Challenges	Reactionary, deficit model which can be insufficient for current students' needs and difficult to monitor. Due to the overlapping roles of the personal tutor and student support services, it can be difficult for staff and students to know where the boundaries of the tutor role lie. Inconsistency of experience due to variation in confidence of students and engagement of tutors. It may be hard for students to access their tutor at short notice.	Deficit model. The way teaching and support roles complement and overlap may be problematic. Students may see tutoring as an additional extra and engagement with professional advisors can be lower. Professional tutors are not a specialist in the subject area, which is something students want.	Student populations are not settled and progress at their own pace, which may differ from planned curriculum support. Student buy-in and engagement can be problematic.	It can be difficult for students to access tutors because they have busy professional lives. Because tutors/mentors are external to the university, they may have limited knowledge of the university and it can be difficult to monitor. Matching students to a professional mentor based on interests can be difficult.	Reactionary, deficit model. Students do not have a named personal tutor.
References	Gubby and McNab (2013); Small (2013); Grey and Lochtie (2016); Grey and Osborne (2020); Ayton and Walling (2022); Lees and Woods (2022); Bosch and Jacobi (2025).	Simpson (2006); Grey and Lochtie (2016); McFarlane (2016); Laycock (2017); Yale (2019); Grey and Osborne (2020); Alberts (2021); Higgins et al (2021); Robinson (2022); Sallai (2022); Smith (2022); Cai and Gellai (2024).	Thomas (2006); Thomas (2012); Grey and Lochtie (2016); Mynott (2016); Grey and Osborne (2020); Assender and Leadbeater (2022); Dunbar-Morris (2022); McIntosh et al (2022); Robinson (2022); Bosch and Jacobi (2025).	Hughes (2004); Nimmons et al (2019); Scerri et al (2020); Alberts (2023); Alberts (2024b); Goh and Richardson (2024).	Sallai (2022); University of Bristol (2022); Alberts (2023).

(expanding on Earwaker, 1992)

How might the models be applied?

For institutions, there is no single or correct approach when it comes to building a robust personal tutoring infrastructure. There is considerable diversity in the sector, and also within each model, which may affect their application and effectiveness (Grey and Lochtie, 2016). Moreover, as the student population is becoming more diverse, it is important that the provision of personal tutoring is tailored to the needs of students within a particular institution (Atkinson, 2014), within a particular school or programme (Battin, 2014) or even to the individual student (Banahene, 2024). While Table 1.4 outlines discrete models, in reality, institutions frequently combine elements of the different models to gain benefits from a number of models and provide an effective personal tutoring system that is appropriate to their context (McIntosh et al, 2022; Pownall and Raby, 2022; Robinson, 2022; Sallai, 2022).

Many institutions now also have a senior tutor or lead personal tutor who is responsible for various aspects of personal tutoring. Often, senior tutors provide leadership, coordination and oversight of the personal tutoring system by monitoring and evaluating tutoring provision, liaising with central services and providing advice, guidance and training to their colleagues (Alberts, 2025). Senior tutors also provide information on personal tutoring to students and may act as an additional point of contact for them, often when a student has more complex needs (Owen, 2002; Alberts, 2025). In some universities, senior or enhanced personal tutors have been trained to work specifically with students who are 'at risk', either academically or pastorally. We address the limitations of using terms such as 'at risk' or 'vulnerable' to label students in Chapter 5 and advocate that the context in which we use these is paramount. It is clear that the personal tutoring infrastructure must reflect the structure and culture of the institution and evolve alongside it. It must be noted that if the work of personal and senior tutors is not fully integrated with that of academic departments or schools (with effective referral arrangements and useful data available to tutors), there is a danger that students who need support may get lost in the system.

Learner analytics and dashboard systems (explored further in Chapter 5) can help to inform planning and decision-making as well as identify students who need, or are predicted to need, assistance. They can also identify students who would benefit from participating in specific interventions. These systems are useful in that they offer a series of flags to enable tutors to explore student support needs. That said, the data that these systems provide should not stand alone – they must be contextualised. Dashboard systems should not drive the tutorial process itself; rather, they add value when they are part of a much broader and robust decision-making approach, one in which tutors use the data to support their students and assist them in having exploratory conversations. This approach ensures that human and social interaction prevails in the personal tutoring process (Grey and McIntosh, 2017).

Well-being has become a strategic priority across the sector and as a result, increasingly institutions are adopting a 'whole institution approach' to student support (UUK, 2017; Hughes and Spanner, 2024), which includes all staff and services at an institution and benefits all students (Thomas et al, 2017; Brown and Thomas, 2022; McIntosh et al, 2022). It is our view that effective personal tutoring is indeed part of such a wider, holistic approach to student support. Figure 1.4 outlines the blended model of tutoring which combines the proactive elements of the models and, at the same time, celebrates the partnership working that should take place between tutors, students and professional services, while being aware of the boundaries discussed in Chapter 4.

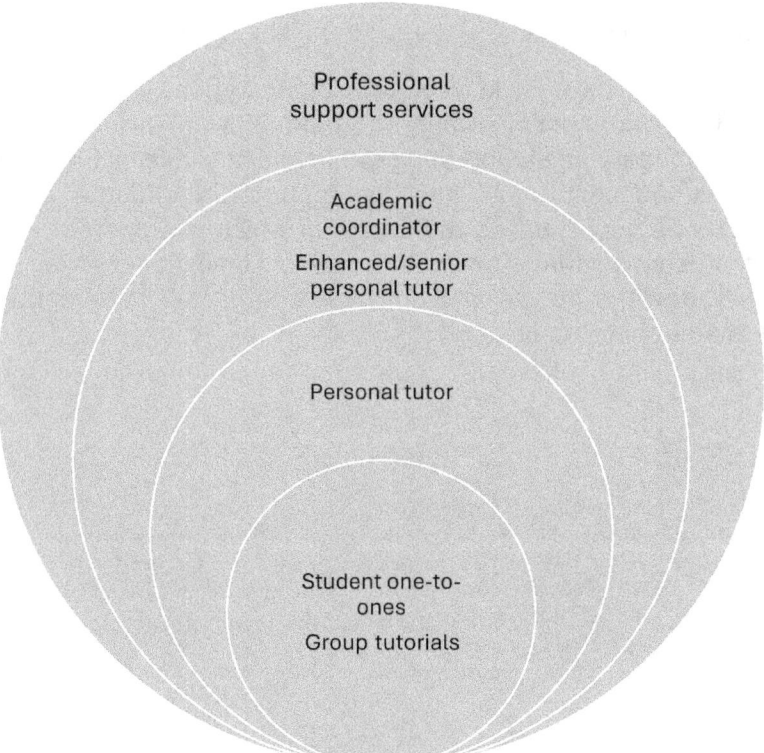

Figure 1.4 *An integrated model of personal tutoring*
Reproduced with permission (McIntosh, 2018)

It is recommended that in effective integrated or blended models of personal tutoring:

- academic tutoring is supported by professional services including, but not limited to, the library, student services, academic registry and the students' union;
- tutoring is coordinated in each school or department and senior tutors may be appointed to support students who are deemed to be 'at risk' and may also coordinate and champion tutoring;
- academic tutoring is integrated within programme structures, underpinned by a robust tutoring curriculum which reflects the demands of the programme and is aligned with the student lifecycle. Tutoring spans all year groups, is structured and provided in both a group and one-to-one setting, facilitating student transition and helping students to connect with their programme and with each other.

Critical thinking activity 4

1. Which of the models outlined in Table 1.4 best describes personal tutoring in the institution you work in? Do you recognise the challenges associated with that model?
2. How does the personal tutoring approach in your institution compare to the blended approach suggested in Figure 1.4?
3. What changes, if any, would you consider in light of these?

Whatever the model of tutoring in your own organisation, it is clear that students crave structured and consistent support (Small, 2013). This can only come from understanding the model you are operating within and maximising its potential benefits. Ensuring you, and your institution, fulfil the features of effective practice listed in Figure 1.5 may be as important as the model in which you operate. This broad, holistic model of student continuation and success highlights the key principles and processes involved in the design and delivery of impactful interventions to support students and enable their learning.

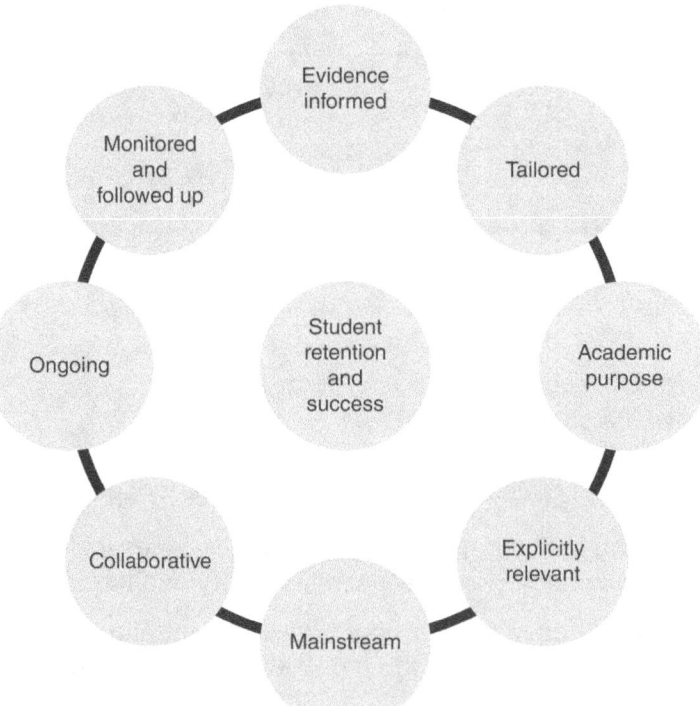

Figure 1.5 *Features of effective practice*
Reproduced with permission (Thomas et al, 2017)

Summary

This chapter has focused on defining personal tutoring. It has explored the similarities and differences between personal tutoring and coaching and how effective personal tutoring encompasses these complementary principles. Whether you are an experienced lecturer or a new academic, you will usually be expected to support student success beyond the context of the classroom and this is where personal tutoring can make a huge impact on a student's progression. Through examples and the two theoretical models in Figures 1.1 and 1.3 we have looked at the different types of support a personal tutor can offer to students. 'Success' will look different for each student, because they all come from different backgrounds, have varying levels of skills and abilities, and each face different challenges both within and outside the classroom.

Remember that developing the personal tutoring principles by regularly practising them and reflecting on their impact alongside your lecturing skills will make you a more effective practitioner overall, which will positively impact your students' progress and success.

We have also considered the rationale for, and the relative advantages and disadvantages of, various models of student support, and have encouraged you to think about which model (or blend of models) your institution, school or department adopts. In the following chapter, we consider the relationship between teaching and personal tutoring.

Critical reflections

1. To what extent do you believe your PG Cert HE, induction, training and development have focused on improving your personal tutoring practice?
2. Think about the importance your current institution places on personal tutoring and explain how you have arrived at that judgement. If you have experience of more than one institution, then, using examples, compare and contrast the two institutions' approaches.
3. Discuss what impact you feel a significant improvement in personal tutoring practice could have on:
    a. students' progress;
    b. a department's performance;
    c. an educational institution's performance.
4. From your experience, compare and contrast the benefits and importance of traditional classroom teaching and personal tutoring.

2 The pedagogy of personal tutoring

Chapter aims

This chapter helps you to:

- understand the relationship between teaching and personal tutoring;
- explore the pedagogy of personal tutoring and its features;
- consider the importance of relational pedagogy and co-creation with students;
- understand the impact of advising theory on the pedagogy of personal tutoring;
- explore coaching and mentoring approaches as personal tutoring pedagogy.

The relationship between teaching and personal tutoring

To understand the pedagogy of personal tutoring, it is important to examine how it overlaps with teaching. As mentioned in the introduction, academic staff are increasingly asked to perform more duties and carry out additional responsibilities, and it is often difficult to separate out personal tutoring from other parts of teaching. One thing, however, is clear – advising *is* teaching; it should not be something separate or 'bolted on' to pedagogic practice. Freire (1998) has written about the close alignment between learning and teaching and the importance of ensuring that this is a dialogic and reciprocal process: 'Whoever teaches learns in the act of teaching, and whoever learns teaches in the act of learning' (p 31). Thus, the dimensions of teaching and personal tutoring should be reconceptualised to acknowledge this. Stenton (2018) brings pedagogy to personal tutoring principles and practice and defines tutoring as both (1) a dialogic encounter – there is no need to switch out of *teaching mode* and into *student support* mode, they are part of the same approach and (2) that 'learning talk' is the foundation of academic practice. As such, Stenton outlines that personal tutoring should be framed as students learning to *think* about themselves in relation to their subjects. The topic of advising as teaching, with a synoptic overview of the curriculum, was explored in more detail in 2005 by Lowenstein and is discussed later in the chapter. Working with students directly remains one of the most rewarding, and challenging, parts of the role and requires academics to adopt specific pedagogical approaches that help to provide students with academic and pastoral support. This chapter outlines the core features of personal tutoring pedagogy and identifies pedagogical approaches that are in alignment with a student-centred approach to teaching.

Most academics working in HE are mindful of students' welfare and support needs, and this can only be honed by focusing on developing advising pedagogies that help support the whole student. That said, the pedagogy of personal tutoring, and more specific pedagogical approaches that inform it, is not well articulated, understood or researched (Walker, 2020; Lochtie et al, 2022). Historically there has been a lack of evidence-informed practice on which to draw (McIntosh and Grey, 2017), and while this situation is steadily improving for other aspects of personal tutoring such as skills and training (Walker, 2025), a focus on advising or tutoring pedagogy remains a neglected area. It is therefore important to outline the core features of advising pedagogy to recognise that supporting students in a consistent and well-structured way can be a particular challenge for individual personal tutors. While personal tutoring is often discussed as part of PG Cert HE programmes, it is often not covered comprehensively and usually remains devoid from other discussions about pedagogic practice, including the Scholarship of Teaching and Learning (SoTL). The most direct experience of personal tutoring pedagogy gained by tutors is therefore acquired while performing the role itself, 'thinking on one's feet' and very much in practice. More work needs to be done to talk about the Scholarship of Student Success (SoSS) which includes approaches to advising and tutoring pedagogy, and the critical use of reflective practice techniques. As this chapter outlines, a personal tutoring pedagogy incorporates those approaches which are typically dialogic in nature including relational pedagogy, co-creation, advising theory, transition pedagogy and coaching approaches. This chapter considers these specific pedagogical approaches and how they can be combined to constitute a pedagogy of personal tutoring.

How effective personal tutoring principles link to effective teaching

The principles of being an effective academic teacher, such as listening and relating to people, as well as sound pedagogical skill and subject expertise, are closely aligned with the principles of being an effective personal tutor (Owen, 2002; Braine and Parnell, 2011). For example, both the lecturer and personal tutor demonstrate a commitment to students through respecting their uniqueness and individuality and therefore provide appropriate learning experiences as well as aiming to motivate and inspire students to achieve their potential. In alignment with the view that advising is teaching, personal tutoring principles are also part of sound pedagogical practice, and most new and experienced tutors use these approaches many times throughout their working day. Even though these are principles that students find particularly helpful, they tend to be the least written about and are not always covered in staff induction.

As access and participation in HE have widened over recent years, the need for a more holistic approach to student support, and indeed a well-articulated pedagogy of personal tutoring, has become greater, with a particular focus on student success, including, but not limited to, student engagement, transition, advice and student learning development (Whittaker, 2008; National Union of Students, 2015; Department for Education, 2017; Thomas et al, 2017; Webb et al, 2017). A holistic approach to personal tutoring is at the heart of student guidance and support, and this is highlighted as a key benchmark in the literature (Watts, 1999; Grant, 2006; Stephen et al, 2008; Thomas et al, 2017). It is the holistic and supportive model of personal tutoring that we advocate in this book (see Figure 1.4).

Successful academics aim to put each student at the centre of their pedagogical practice, whether that is when planning a lesson, marking an assignment or even having a departmental meeting with colleagues. In today's modern, fast-paced, target-driven and ever-changing educational landscape, personal tutors, whether you agree with it or not, are expected to support students' success more holistically, in curricular, co-curricular and extra-curricular domains. Whatever your pedagogical approach, you are trying to help students to get from point A to point B more quickly than they could do by themselves. Point B is student success, although 'success' for each student looks very different and, probably *should* look very different. This is where highlighting how personal tutoring pedagogy aligns with effective personal tutoring principles, to enable you to help your students achieve more, not only in terms of passing an exam or achieving a good mark on an assignment but also in terms of developing the *whole* student, one who can confidently overcome all of the many and varied challenges they encounter.

Critical thinking activity 1

1. What are your thoughts on the relationship between your teaching practice/pedagogical approach and your role as a personal tutor?
2. Is personal tutoring in your institution well-defined, pedagogically informed and explicitly linked to your teaching practice?

Exploring the pedagogy of personal tutoring and its features

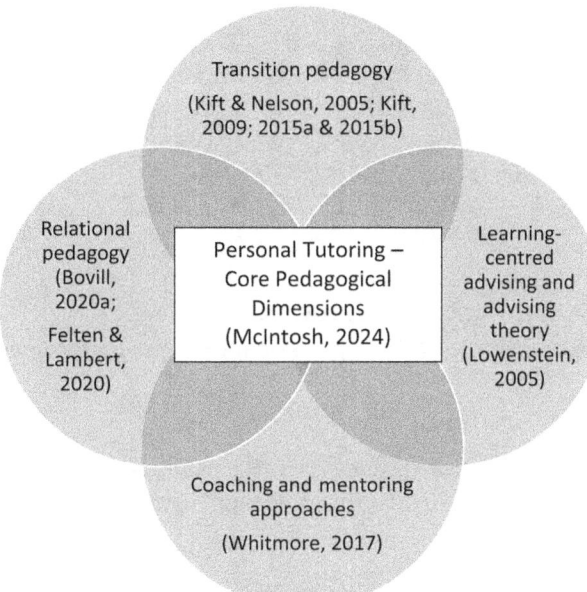

Figure 2.1 *Personal tutoring – core pedagogical dimensions*
(Visualisation re-created with permission by McIntosh, 2024)

As mentioned earlier, it is important to understand that effective teaching and personal tutoring pedagogy overlap and naturally become blurred as you face different situations and challenges both within and outside of the classroom. Figure 2.1 provides a visualisation created by McIntosh (2024) which outlines the core features of personal tutoring pedagogy and how this relates to other defined pedagogical approaches. The likelihood is that personal tutoring pedagogy will be aligned with your teaching and assessment activities. When working with students for the first time as new academics, we have a tendency to be overly analytical and critical of our teaching practice. This is natural and also positive in moderation because it shows the commitment to improve. The fundamental principles of becoming an effective personal tutor are built upon a pedagogical approach that is focused on training, developing practical experience and actively reflecting on that experience. If you continue to apply the personal tutoring principles in different situations and with different types of students and reflect on the impact, then you will embrace the fundamental tenets of personal tutoring pedagogy.

The NACADA Concept of Academic Advising

Before we can explore the fundamental features of personal tutoring pedagogy, it is firstly necessary to discuss how pedagogy relates and aligns to both learning outcomes and the curriculum. NACADA (the Global Community for Academic Advising) has created the Core Concept of Academic Advising (2006), and this is a useful starting point, see Figure 2.2.

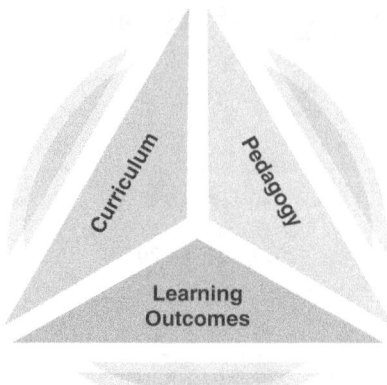

Figure 2.2 The NACADA Core Concept of Academic Advising
(Reprinted with permission from NACADA: The Global Community for Academic Advising (www.nacada.ksu.edu))

The core concept was created 'for the good of the profession', via a lengthy consultation in 2005 and, through that exercise, the three components of advising were identified. The core concept recognises that:

> *regardless of the diversity of our institutions, our students, our advisors, and our organisational structures, academic advising has three components: (1) curriculum (what advising deals with), (2) pedagogy (how advising does what it does), and (3) student learning outcomes (the result of academic advising).*
>
> (NACADA, 2006)

The core concept highlights that:

> *academic advising, as a teaching and learning process, requires a pedagogy that incorporates the preparation, facilitation, documentation, and assessment of advising interactions. Although the specific methods, strategies, and techniques may vary, the relationship between advisors and students is fundamental and is characterised by mutual respect, trust, and ethical behaviour.*
>
> (NACADA, 2006)

We shall explore these features further on in this chapter and also in the rest of the book. Personal tutoring pedagogy must therefore sit alongside learning outcomes and the curriculum in order to be effective. Learning outcomes are as pivotal to advising and personal tutoring as they are to any other aspect of teaching, especially given that it is important to ascertain how students' learning develops through a facilitated advising process and, as mentioned earlier, to document and assess how the student learns to think about themselves in relation to their subject.

The importance of providing a synoptic overview of the students' curricular experience is a fundamental tenet of advising theory, which will be discussed later. The features of a personal tutoring curriculum are discussed in Chapter 6 but are equally a feature of advising theory, especially in terms of scaffolding the learning experience and exploring key thematic concepts across different modules or units of learning. Since its publication in 2006, the core concept continues to be a key feature of applied advising practice globally. Troxel et al (2021), writing on *transformations in academic advising as a profession*, reflect on the impact of the core concept in relation to student success. They argue that advising is 'uniquely placed within the academy as a bridge between the curriculum and the co-curriculum and draws from multiple theories and disciplines to ground scholarship and practice in the field to support student success' (p 24). Troxel et al refer to the work of the NACADA core competencies (2017) which have continued to build on the foundational core concept 'to identify the broad range of understanding, knowledge, and skills that support academic advising … the core competencies consist of three categories (conceptual, informational and relational)' (p 26). It is the relational competencies that relate most closely to the features of personal tutoring pedagogy and are explored in more detail later.

Advising theory and learner-centred advising

In the same way that the NACADA core concepts underpin personal tutoring pedagogical practice, advising theory is equally important to understanding the features of personal tutoring pedagogy. As mentioned previously, advising *is* teaching and, in 2005 Lowenstein asked the critical question: 'if advising is teaching, what do advisors teach?'. As teaching is only one of the structuring components of learning (Wenger, 1998), equally personal tutoring is one of the structuring components of teaching. In an article based on advising theory, Lowenstein (2005) explored the different modes of advising, where he advocated for a learner-centred approach as favourable to the dominant developmental advising paradigm. Indeed, the learner-centred approach of advising is far more attuned with relational advising and tutoring pedagogy, where much more can be done to put the learner at the centre of the advising approach, again facilitating the idea that advising pedagogy is about the student as an active participant in their learning and learning to think about themselves in relation to their goals and the subject. For Lowenstein, advising pedagogy is where the advisor 'plays a role with respect to a student's entire curriculum … [and] also helps the student to understand and create the logic of the student's curriculum' (2005, p 123). In order to understand the different models at play here, Table 2.1 summarises the core features of the three dominant advising approaches. This will be helpful to you during the discussion of the features of personal tutoring pedagogy later on in the chapter.

Table 2.1 The features of prescriptive, developmental and learner-centred advising models

Prescriptive advising (basic, transactional) (based on Crookston, 1972)	**Developmental advising (adaptive)** (based on Crookston, 1972)	**Learner-centred advising (optimal, dialogic)**
• Monologue • Student is passive • Transactional • Information • Facts and rules, policies, procedures, administration	• Dialogic • Student is passive to active • Goal is to enhance the student's development, a goal beyond just providing information. • Focus on modular lenses to learning/curriculum	• Dialogic • Student is active • Relational • Engaging • Transitional support • Student in centre, leading • Co-created • Contextualised – goal is to focus not only on logic of curriculum but on process of learning. • Developing higher-order thinking skills. • Provides perspective on whole curriculum and making meaning of subject. • Coaching approaches

Source: McIntosh (2024), adapted from Lowenstein (2005).

The learning-centred model of advising is most aligned with the main features of personal tutoring pedagogy. It is cognisant of the fact that, as Lowenstein states:

> *learning transpires when a student makes sense of his or her overall curriculum just as it does when a person understands an individual course [in the UK, a module or unit], and the former is every bit as important as the latter.*
>
> (2005, p 127)

Furthermore, the insights coming from the learner-centred model relate not just to the subject matter but to the individual; they are lifelong and interdisciplinary and they allow students, in active dialogue, to connect the thematic areas of a subject to make meaning. In that respect, a skilled advisor harnesses personal tutoring pedagogy to: (1) put the curriculum into perspective, (2) take an interdisciplinary and thematic approach to subject content, (3) scaffold and sequence learning to ensure a seamless journey across all levels, (4) consider meta-skills and high-level skills development such as design thinking and problem solving and (5) assist students to develop personally and professionally. It is now important to examine the learner-centred model in relation to the main features of personal tutoring pedagogy.

Relational pedagogy and co-creation with students

In their article on transformations in academic advising, Troxel et al refer to the work of Drake (2011) who stated that academic advising is about 'building relationships with our students, locating places where they get disconnected, and helping them get reconnected' (p 8). This quote sums up beautifully one of the most fundamental features of advising and tutoring pedagogy: as a dialogic and relational one. It is through relational and dialogic approaches to pedagogy that students are supported and challenged to embrace these connections. This can be further facilitated through co-creation. In her book *Co-creating learning and teaching, towards relational pedagogy in higher education*, Bovill (2020a) established relational pedagogy as the foundation for co-creating learning and teaching. Again, there is an emphasis on moving away from the passive and transactional to the active and dialogic, learner-centred approach, with student engagement at its heart. For Bovill, 'relational pedagogy puts relationships at the heart of teaching and emphasises that a meaningful connection needs to be established between teacher and students as well as between students and their peers, if effective teaching is to take place' (p 3). Bovill writes that co-creation occurs 'when staff and students work collaboratively with one another to create components of curricular and/or pedagogical approaches' (pp 3–4). If we compare this to the features of learner-centred advising as advocated by Lowenstein, contemporary personal tutoring pedagogy is situated fundamentally in the learner-centred approach, with relational pedagogy facilitating the connections and relationships between tutors and students and students themselves.

We argue that relational pedagogy is as fundamental to personal tutoring as it is to teaching and, furthermore, that personal tutoring pedagogy must also demonstrate the features of co-creation in order to be effective. As mentioned in McIntosh and May (2025) 'There are several definitions of co-creation in global higher education settings, many of which seek to understand the process by which staff and students work together to develop meaningful and engaging learning experiences' (p 21). Personal tutoring pedagogy also incorporates practice which connects students to their peers and nurtures peer-to-peer relationships; in other words, it is a pedagogy that promotes group-focused advising as well as approaches to advising individual students. Bovill also focuses on the important element of building trust (which resonates with the NACADA core concept description of advising pedagogy). For Bovill, relational pedagogy is also aligned with critical pedagogy, originally developed by Freire and pioneered by Giroux who critiqued existing approaches to teaching and focused on making the case for more learner-centred approaches which allowed students 'to make more choices and decisions about their learning, a more dialogic student-teacher relationship, and a shift to viewing the learner as a competent contributor to education' (Giroux, 1983 in Bovill, 2020a). In relation to Lowenstein's discussion of learner-centred approaches to advising, there is a clear link between relational and dialogic approaches and helping students to make and construct meaning in relation to their subject; hence, we argue again here that advising and tutoring pedagogy are significantly informed by constructivist theory as well as relational and co-created pedagogy. McIntosh and May's *3 C's model of co-creation* is also informed by constructivist learning theory, which is informed by the work of Vygotsky (1978). The three core features of their model of co-creation in this space focus on: (1) community, (2) collaboration and (3) cohesion:

> *These three core features coalesce around high-quality relationships and relational pedagogic practice to impact student belonging and connectedness in the academy and support improved student outcomes. The model is research-informed and can be applied in a variety of higher education settings ... The model is built on a traditional Freirean philosophy of pedagogy and other models of relational and relationship-rich education (Lyle, 2019; Bovill, 2020a; Felten and Lambert, 2020). It is also built upon social constructivist learning theories (Vygotsky, 1978; Lave and Wenger, 1991), giving prominence not only to relational pedagogies, but also to the context and culture in which they occur.*
>
> (McIntosh and May, 2025, p 19)

As mentioned previously, in recent years, the concept of relational pedagogy has evolved, and is often now discussed in terms of 'relationship-rich education' (Felten and Lambert, 2020). For Felten and Lambert, 'relationships are the beating heart of the undergraduate experience' (p 1), fundamental to persistence, success and institutional culture. At the centre of relationship-rich education are student belonging and connectedness and, for Felten and Lambert, the institutional culture should be orientated around students being encouraged to question meaning for themselves, and to develop a web of connections. Advising is a fundamental part of relationship-rich education because it can help to facilitate these connections (between the subject matter and the student) and also to encourage dialogue among students themselves. Most of this involves getting the 'basics' right and, as Bovill outlines, the foundation of co-creation and the development of relationships must be based on dialogue, trust, respect, learning names of students, as well as active listening (Bovill, 2020a, pp 45–47). According to Katz (2021): 'co-creating with students is a process ... based on constructivist learning theory, which says learners construct knowledge and meaning from lived experiences rather than from passively taking in information ... meaningful learning opportunities are made possible by honouring student voices'. This has many synergies with coaching, which will be discussed later in the chapter.

Again, co-creation is a feature of the learner-centred advising model, with an active focus on the learner at the centre and focused on meaning-making and building connections between units of the curriculum. The aforementioned research-informed *3 C's model* (McIntosh and May, 2025) was designed to underpin the elements that are fundamental to co-creation by fostering both dialogue and the development of staff and student relationships in UK HE. The model is especially relevant to recent developments in academic advising and personal tutoring and can be applied in various HE contexts, of which advising is one. It is suggested here that, as a result of employing relational approaches as part of personal tutoring pedagogy, co-creation occurs and has a transformational impact on community, collaboration and cohesion. Co-creation can ensure that advising and student support are embedded in curricular, co-curricular and extra-curricular contexts where students are supported to reflect on their academic, personal and professional development. The 3 C's are essential preconditions for this work, where new approaches have been adopted in the development of a personal tutoring curriculum (see Chapter 6), with synoptic learning outcomes designed to support student mental health, well-being and employability across their academic programme (McIntosh, in prep). For example, a curricular approach to advising pedagogy can ensure that all stakeholders, including specialist professional support services and academics, as well as students, are involved in group advising and delivery approaches within the classroom. Here, students benefit from being connected to broader employability and mental health/well-being and library professionals as part of their curricular learning experiences.

A personal tutoring curriculum is also intended to support collaborative approaches to the development of students as learners and to develop both an individual learner and a cohort identity (Whannell and Whannell, 2015), where a community of learners supports the development of co-creation. Again, there are many alignments here with the learner-centred model advocated by Lowenstein. Recent innovations in advising are also cognisant of employing a relational pedagogy which, as discussed previously, is critical to the creation of learning communities. With the 3 C's as pre-conditions for co-creation, more dialogue can be encouraged between students, academic colleagues and professional colleagues regarding the development of the learner.

Transition pedagogy

Transition pedagogy is another fundamental feature of advising and tutoring pedagogy. In 2005, in the Australian context, transition pedagogy emerged as 'a guiding philosophy for intentional first year curriculum design and support that carefully scaffolds and mediates the first-year learning experience for contemporary heterogeneous cohorts' (Kift, 2009, p 4). In 2015, Kift (2015b) advocated a 'whole of institution' approach to first year transitions where all stakeholders are involved in embedding a culture of First Year Experience (FYE) and 'getting the context right for staff [helps] to get the context right for students' (Hunt and Peach, 2009, p 14). Transition pedagogy investigates the scaffolding process for student success framed around six principles of first year curriculum design: (1) transition, (2) diversity, (3) design, (4) engagement, (5) assessment and (6) evaluation and monitoring. These six concepts are closely aligned with the learner-centred model of advising and the other features of advising and tutoring pedagogy. If learner-centred advising is associated with a synoptic view of a student's curriculum, a focus on transitionary experiences (into HE and into higher years of study) is critical. A personal tutor is well-placed to support students to understand the transition points in their student journey and to support important dialogue around these key adjustment points. Chapter 6 discusses in more detail the importance of transitioning into university life, effective transitional support and the role of the tutor in transition. For the purposes of articulating an advising and tutoring pedagogy, a successful learner-centred design will be cognisant of transition and the diversity of the student body (understanding the adjustment points for learners with different contexts and factoring that into their approach). The book considers some key tutoring activities that can be incorporated into your pedagogic approach around transition (Chapter 6) and inclusion (Chapter 5). Engagement, another fundamental principle of transition pedagogy, is also a key feature of learner-centred advising and, as discussed previously, when combined with a focus on co-design with students, can facilitate a student learning to think about themselves in relation to their subject and to their own development. In terms of incorporating assessment and evaluation, the alignment of personal tutoring pedagogy with learning outcomes and the curriculum (as underpinned by the NACADA core concept) is a robust way of ensuring that the connections between the different elements of the curriculum are made, and that the personal tutor can assess a student's development in that regard. Personal tutoring must have its own personal development goals. Chapter 8 explores reflective practice and professional development in advising and tutoring, which are both critical to ensuring that one's advising approach is evaluated over time. There are some useful UK models which consider transition and adjustment, including Morgan's *Student Experience Transitions model* (2022) which is also discussed and applied in Chapter 6. Morgan's model serves as a useful framework to underpin your personal tutoring pedagogy. It also provides a learner-centred model around the stages of the student journey from pre-arrival, arrival, welcome and induction, adjustment to higher levels of study and, importantly, outduction into further study or a graduate role. McIntosh and Barden's (2019) *early intervention model* is also useful in understanding other infrastructure required to support personal tutoring, including the importance of onboarding and induction and peer support.

Coaching and mentoring approaches

Finally, coaching, specifically solution-focused coaching, is another core feature of personal tutoring pedagogy. There are many definitions of coaching but one of the most widely recognised is 'coaching is unlocking a person's potential to maximise their own performance. It is helping them to learn rather than teaching them' (Whitmore, 2017, p 11). Coaching approaches are also discussed in Chapter 1. For Passmore and Fillery-Travis (2011), coaching is a 'dialogue between a facilitator (coach) and a participant (coachee), where the facilitator uses open questions, summaries and reflections which are aimed at stimulating the self-awareness and personal responsibility of the participant' (p 74). The solution-focused approach to coaching is, as the title suggests, essentially trying to make greater progress with the student by focusing on where they want to get to and understanding what skills and knowledge they need to get there, rather than spending excessive amounts of time exploring the problem or issue they may be facing. Again, there are many synergies here with Lowenstein's learner-centred model of advising, and thus coaching connects also with relational, dialogic and transitional approaches to advising and tutoring support. One of the principal features of a solution-focused coaching approach, and one of the reasons why we advocate its use as a core pedagogical practice with students through your personal tutor role, is that it can significantly reduce any inferiority students feel about themselves or their current situation. Furthermore, in terms of emotional well-being, experience shows that this approach helps students to think more optimistically, behave more confidently and engage with their goals, which become more self-generated. As discussed in Chapter 1, not all personal tutoring is coaching but coaching can be an important developmental activity to be conducted as part of the tutor–tutee relationship (Gurbutt and Gurbutt, 2015). We explore solutions-focused coaching here because it aligns effectively with the dimensions of learner-centred practice, where dialogic and relational approaches are paramount, and can facilitate and enable the student to connect the dimensions of the curriculum and embrace lifelong learning.

The solution-focused approach grew out of techniques from the world of therapy in America in the 1980s. Solution-focused brief therapy was developed by American social workers Steve De Shazer, Insoo Kim Berg and their team at the Milwaukee Brief Family Therapy Center. Through their practice and research, they discovered that their clients made much greater progress over a shorter period of time when the conversations focused more on the clients' future goals, a positive view of the future, and on their own strengths and competencies. From these early days, the solution-focused approach has grown and is now used successfully in a variety of settings, such as business consulting, hypnotherapy, counselling and coaching within the commercial world. Coaching is becoming increasingly important to student success in the United States and has the potential to deliver real benefit in UK HE by:

- increasing motivation and engagement;
- developing personal or professional competencies;
- aiding retention;
- assisting academic, personal and social success.

(European Mentoring and Coaching Council, n.d; Gurbutt and Gurbutt, 2015; Calcagno et al, 2017; Ralston and Hoffshire, 2017)

In recent years, solution-focused coaching has been used as a catalyst for personal development and applied to understanding the coaching experiences of non-traditional students as well as to understanding the value of coaching and mentoring for minority groups: see, for example, Lancer and Eatough (2018), Spencer (2021) and Hillman et al (2024). Solution-focused coaching also has links with cognitive behavioural therapy (CBT), which has also led to the development of another strand of coaching called cognitive behavioural coaching (CBC). CBT and CBC are similar, but CBC focuses on achieving personal and professional fulfilment, not an understanding of psychological disturbance, which is a core component of CBT (Neenan, 2009). CBC and solution-focused coaching are also similar; however, CBC is a fusion of CBT, rational emotive therapy, solution-focused approaches, goal-setting theory and social cognitive theory (Palmer and Szymanska, 2018). Even though there are similarities between solution-focused coaching and CBT, the main difference is that solution-focused coaching primarily focuses on goal achievement rather than healing. When considered in the context of a learner-centred model of advising and tutoring, the importance of goal-orientation becomes very clear – helping the student to understand the curriculum and meet learning outcomes.

There are two different approaches that you can adopt when helping students to solve their problems: the problem-focused and solution-focused approaches. In tandem with the learner-centred advising model, the solution-focused approach is more effective as a pedagogical practice, in enabling students to develop self-efficacy, self-reliance and improve independent learning (these are highly desirable outcomes in terms of articulating a personal tutoring pedagogy). Table 2.2 outlines the differences between the solutions and problem-based approaches to advising.

Table 2.2 Different approaches to helping students solve their problems

Problem-focus approach	**Solution-focus approach**
Understand and diagnose the problem.	Recognise what solution or outcome the student would find desirable or is needed.
Know what causes the problem.	Find know-how and resources; in other words, skills or previous experience, which will help the student to work towards the solution or agreed outcome.
Use this information to address and fix the problem.	Taking into account the student's know-how, exploring the solution and agreeing a small action, or actions. Often the problem that the student was facing will either reduce or seem less significant to them and together you may discover a new way to overcome it.

(Adapted from Jackson and McKergow, 2007)

There are a number of factors that can influence the effectiveness of both approaches in terms of using them in your pedagogical approach, as part of the learner-centred process. These are:

- the focus or desired outcome of the conversation;
- the degree of rapport and depth of relationship you have with the student;
- how much time you have for the conversation;
- the level of motivation and emotional intelligence that the student possesses.

All the factors above point to a solutions-focused approach being better aligned with a learner-centred approach to advising and tutoring, which is inherently dialogic and relational versus a developmental or prescriptive model of advising, which are more problems-focused and transactional.

Key characteristics of using solution-focused coaching with students

Table 2.3 illustrates some of the key characteristics that will help focus the way you view and use solution-focused coaching in your day-to-day pedagogical practice with students and in your personal tutor role.

Table 2.3 Key characteristics of using solution-focused coaching with students

Key characteristic	Explanation
Positive change can occur	Solution-focused coaching works on the assumption that positive change can occur with students and that this change can happen quickly. This ascribes to the relational nature of the learner-centred model.
Clear goals and self-directed action	You should work with the students to define specific goals (Gurbutt and Gurbutt, 2015; Gannon, 2025). The impact of a good coaching conversation doesn't stop when it stops. Set a clear expectation that the students must be self-directed and take the responsibility to implement actions to achieve these goals outside the coaching conversations. This will help the student to reach a synoptic view of their learner experience, facilitating the connections between concepts and learning across their curriculum.
Develop solutions and focus on the future; not dwelling on problems within the past or present	Listen to any issues or problems in order to communicate empathy and develop rapport with your students. Quickly move the conversation on to exploring future goals, past successes and what skills, knowledge and abilities they have. Again, this is a learner-centred approach where the student is in the driving seat, able to determine (with your support) their goals and course of action.
Students' experience, expertise and resources	A solution-focused personal tutor is an enabler and facilitator. There is a belief that students are likely to already have the answers and the ability to take themselves forward, and as their personal tutor it is your role to help them notice this. This is learner-centred in its nature. When students feel they have worked something out for themselves, there is a greater chance that they will ask themselves the same questions in the future and coach themselves. The best coaches in some ways become invisible. The learner-centred model supports the student to achieve an element of self-actualisation through the support and scaffolding provided via their personal tutor (Gurbutt and Gurbutt, 2015; Gannon, 2025).
Reframe the students' perspective and help them to notice positives	Possibilities include reframing and helping them to notice: • a distant possibility as a near possibility; • a weakness as a strength; • a problem as an opportunity.

Reframing

Reframing students' perspectives isn't always an easy task, particularly if they have a negative belief about themselves or their situation, but experience has shown that it is an effective tool for pedagogical practice and one that you can hone over time and in dialogue with the student. The new framing of their perspective needs to be felt, and it usually needs to have an emotional impact and be more emotionally compelling than their old view. Try using the phrase 'Let's look at it another way' and encourage them to reframe their thoughts by exploring the situation through dialogue. Sometimes the student might not be in the right frame of mind to have the view 'reframed'. A receptive mood is usually necessary; otherwise, the effort may be wasted. Reframing can affect students' emotional state, hopefully making them happier, more positive and optimistic. Negative emotions are not always detrimental to their academic progress. However, Huppert (2009) found that particularly in the fields of positive psychology and neuroscience, people who have more positive emotions or are more regularly in a positive mood tend to:

- engage with goal pursuits that are more self-generated and consistent with personal values;
- have a broader focus of attention; in other words, they can see the 'bigger picture';
- generate more ideas in problem-solving tasks;
- build enduring coping resources, which leads to resilience;
- evaluate themselves and others more positively.

Helping students to notice

One of the main ways of identifying when students notice something new about themselves or their situation is by noticing a visible change in their facial expressions and/or body language. The best way to enable students to really notice something about themselves is through careful and considered questioning, rather than telling them what they should notice. *Telling* students can sometimes work, but this has limited impact. *Enabling* students to notice crucial aspects of themselves or their situation – in other words raising their self-awareness – is key as this helps to develop more enduring ownership of their situation and self-reliance, which in turn promotes greater self-efficacy. Both of these things are relational and dialogic in their very nature.

Critical thinking activity 2

1. What are your thoughts on the four dimensions of personal tutoring pedagogy cited in this chapter?
2. What particular dimensions do you use most often in your capacity as a personal tutor? Which ones do you want to develop further?

Summary

This chapter has discussed the main features of personal tutoring pedagogy and how they relate to Lowenstein's learner-centred model of advising and the NACADA core concept of advising (see Figure 2.2). Through employing the features of specific pedagogical approaches such as relational pedagogy, co-design, transition pedagogy and solutions-focused coaching, the chapter has demonstrated how an effective and dynamic student-centred approach can be facilitated. It has also demonstrated how these pedagogical approaches coalesce to form a coherent strand of personal tutoring pedagogic practice which both supports student learning and contributes to student success.

Critical reflections

1. To what extent do you feel you are already using a learner-centred approach to personal tutoring pedagogy and similar tools or approaches with your students before reading this chapter?
2. Considering your experiences so far, explain the situations when you feel which particular features of learner-centred advising and tutoring pedagogy would be:
    a. most useful and effective;
    b. less useful and effective;
    c. situation-dependent.
3. To what extent do you feel that the approaches to learner-centred pedagogy fit within the culture, policies and aims of your current institution? If you have taught in more than one institution, use examples to compare and contrast the most recent two.
4. If you find that the tools and techniques from this chapter improve your skills, your performance and your effectiveness as a personal tutor, what could you do to increase their use with the following?
    a. Other staff within your institution.
    b. Other early career academics on your PG Cert HE.

3 Core values and skills of the personal tutor

Chapter aims

This chapter helps you to:

- understand the core values and skills of the effective personal tutor and be able to distinguish between them;
- consider approaches to embedding the core values within your teaching and personal tutoring practice and apply them to different situations;
- develop techniques to improve your personal tutoring core skills and apply them to different situations.

Introduction

This chapter explores the core values and skills of the effective personal tutor in two separate sections. It does so by exploring typical scenarios that you are likely to face.

Section 1: What are the core values of the effective personal tutor?

We have already explored the ways in which students can be supported. Here, we look at the core values which should become increasingly evident in your day-to-day actions, behaviour and approach. This section does not aim to explore extensively professional values in academia or in HE more generally as they are detailed elsewhere (for example, Department for Education, 2017; Advance HE, 2023; QAA, 2023). Instead, it aims to build upon them in order to focus specifically on the values of an effective personal tutor. The core values of the effective personal tutor are:

DOI: 10.4324/9781041055266-4

- working in partnership with students;
- approachability;
- authenticity;
- being inclusive and valuing students as individuals;
- being non-judgemental;
- compassion;
- diplomacy;
- high expectations.

What is a core value and how do I know what mine are?

Embodying the core values of the personal tutor, when compared with other positive values, is fundamental to providing effective student support. Furthermore, when values underpin core skills (Section 2 of this chapter, beginning on page 50) and key activities (Chapters 5 and 6), they can have a significant impact on student outcomes.

So, what is a value and how does it relate to your personal tutor role? Values are things that you believe are important to the way that you live and work; core values are those which hold the greatest amount of meaning to you. They are central to the decisions you make in the lecture theatre, seminar room and while working one-to-one with your students. Another way to look at it is that your values are your guiding principles which shape your priorities and in many cases dictate your day-to-day behaviours and approach to people and work. Your values can be seen in the actions you take and in the way you respond to dilemmas, challenges and adversity. These should be in line with the 'underlying values of higher education ... the joy and value of knowledge pursued for its own sake; the pursuit of the good ... the fundamental importance of freedom of speech and vigorous disagreement based on mutual respect' (Department for Education, 2017, p 8).

A core value is only truly a core value if you *live* by it and it can be seen in your actions (at least the majority of the time). When the things that you do and the way you behave match your core values, then you are likely to feel satisfied and content. For example, if you value working with people and you sit in front of a computer screen from 9am to 5pm every day you are less likely to be satisfied with your profession. This is because it is important for your core values and actions to align in order for you to feel that you are doing valuable work. At this point, it is useful to consider the reasons why you chose to pursue a career in HE and academia.

Usually, values are perceived as quite abstract as well as difficult to identify and explain to others. When you discover your own core values, you discover what is truly important to you. A good way for you to try to understand your values is to think deeply about the following questions from a work-life and personal perspective.

Critical thinking activity 1

Identify examples of when you were the most happy, proud, fulfilled and satisfied at work.

1. For each example, indicate why you felt that way.
2. What factors contributed to you feeling like that?
3. Now, try to encapsulate each of those examples into a descriptive word or words. For example, achievement, balance, generosity, happiness, mastery, self-reliance, teamwork.
4. Write these down in no particular order. Compare them as pairs and ask yourself: 'If I could satisfy only one of these regularly, which one would I choose?' Keep doing this until they are in order.

The words that you have listed could be seen as your individual core values. Identifying your core values is not an easy task. When working with students there can be many conflicting pressures and choices to make, and when many of the options seem reasonable it is reassuring to rely on your core values, as well as the values of the institution you work for, to guide you in the right direction.

How to develop the personal tutor core values

The values of an academic department or programme rarely, if ever, appear on a meeting agenda. For you to understand the core values of the personal tutor, you need to see the values in action and the following case study and related activity allows you to do this.

CASE STUDY

Aashna's story

Aashna is in her second year of teaching psychology at a high-ranking university.

1. Aashna's first year tutees are due to give a presentation in their 'Brain and Cognition' module and many students are feeling nervous about it. Aashna arranges for the students to have a practice session during a group tutorial. However, when it is time for the group tutorial, only two students turn up. Aashna goes ahead and the two students practise their presentation. After the tutorial, Aashna emails each of the absent tutees to remind them they have missed the tutorial and explain that their absence affected other students' ability to practise. She also checks in with students as to why they did not attend and asks if they need any support.
2. During the first week of term, Aashna meets with all her new first-year students. Aashna starts the tutorial by talking to the students about her academic background,

her interests and what she loves about psychology, and how she came to be a lecturer. She asks students about their interests, why they have chosen psychology, what they hope the degree will give them, and if they have signed up for any student societies. Aashna makes a note of the students' interests and makes an effort to learn the names of her tutees.

3. Ahead of a scheduled one-to-one, Aashna uses her university's learning analytics dashboard to monitor her tutees' progress and engagement. Finn, one of Aashna's tutees, has consistently been absent from lectures and seminars for two of his modules. In the tutorial Aashna asks what is preventing Finn from attending some sessions. Finn explains that he struggles to pay his rent each month, and that he has had to take on extra shifts to make ends meet. Finn says he tries to catch up on lectures using the recordings, but that he is finding this difficult to do and is falling behind. Aashna helps Finn develop a plan to catch up with his lectures. She makes Finn aware of their university's hardship fund.

Critical thinking activity 2

» *In each case decide which core value (from the personal tutor core values list at the start of this section) you believe Aashna is embodying and identify the positive benefit being created from this approach.*

Discussion

In the previous scenarios, Aashna can be said to display the following core values of the personal tutor.

1. High expectations – Aashna challenges her students by expecting maximum effort and application as well as expecting a level of independence. Student achievement is closely linked to the expectations that tutors place on them (Rubie-Davies et al, 2020). Students who are expected to learn more or perform better generally may be more likely to do so, while those held to lower expectations may achieve less. Lowering expectations of students can become a self-fulfilling prophecy. The way to avoid this is to raise expectations for all areas of a student's life and ensure they receive the support they need to reach those high expectations. This is linked to the notion of independent learning (see Chapter 6) and will positively affect their grades and career prospects, as well as the success rates of the institution.

2. Being inclusive and valuing students as individuals – Aashna makes an effort to get to know each of her tutees as individuals, by remembering their name, their interests and their specific circumstances. It is important to students that universities are student-focused and personal tutoring is an important element of that. Students want to feel that they matter and are known to, and supported by, the university, are valued as individuals and not as just another student (Flett et al, 2019; Gravett et al, 2021).

Students are not a homogenous group and it is important to differentiate between students' values, interests, background and goals and to be inclusive in personal tutoring practice (McGill et al, 2020; UKAT, 2020; Advance HE, 2023). As tuition fees have risen so have student expectations of tutors and support services. At the same time student numbers have grown and resources have become stretched. Tutors often struggle to meet demand and to balance the needs of all their students, particularly when cohorts are large and the curriculum has many assessments. There is a danger that the massification of HE will involve treating students like a number, or as 'customers' who are paying for the privilege of being at university. An effective personal tutor is aware of this challenge and can work towards bridging this gap by valuing students as individuals, even if student–staff ratios are high. There are ways of managing this workload effectively, via group tutorials, which will be discussed later.

3. Compassion – rather than reprimanding Finn for his attendance record, Aashna allowed Finn to tell his side of the story. For students, it is crucial that their personal tutor is concerned, caring and supportive (McGill et al, 2020; UKAT, 2020; Yale, 2020a, 2020b, 2020c; Alberts, 2022b; Bell, 2022). If students feel their tutor does not care, the relationship is given no value and can feel like a waste of time (Yale, 2019). In this case, Aashna's compassion helped Finn to tell his story. It allowed Finn to access the university's hardship fund and developed his relationship with Aashna as personal tutor.

The remaining core values from the list are explored in Table 3.1.

Table 3.1 Remaining core values of the effective personal tutor

Core value	Explanation	Typical context
Approachability	Being seen as friendly and easy to talk to is an essential skill for a personal tutor (Ghenghesh, 2017; Yale, 2019; Hayman et al, 2020; Yale, 2020c; Stuart et al, 2021; Bell, 2022). Without approachability, students may find interactions disappointing and hurried; they may be discouraged from seeking support from a tutor who appears to be busy and even drop out if they feel they are not able to engage meaningfully with them (Dobinson-Harrington, 2006; Yale, 2020c).	When an experienced tutor works with students on a one-to-one basis, they can often see when something isn't quite right. It is possible to use verbal or non-verbal cues to explore this, for example, a lack of eye contact, negative body language and/or demeanour. Tutors can become more approachable to a student and encourage them to open up by focusing on the following: • having open and welcoming body language; • having the confidence to ask how students are, using general and open questions, for example, 'how are you?', 'how are things?', 'what is on your mind?'; • telling students about their own background and experience; • reiterating the importance of trust in the tutor–tutee relationship. This can take time to establish so clear boundaries and a focus on confidentiality should be paramount and should include a frank discussion about disclosure and a duty to declare (for example, if the tutee is at risk of harming themselves or others).

Table 3.1 (Cont.)

Core value	Explanation	Typical context
Diplomacy	Diplomacy is an important skill as personal tutor and can be useful to engage and work positively with students (Wootton, 2007).	Difficult situations may arise between students, or between a student and another member of staff. An experienced tutor would use their communication skills to sensitively and tactfully mediate and de-escalate tense situations and help the student reflect.
Being non-judgemental	As part of their training, tutors should be encouraged to avoid making judgements about students' lives based on their own values and university experiences (Wisker et al, 2007; Swain, 2008; McGill et al, 2020). The UK HE sector is built upon the belief that all students, regardless of background, should be supported so they can access, progress within and succeed in HE, and the tutor should embrace this wholeheartedly (Advance HE, 2023).	It can be challenging for a tutor, no matter how experienced they are, to completely reserve judgement when it comes to students. The core value of being non-judgemental means striving to overcome the need to label students, giving them the opportunity to engage with you and develop a healthy rapport. In order to be successful in their own right, students need to be given autonomy, the freedom to make mistakes and to learn from them, and be provided with the tools and support to cope with setbacks. Unfortunately, tutors often witness students struggling and feel powerless to prevent their distress. However, being an effective personal tutor involves motivating and inspiring students to achieve their potential. In order for a student to achieve this, and hopefully improve their behaviour or attitude, it is important to engage with them, individually and in groups, as often as you are able to do so.
Working in partnership with students	Increasingly, institutions and academics are seeing students as partners in the education (McIntosh and Cross, 2017; Gravett et al, 2020; Matthews and Dollinger, 2023).	The tutor–tutee partnership is a two-way relationship with a shared and negotiated agenda founded upon mutual recognition and respect (Wootton, 2006; Stephen et al, 2008; Yale, 2019; Yale, 2020c). This relationship can be further facilitated by displaying to students that you understand the pressures they face, that you too have been a student and, on occasion, you also have challenges to overcome in your work (for example, when receiving negative feedback about a proposed journal article submission). This approach also allows you to role model good behaviour and demonstrate a positive attitude in response to stressful situations.
Authenticity	Students must see their personal tutor as someone who appears authentic. This includes the appetite to support students selflessly and is essential when developing a healthy tutor–student relationship (Yale, 2019; UKAT, 2020; Alberts, 2022b; Gravett and Winstone, 2022).	Students are perceptive and can tell when a personal tutor is authentic and that their concern for them is genuine. Tutors are likely to have greater impact upon students if they feel that the help, advice and support the tutor is providing is honest and given as objectively as possible.

Individual and shared core values

Having established what the core values of the personal tutor are, you are hopefully thinking 'I believe I have a lot of these values (or similar ones) and I believe I show them through my actions a lot of the time when working with students'. To really have an impact on student support and, ultimately, students achieving their potential, these values need to be shared and shown consistently by other staff, as well as being recognised and promoted by middle and senior managers.

Core values directly affect employee actions, behaviour and organisational culture. Therefore, having positive and shared core values that everyone buys into (staff and students) is one of the key ways to improve consistency of performance. A study (Guiso et al, 2013) 'found that there is a relationship between a culture of strong values ("high integrity") as perceived by employees and organisational performance. That is to say, the values need to be "lived" throughout the organisation' (The Great Place to Work Institute, 2014, p 5).

Critical thinking activity 3

» *What three actions could you take to embed the core values of the personal tutor into your work with students either within the class, in a group tutorial or working one-to-one?*

Discussion

Compare your answers to the following suggested ideas for embedding the core values of the personal tutor into your work with students:

- explain the core values to your students;
- display the core values in your module handbooks or Virtual Learning Environment (VLE), or website, with examples of actions that embody them;
- tell students what they can expect from you (in other words, to display the core values).

Section 2: What are the core skills of the effective personal tutor?

Now that you have a firm grasp on core values in effective personal tutoring, let's examine core skills. The core skills of the effective personal tutor are:

- active listening and questioning;
- building genuine rapport with your students;
- challenging;

- consistency;
- critical thinking;
- decision-making and problem-solving;
- developing independence and resilience;
- digital literacy;
- proactivity, creativity and innovation;
- reflecting back and summarising;
- role modelling;
- teamwork;
- working under pressure.

What is a core skill?

A skill refers to the ability to do something well. In addition, examples of synonyms for skill include expertise, adeptness, mastery, competence, efficiency, experience and professionalism, to name but a few. These highly descriptive words are connected with taking action or doing something, but also ensuring you do it well.

You use your core skills in the day-to-day actions you take to support your students. Having the right skills is important to be able to carry out your job, but it is your core values that drive you to take those actions repeatedly. So, to have the greatest impact and to develop into an effective personal tutor, you need to have and use both the core values and skills together.

Different categories of personal tutor core skills

The core skills of the personal tutor can be broken down into different subgroups as seen in Figure 3.1.

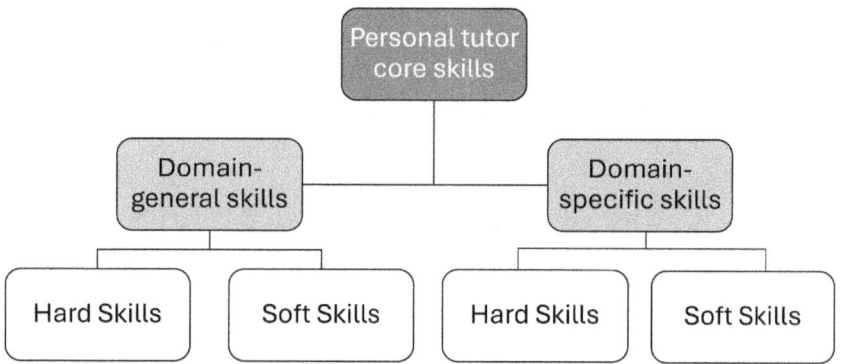

Figure 3.1 *Different categories of personal tutor core skills*

The first way to divide the core skills is into domain-general and domain-specific. Domain-general skills are common skills that may not necessarily be directly related to your personal tutor role and which you would find useful for most jobs, for example, good communication, time management, problem-solving and organisational skills. Domain-specific skills are those that are more directly related to your personal tutor role.

Hard and soft skills

A further way to divide the core skills is into 'hard' and 'soft' skills. Table 3.2 gives examples of these.

Table 3.2 Hard and soft skills examples

Hard skills	Soft skills
Effective curriculum planning.	Building rapport.
Conducting effective research.	Decision-making.
Effective scheduling and time management.	Reflecting back and summarising.
Helping students develop applications for postgraduate study.	Active listening and questioning.

Zepke and Leach (2010) argue for curriculum outcomes to include key skills which are hard (communication, application of numbers, information technology, problem-solving, improving personal performance and working with others) and soft (social skills, coping with authority, organisational skills such as personal planning, analytical skills such as exercising judgement and personal skills such as insight, motivation, confidence, reliability and awareness of health). Soft outcomes do not measure success objectively; they measure it according to students' perceptions of the progress made towards their own goals or that of their programme (Zepke and Leach, 2010). Hard skills are normally related to a specific task or action, for example, planning a group tutorial or undertaking a one-to-one, and we look at both of these in detail in Chapter 5. In terms of recruitment and selection, the hard skills are essential for getting an interview, but it is usually the soft skills (which are personality driven) that will get you the job because educational institutions target practitioners who will be a good fit within the department and make a good impression on students.

How to develop the personal tutor core skills

This section focuses on developing the core skills that are required when delivering effective personal tutoring. Table 3.3 outlines some background or explanation to the personal tutor core skills.

Table 3.3 Core skills of the effective personal tutor

Core skills	Explanation and/or example
1. Building genuine rapport with your students	Developing a harmonious relationship with a student in which each person is able to communicate effectively and understand the other's feelings or ideas.
2. Active listening and questioning	Asking intelligent questions and listening to/observing the responses is integral to ensuring that tutoring aids retention (Dobinson-Harrington, 2006; Wisker et al, 2007; McGill et al, 2020). It is also important to the student that their tutor listens actively and is able to interpret clear verbal and non-verbal messages.
3. Challenging	Students are more likely to succeed if tutors challenge them to achieve more (Mayhew et al, 2010). Challenging may be possible in discussion sessions, when setting goals and milestones or when encouraging them to embrace autonomous and independent learning (Mayhew et al, 2010; Thomas et al, 2015; Ralston and Hoffshire, 2017). Guiding students to think more carefully about their situation and challenging the assumptions that they make may help them to see things they may otherwise fail to recognise.
4. Reflecting back and summarising	It is important to help students to reflect upon their motivations, aspirations and needs alongside their assessment feedback in order to make sense of their academic progress (Stephen et al, 2008; Calcagno et al, 2017). Showing students you understand what they have said by listening actively and paraphrasing it back to them will not only help your students to learn but also help you to continually reflect upon your own experience as a practitioner (Wisker et al, 2007; Small, 2013).
5. Developing independence and resilience	The quality of the academic environment is critical in helping students foster the resilience they need to succeed. The ability to embrace and learn from failure can be developed by personal tutors if they possess the innovative pedagogies required to do so. As nurturing strong, independent learners is a traditional value and mission of HE, academics need the skills and knowledge required to help students understand and practise effective independent learning (Thomas et al, 2015).
6. Teamwork	The ability to work effectively with your colleagues is paramount (McGill et al, 2020). It is also likely to grow in importance as you progress throughout your career and develop your academic programme (McCabe and McCabe, 2010; Advance HE, 2023). The challenges of working as part of a tutorial team and good practice in doing so are explored in Chapter 4.
7. Decision-making and problem-solving	Thinking through and making difficult decisions, even when there doesn't appear to be a clear consensus or solution.
8. Role modelling	Serving as a role model, academically, professionally and in terms of reflective practice, is an important part of being a personal tutor (Small, 2013). Embracing positive core values sets a healthy precedent for students; it also maintains professional boundaries and helps students to see what professionalism looks like.

Table 3.3 (Cont.)

Core skills	Explanation and/or example
9. Proactivity, creativity and innovation	Creativity is a requirement to succeed as a tutor and innovative practices are an indicator of success in student retention. Effective personal tutoring needs to be proactive because students prefer any interaction to be instigated by the tutor (Stephen et al, 2008; Thomas and Jones, 2017; Alberts, 2022b). However, a balance between proactive tutoring and student choice/autonomy is also required, especially in the face of competing daily pressures faced by both tutors and students (Augustus et al, 2023; Wakelin, 2023). The management of boundaries and the discussion of expectations is very important here. Boundaries and independent learning are explored in Chapter 4.
10. Working under pressure	Tutors are often exposed to many emotional situations, including listening to some distressing circumstances involving their students. This may leave both tutors and students feeling anxious and overwhelmed (McFarlane, 2016; Augustus et al, 2023; Wakelin, 2023). The time to support students in this way may not necessarily be included in their timetable or the time allocated may not be sufficient, forcing tutors to work beyond their contract to provide the best support they can (Havergal, 2015). In the face of these significant challenges tutors need to remain calm in order to stay effective and be sure to ask for help and support from others in order to perform their role.
11. Consistency	Tutors need to be a consistent and reliable point of contact and so must be transparent in letting students know when and how to contact them. If tutors advertise certain times when they will be available to students in their office they have to make sure that these times are consistent and communicated to students properly. If these circumstances change they must offer a clear alternative (Swain, 2008; Ross et al, 2014).
12. Critical thinking	It is vital that academics demonstrate and model to students a critical thinking approach to the management of information and help them to appreciate the dialectic processes of constructing knowledge (Thomas et al, 2015).
13. Digital literacy	Digitally fluent tutors use data and technology to inform and support their tutoring. Technology has made many of the tasks of personal tutors more efficient (Troxel et al, 2021) and use of technology can lead to improved sharing of information, richer interactions with students, and building of stronger tutor-tutee relationships (McIntosh and Grey, 2017; Lowes, 2020; Advance HE, 2023; Pinnell and Hamilton, 2023). Learning analytics and predictive analytics are useful for personal tutors to target interventions at students who may be struggling. Over the coming years, generative AI is likely to become an increasingly important tool for personal tutors (Essien et al, 2024; Wardle et al, 2025). Offering online alongside in-person tutorials can increase students' engagement with tutorials and the use of technology also promotes innovative pedagogical practice, such as using a flipped approach to personal tutoring (Steele, 2016).

Table 3.3 (Cont.)

Core skills	Explanation and/or example
14. Mentoring	Through mentoring a personal tutor can focus on the personal development of the student. By giving advice, the tutor facilitates the student's learning, development of new skills and personal growth (Mullen and Klimaitis, 2021). Mentoring is particularly effective during transitions (Mullen and Klimaitis, 2021). The mentoring approach in personal tutoring is discussed in Chapter 2.

As a personal tutor, you need to choose which of these core skills, or which skill combinations, are appropriate for particular contexts and specific students. It is through practice and reflection that tutors can develop the experience to understand when one skill is more appropriate than another. The next two critical thinking activities explore two particular skills.

Building genuine rapport

Students place great importance on the quality of the relationship with their personal tutor and this can have a positive effect on their learning and progression (Braine and Parnell, 2011; Small, 2013; Yale, 2020a). Focusing on cultivating a healthy rapport can help to focus a student's attention, improve their enjoyment in learning and increase the time they spend engaging in study. It can help to buffer against some of the stresses and difficulties of starting university (Barefoot, 2000; Ross et al, 2014; Yale, 2019), and can improve students' confidence (Yale, 2020a). A good tutor-tutee relationship improves the overall student experience (Braine and Parnell, 2011; McFarlane, 2016), and satisfaction with their degree programme (Palmer et al, 2009). Tutor–student rapport can increase student engagement levels both inside and outside of the classroom, including developing confidence in public speaking and asking questions of tutors, as well as improving student motivation levels (Starcher, 2011).

Building this relationship and establishing a rapport with students is therefore an essential part of being an effective personal tutor (Wisker et al, 2007; Swain, 2008; Braine and Parnell, 2011). If students have a strong, positive rapport with their tutor and with their cohort they are more likely to understand, and be responsive to, tutor opinions and influence. Relationships should be close, supportive, personal, safe, confidential (unless appropriate to disclose), trusting and empowering (Stephen et al, 2008; Small, 2013; Calcagno et al, 2017; Thomas et al, 2017). This may be something that comes naturally to some practitioners but can take more time and effort for others. Rapport is affected by the tutor's natural personality as well as the student's nature and the context within which they work together. For example, exploring and understanding the difference between seeing students in classes and also meeting them in one-to-ones and group tutorials can greatly affect how rapport is developed. It is important to realise that the skill of building rapport can be learned and improved over time. This is an important skill to develop because a student's relationship with their personal tutor is the embodiment of a student's overall relationship with the institution (Yale, 2019).

Critical thinking activity 4

» *Below are some techniques for building rapport with your students. Think about them in general terms and, from your own opinion and experience, rank the strategies one to six, with one being the technique you view as the most effective and six as the least effective. Are there any more techniques that you can add?*

Building rapport techniques	Rank 1–6
Making and maintaining sensitive eye contact	
Learning students' names and how to pronounce them correctly, and using this in conversation	
Smiling and using open body language	
Learning about students' hobbies, interests and aspirations	
Having informal chats with students before or after your teaching or tutorials	
Validating through active listening and asking open-ended questions	

Now that you have your personalised rank of techniques, start with number one and work through the list by practising and reflecting on the impact with your students.

Decision-making and problem-solving

As you develop your career as an academic and personal tutor, you may find that sometimes you can find yourself 'between a rock and a hard place', facing conflicting pressures. Using creative problem-solving to make difficult decisions can be one of the most challenging parts of the tutor role, even when decisions are clouded by feelings and seemingly without clear consensus or solution (McCabe and McCabe, 2010). Conflicting tutoring ideologies may exist when seeking to meet the needs of the student, your career (by focusing on high-profile research activity) and the institution (Dobinson-Harrington, 2006; Watts, 2011).

Below are some scenarios. It is possible that you could find yourself in similar situations as students progress through their studies. These scenarios are deliberately described as being at specific points in the student lifecycle. Lifecycle stages will be discussed in Chapter 6.

1. It is December, and one of your second-year undergraduate student's mental health is deteriorating. She disclosed her ongoing struggles with anxiety and depression to you in the first year, and you referred her to the student support service for help.

She is a capable student, but during the second year her attendance has been poor and she has missed several assessments. You feel that it would be beneficial for the student to suspend her studies to focus on her mental health, and your department is planning to start a withdrawal procedure. You are also aware that when she suspends, she will no longer be able to access the university's counselling service and will instead have to access treatment through the NHS for which there is a long waiting list in your area.

2. It is January and Wuhao, one of your MSci Biochemistry students, is behind. He has missed several assessments, although he did submit the assessment for your module. He has low attendance and has missed some crucial lab sessions. Your colleagues say he is disengaged in class, although you think he works well in your module. In your opinion, Wuhao has found it difficult to move to the UK and has struggled to settle into the university. As a personal tutor you have tried to support his integration during your one-to-ones, but he seems increasingly isolated. Most of your colleagues say that he should be removed from the course. The retention rates on this programme have been very poor for the last three years.

3. Ella, one of your first year Business Management and Sustainability students, has poor attendance and has received low marks. One of the reasons she has given for this is that she is a carer for her mother who has recently had various hospital appointments for her ongoing health condition. Ella commutes to university from her home, which is over an hour away by public transport. Ella only travels after 09:30 to avoid the expensive rush hour tickets, and therefore usually misses one of her early seminars. Rail works and travel delays also means she's regularly late or absent from classes. At an exam board you have been asked by the chair to recommend whether she should be allowed to re-sit the two modules she failed, and do so alongside taking her second-year modules, or whether she should either interrupt/suspend her studies or terminate them completely.

Critical thinking activity 5

1. For each scenario, consider the following questions.
    a. What decisions or actions would you take?
    b. What factors would you need to consider?

As you hopefully appreciate, there is not always a perfectly correct answer; there is only what is the best option for that context at that time. Doing what is right for the student should be your first priority. However, this is easy to say. Your views may be in conflict with those of the institution. The ideal situation is when the institution always puts the students' interests first through its shared values, policies and decisions. The institutional self-assessment system at the end of this chapter and those that follow illustrate ways in which 'bigger picture' issues can be influenced and prompt you to act.

Professional standards and recognition

Professional standards contain the skills and competencies needed to be an effective personal tutor and are therefore useful to help identify which areas to focus on in skills development. They are also a standard against which to measure effective practice. Used in the UK and beyond is the Professional Standards Framework for Teaching and Supporting Learning in HE (PSF 2023) which underpins Fellowship of Advance HE accreditation (Advance HE, 2023) and, typically, postgraduate certificates in learning and teaching. Generally, at least one of these is a contractual requirement for teaching in HE. The PSF 2023, however, lacks detail on personal tutoring and therefore there was a need for professional standards specific to personal tutoring (Walker, 2020). NACADA (2017) developed core competencies for academic advising, which subsequently informed UK professional standards for personal tutoring through UKAT. UKAT has developed a Professional Framework for Academic Advising & Personal Tutoring (UKAT, 2023), which sets out core skills and competencies of personal tutoring. For individuals or institutions that are interested in formal recognition of their student support through advising and tutoring, UKAT offers professional accreditation, on three different levels, depending on an individual's role in the delivery or leadership of personal tutoring (UKAT, n.d.).

Other relevant professional standards frameworks include the National Occupational Standards (NOS) for Personal Tutoring in Further Education (The Further Education Tutorial Network (FETN), 2013), and the Advance HE Competency Framework for Responding to Students in Distress (2025). Professional standards and recognition are discussed in more detail in Chapter 8.

Summary

The core values of the effective personal tutor are your guiding principles which shape your priorities and, in many cases, dictate your day-to-day behaviours and approach to people and work. It is important to take time to reflect on your core values to make sure these are consistent with students' best interests. These principles are about putting your own agenda aside to focus on the best method(s) for supporting your students. Your values are reflected in how you support students and can be shared by your colleagues, department and institution. When positive values are shared, this improves the organisational culture and ultimately the institution's key performance indicators.

Core skills are your key abilities which are expressed through the day-to-day actions you take to support your students. All personal tutor core skills can be learned and improved with practice and reflection. While having the right skills is important to be an effective personal tutor, it is your core values which will drive you to take those actions consistently.

Critical reflections

1. Compare and contrast the similarities and differences between your own values as an academic and the core values of the personal tutor.

2. To what extent do you believe your PG Cert HE or induction focused on improving your core skills? What, if anything, do you think could be done to improve this?
3. Evaluate whether effective hard skills or soft skills have the greatest impact upon students' success.
4. How well do your students display the core values of the personal tutor or similar positive values? What factors do you believe are influential in this?
5. To what extent does your current institution explain and promote its shared core values to its staff? If you have experience of more than one institution, compare and contrast the two institutions' approaches to its shared core values, using examples.

Personal tutor self-assessment system

What it is for

The personal tutor self-assessment system is designed for you and your institution to self-score current performance and identify targets for improvement against each of the book's chapter themes. You can use it to continually reflect and judge where you and your institution are against particular standards. You will achieve a score at the end of each chapter leading to a cumulative score at the end of the book. This final score will rate you and your institution separately.

How to use it

To identify current standards you should choose the level that best describes you and your educational institution. These can then be used to set targets for future development. Bear in mind when doing this that the levels are sequential and incremental. The content of the level below is not repeated and it is assumed this has already been achieved. For example, to achieve the intermediate level you will have achieved the minimum standard and beginner level.

The personal tutor core values and skills are repeated below to aid this chapter's self-assessment.

Core values:

- high expectations;
- approachability;
- diplomacy;
- being non-judgemental;
- compassion;
- working in partnership with students;
- authenticity;
- being inclusive and valuing students as individuals.

Core skills:

- building genuine rapport *with* your students;
- active listening and *questioning*;
- challenging;
- reflecting back and *summarising*;
- developing independence *and* resilience;
- teamwork;
- decision-making and problem-solving;
- role modelling;
- proactivity, creativity and innovation;
- working under pressure;
- consistency;
- critical thinking;
- digital literacy.

Core values and skills of the personal tutor • 61

PERSONAL TUTOR SELF-ASSESSMENT SYSTEM: Chapter 3 Core values and skills of the personal tutor

	Minimum standard 1 star	Beginner level 2 star	Intermediate level 3 star	Advanced level 4 star	Expert level 5 star
Individual (core values)	My day-to-day actions with students generally display over half of the core values.	I am conscious to display all of the core values through my interactions with students in lessons, group tutorials and one-to-ones.	I often reflect upon the impact that the core values have on the performance of my students. The reflections inform my personal development targets.	Feedback I receive on my classes, group tutorials and one-to-ones reflect the core values.	I explain and promote the impact the core values have on my students, both within and outside of my curriculum team.
Individual (core skills)	I regularly use over half of the core skills in classes, group tutorials and one-to-ones, as well as with colleagues.	I use all of the core skills. They have a clear and positive impact on the relationships with my students and colleagues.	I often reflect upon the impact that the core skills have on the performance of my students. The reflections inform my personal development targets.	Feedback I receive on my classes, group tutorials and one-to-ones reflect the core skills.	I explain and promote the impact the core skills have on my students both within and outside of my programme team.
Institutional (core values)	My institution's values are similar to, or in some cases the same as, the core values. These are shared with new and existing staff at least twice within an academic year.	Deans and Heads of School discuss the core values in meetings. Discussions take place about how staff can embed these into their day-to-day activities, for example, in schemes of work, lesson plans and one-to-ones.	All staff have a constructive appraisal which, in part, reviews how the core values are being embedded into every employee's activities.	All staff have a clear understanding of the core values and the importance of embedding them into their day-to-day work.	Student voice feedback shows that the majority of students feel the core values have a positive impact on their learning, progress and well-being.

PERSONAL TUTOR SELF-ASSESSMENT SYSTEM: Chapter 3 Core values and skills of the personal tutor					
	Minimum standard 1 star	Beginner level 2 star	Intermediate level 3 star	Advanced level 4 star	Expert level 5 star
Institutional (core skills)	Most staff use over half of the core skills with students. Evidence of this is shown through student voice feedback.	All staff receive regular training to develop the core skills and are encouraged to take ownership of this process.	Feedback from line managers routinely comments on employees' use of the core skills with students and colleagues. This feedback informs the appraisal process.	The core skills are consistently and routinely improved through varied strategies. Staff are encouraged to implement ways of assessing how effective the core skills are at improving student outcomes.	Student voice feedback shows the majority of students feel that the core skills employed by staff benefit their learning, progress and well-being.

4 Setting boundaries

Chapter aims

This chapter helps you to:

- identify the following types of boundaries along with their rationale
    - expertise and referral;
    - temporal;
    - independence and engagement;
- establish the necessary boundaries between
    - personal tutors and central services;
    - personal tutors and students;
    - personal tutors and academic colleagues;
    - students and their peers.

Introduction

To perform the personal tutor role effectively it is vital you know your limits and establish firm, clear boundaries to guide your tutoring practice (Luck, 2010; Shaw, 2014; Stenton, 2017; Walker, 2020, 2022). When carrying out tutorial support you are nurturing individuals and small groups of students and this inevitably means that, at times, you will become closely associated with students' emotional and overall well-being. While this type of support is undoubtedly what will make you an effective personal tutor, it does come with a 'health warning'. It exposes you to some of the dangers of getting too close to the issues and by implication, at times, to the students themselves (Luck, 2010). Also, if boundaries are not considered and adhered to, your role as tutor may sometimes feel as though it is morphing into that of social worker or even counsellor (Hughes and Bowers-Brown, 2021; Augustus et al, 2023). The massification of HE, the diversification of the student body, the cost-of-living crisis and an increase in students with complex needs means academics are increasingly called upon to support students experiencing mental health problems and increasing levels of stress (Hughes et al, 2018; Brewster et al, 2022; Augustus et al, 2023). At times like this, boundaries are critical and must be discussed and implemented appropriately. Support for academics to cope with this pressure and to perform their tutoring role effectively must also be forthcoming (Hughes et al, 2018; Brewster et al, 2022; Walker, 2022; Augustus et al, 2023). Advance HE (2025) has outlined good practice for institutions to support staff in responding appropriately to students in distress. One such recommendation is that institutions should have regular, open discussions with staff about the boundaries of their roles, and what the university can do to support staff to maintain those boundaries. Different institutions may place varying boundaries around the tutoring role. You may find the boundary lines drawn by your institution may differ from the examples given here. While the location of the boundary may be important, the manner in which it is agreed, communicated and embedded is even more so.

Clear boundaries, wherever they lie, apply to both academics and to students. In other words, an understanding and articulation of boundaries is absolutely necessary for the benefit and protection of both the student and the tutor. On the student side, recognising boundaries avoids over-dependency and helps develop coping mechanisms (Grey and Osborne, 2020). Effective tutoring should always provide comprehensive support for students while also ensuring they take responsibility for themselves and develop as autonomous and independent learners. A tutor who is overly involved with a student's progress, and who attempts to remove some or all of the challenges they face, potentially stifles opportunities for them to learn, solve their own problems and develop the coping strategies necessary to navigate their learning journey and wider student life. These skills are essential for a student's growth and are key to helping the student develop in confidence, self-esteem and autonomy.

From a tutor's perspective, boundaries can help you to achieve a healthy balance. They can ensure that you are looking after yourself and are able to compartmentalise both your personal and professional responsibilities. This is even more crucial when you are exposed, on a regular basis, to students' distressing or emotional circumstances (Shaw, 2014; McFarlane, 2016; Augustus et al, 2023; Alberts, 2025). If you do not consider or set healthy boundaries then you risk compromising your own emotional well-being and this can easily lead to exhaustion and/or impact on your energy levels, sleep patterns and home life (Hughes et al, 2018; Hughes and Bowers-Brown, 2021; Brewster et al, 2022; Augustus et al, 2023; Alberts, 2024a, 2025). If you feel that this is something you are struggling with then it is important to acknowledge your feelings by confiding in a colleague in order to 'offload' in a constructive way and seek reassurance (Small, 2013; Walker, 2022; Yale and Warren, 2022). Many institutions have someone who oversees personal tutoring provision, such as a senior tutor, who can help navigate the boundaries of the role (Alberts, 2025). Otherwise, a mentor or trusted colleague can provide you with support to unpack these issues and this is discussed in more detail in Chapter 8.

Alberts (2022b) states that care and authenticity are vital components of the tutor–tutee relationship, and this can be demonstrated through proactivity in the personal tutoring relationship. Students can often feel that they are a burden to their personal tutor, so being proactive in reaching out can help them to see that they are not a burden and their tutor cares for them. It should therefore be recognised that personal tutoring is a form of emotional labour.

What is emotional labour? For the purposes of this book, it is defined as attentiveness to students' emotional and personal well-being, also described by students as commitment (Anderson et al, 2020). Students may approach you with issues related to their emotional and personal well-being, and this can lead to challenges for personal tutors. Caring for students' personal needs can be tricky, as it can lead to blurring of boundaries between private and professional life and between rationality and emotion (Anderson et al, 2020). However, Anderson et al (2020) conclude by calling for teaching in HE to be recognised as 'cognitive, emotional and embodied work' (p 1); and acknowledge the powerful influence teachers can have on their students. If this is true of teaching in HE, it is even more relevant to personal tutors, who 'nurture the emotional wellbeing of learners through individualised, holistic support' (Stork and Walker, 2015, p 3). As noted in Chapter 1, the personal tutor role often encompasses being a caretaker or counsellor, or maybe just being a listener.

As a personal tutor, it is important to set your boundaries and to signpost students to the appropriate services when necessary. Establishing boundaries need not be seen as a negative or detrimental to the students' experience but can positively allow tutors to focus on their own areas of expertise and refer students to help which may be more beneficial for them (Dunbar-Morris, 2022). You should therefore make sure that you are familiar with the university support systems and services in place so that you can direct students to the help that they need. This should also reduce the burden on personal tutors by sharing the emotional labour with, for example, the university's well-being or student support services.

It is necessary for you and your students to know where your sources of support begin and end (Luck, 2010; Hughes et al, 2018). However, this may not be easy to establish and maintain, not least because institutional personal tutor policies, processes and established practices can be ambiguous, exist only in policy documents and differ considerably from lived experience (Smith, 2008; Stephen et al, 2008; Hughes et al, 2018). The examples and case study provided in this chapter aim to give you an insight into the subtleties needed to enable you to navigate institutional tutoring provision and to put policy and theory into practice. The chapter also explores and navigates the boundaries between you and your students, among you and your colleagues and between the different aspects of your academic role.

What are boundaries?

Boundaries can be best understood by grouping them into different types and by examining examples alongside their rationale (see Table 4.1).

Table 4.1 Boundary types

Boundary type	Rationale	Examples
Expertise and referral boundaries (Hughes et al, 2018; Walker, 2020; Hughes and Bowers-Brown, 2021; Stuart et al, 2021; Augustus et al, 2023; Wakelin, 2023)	Tutors generally do not have the expertise or training and so may not feel comfortable in providing specific types of information, advice, guidance and support. For example, tutors often lack the professional frame of reference to mitigate risks and therefore to respond appropriately to students' complex difficulties (Augustus et al, 2023). At the same time, colleagues elsewhere in the institution may be employed specifically for these purposes (Hughes et al, 2018).	Student Counselling/well-being: Self-harm, sexual assault, (sexual) abuse, (domestic) violence, suicidal ideation, traumatic bereavement, severe depression, alcohol or substance abuse or anything that would benefit from professional mental health support (Hughes et al, 2018; Hughes and Bowers-Brown, 2021; Augustus et al, 2023). Student Funding: A student whose loan has not come through so cannot afford to both eat and travel to campus that week. Accommodation: A student who needs to escape their home for a place of safety so seeks advice (Luck, 2010). Problems with halls of residence or privately rented accommodation. Disability Support: A student discloses that they feel they may have dyslexia but has no previous diagnosis. Careers and Employability: A student wants help with applying for a graduate training programme. Study Skills Support: A student brings feedback on several assignments which show improvement in the structuring is needed.

Temporal boundaries (Gidman et al, 2000; Wilcox et al, 2005; Aultman et al, 2009; Hughes et al, 2018)	Time is a major determinant in how the personal tutor role is undertaken and how effective it will be (Gidman et al, 2000). Tutors have limited time to support struggling students due to competing or even conflicting demands (McFarlane, 2016; Brewster et al, 2022).	A tutee's complex individual pastoral needs take up excessive amounts of tutor time leading to increased pressure and work hours (Brewster et al, 2022; Augustus et al, 2023). Several students approach tutors who are known to be helpful instead of their allocated personal tutor who appears more focused on their research (Stephen et al, 2008; Morris, 2015; Hughes et al, 2018). To be fair and equitable to all students the institution applies strict time limits to tutorial meetings but some students state that they feel rejected and that the support is hurried and disappointing (Yale, 2019, 2020b).
Independence and engagement boundaries (Wisker et al, 2007; Thomas et al, 2015; Yale, 2020b)	The quality of learning in HE can depend on the correct balance of scheduled contact and directed independent learning (Soilemetzidis et al, 2014). If students become overly dependent the relationship can become damaging and the consequences severe (Luck, 2010; Thomas et al, 2015; Hughes et al, 2018). Students generally accept the idea of independent learning but require support to learn autonomously and reflect upon this learning (Dobinson-Harrington, 2006; Harvey et al, 2006).	A tutor strays too far in their support, becomes overconfident in their ability to help and even provides their personal contact details to students, leading to constant phoning/messaging at all hours or even stalking (Luck, 2010; Hughes et al, 2018). It becomes clear that late enrolling students who were not inducted into a shared understanding of independent learning disengage or become disruptive in classes (Luck, 2010; Thomas et al, 2015). You find that those students who are clearly and actively engaged in their studies benefit from their active involvement on the programme (Thomas and Jones, 2017).

Expertise and referral boundaries

Ideally, tutors might prefer to advise only on academic matters, not seeing pastoral advice and guidance as part of their overall tutoring remit or role (Wilcox et al, 2005; Smith, 2008; Hughes et al, 2018). Many tutors have reported feeling uncomfortable, inadequate, anxious and exhausted by this part of their role, leaving them reluctant, or even unable, to offer students any degree of support on personal issues (Hughes and Bowers-Brown, 2021; Stuart et al, 2021; Augustus et al, 2023; Wakelin, 2023).

The increasing prevalence of student mental health problems means that complicated emotional and pastoral issues are becoming an inevitable part of the tutor's role (Hughes et al, 2018; Hughes and Bowers-Brown, 2021; Brewster et al, 2022; Augustus et al, 2023). Situations like this can result in an imbalance between the support that students need and expect compared with the support that tutors can realistically offer (Grey and Lochtie, 2016; Hughes et al, 2018; Yale, 2019). It is impossible to completely dissociate academic and pastoral issues. Invariably, many academic problems may have a non-academic cause, and vice versa (Smith, 2008; Hughes et al, 2018; Hughes and Bowers-Brown, 2021). In this context it is often helpful to look at what issues may be presenting as symptoms of a situation and those which are the likely cause. It is vital then that you acknowledge the wider factors affecting students, especially those relating to all-important social integration, beyond the curriculum, that 'spill over' into the academic context (Stephen et al, 2008; Race, 2010; McFarlane, 2016). It is important that you do not cross the boundaries of your expertise, but rather listen and then signpost or refer to central, professional student services, because if you do provide ongoing support and this goes wrong, you will be judged not against the qualities of a well-meaning academic but as that of a trained and experienced counsellor (Hughes et al, 2018). Many tutors have navigated this by stressing that they are not mental health professionals (Wilcox et al, 2005; Smith, 2008; Hughes et al, 2018). Universities generally expect staff to listen to a student and then signpost and refer, as appropriate, to central professional student services. It is not sustainable for you to support students alone, so it is vital that you and your institution acknowledge the limits of the personal tutor role and encourage students to seek help or access resources from central services (Hughes et al, 2018). Institutions should also acknowledge that despite signposting or referring, students may continue to seek support from their personal tutor (Hughes et al, 2018; Augustus et al, 2023) and that therefore adequate support and training needs to be in place for academics taking on this role (Augustus et al, 2023).

Clear and effective referral

In order to maintain clear boundaries of expertise, a robust referral system to direct students towards appropriate pastoral support is key (Hughes and Bowers-Brown, 2021; Stuart et al, 2021; McIntosh et al, 2022; Wakelin, 2023). As a tutor you are a gatekeeper to specialist support and it is essential that you find out about the services your university offers to students (Grant, 2006; Shaw, 2014). Signposting can be more complex than it initially appears, often involving proactive engagement that identifies the student's needs and matches this with the correct support service before encouraging them to access it (Hughes et al, 2018). It can be particularly difficult to distinguish between regular stress levels, low motivation or academic anxiety and more severe mental health problems, so it is vital that you conduct an effective preliminary listening exercise and, if you do refer on, ensure it is done sensitively without appearing to 'pass the buck' (Grant, 2006; Hughes et al, 2018). Your institution may have a referral threshold framework in place to help you assess possible risk and identify the best route for referral.

The relationship between tutors and central services can be problematic and academics can worry when they do not hear about the outcome, or students come back frustrated by long wait times (Hughes et al, 2018; Hughes and Bowers-Brown, 2021). Clear and efficient routes of support and referral require effective communication between services as exact boundaries may be negotiable (Luck, 2010; Small, 2013; Hughes et al, 2018; Hughes and Bowers-Brown, 2021). Active referrals are recommended whereby you, as tutor, proactively refer students to specialist support colleagues, including passing on any important information the student has agreed can be shared (in accordance with data protection regulations), ensuring they do not have to recount their circumstances again fully to another member of staff. We suggest you retain details of specific services on hand and, where possible, ask the student to arrange an appointment while you are there with them (so that you are not just pointing students to another part of campus). A 'warm' referral, where you go with the student to the service you are referring them to, helps to ensure students do not 'fall between the cracks'. Limited, targeted follow-ups that fit within your and the student's time constraints are also critical (Smith, 2008; Swain, 2008; Shaw, 2014; Grey and McIntosh, 2017; Advance HE, 2025).

The development of stronger partnerships between tutors and central services should provide greater support for you in your role. It is likely that you remain the first person students turn to for advice if they feel less confident approaching centrally based staff that they do not know (Raby, 2020; Augustus et al, 2023). Calls for closer and greater collaboration between academic programmes and central services are growing in number and volume (see Table 4.1), and this may prove to be essential in meeting the evolving challenges that students and tutors face (Thomas, 2012; Grey and McIntosh, 2017; Thomas et al, 2017; Hughes and Bowers-Brown, 2021).

Temporal boundaries

Academics are often expected to simultaneously perform several high-pressure roles, such as lecturer, assessor, researcher and administrator, each of which carry multiple obligations and responsibilities. This tension can lead academics to make difficult decisions as to how they allocate their time and develop their career (Ghenghesh, 2017; Hughes et al, 2018; Hughes and Bowers-Brown, 2021). In many institutions, bringing in grants and publishing research are prestigious and therefore regularly take precedence over teaching expertise in the criteria for academic promotion. In cases like this, students often complain that their education is only a secondary priority to academic research (Morris, 2015).

Academics can easily spend more time on recording metrics or producing a paper trail for tutorials in order to justify their efforts and this starves them of the time they can spend actually supporting learning or struggling students (Luck, 2010; Gubby and McNab, 2013). Tutors often feel responsible for the approximately 30 students (or in extreme cases more than 100) they have been assigned as tutor. On top of this, tutors who feel that they are not well supported may find it particularly difficult to strike the right balance between being accessible to students, when needed, and being too available. This can mean that they become overwhelmed (Ridley, 2006; Grey and Lochtie, 2016). The time spent on tutoring may seem invisible to other colleagues, particularly those in management positions, when it is not properly considered in workload planning models (Hughes et al, 2018; Brewster et al, 2022). Even if the support required falls outside the clear boundaries of their role, tutors may find that referring on conflicts with their core values and natural responsibility that they feel towards students (Hughes et al, 2018). However, to effectively support students' well-being tutors must first take care of and protect their own needs and this includes maintaining these boundaries wherever possible (Levy et al, 2009; Shaw, 2014).

Boundaries with academic peers

Early on in your academic career, you may gain advice and reassurance from your academic peers and/or a mentor. Nevertheless, effective tutoring means that you also need to be firm in establishing boundaries with your academic colleagues and to work with them effectively as a tutorial team (Small, 2013). In a time of significantly increased workloads and institutional change, tutoring can be seen by some as a low-priority task and merely an inconvenient add-on to the important business of teaching and research (Myers, 2008; Calcagno et al, 2017). If students do not receive the support they require from their assigned tutor they may approach you instead, potentially overloading you as any time spent on this will not be factored into your workload (Stephen et al, 2008; McFarlane, 2016; Hughes et al, 2018). This can be an issue for women in particular (Barnes-Powell and Letherby, 1998; Ashencaen Crabtree and Shiel, 2019; Brewster et al, 2022), because students often perceive their female lecturers to be more approachable, caring and nurturing (Barnes-Powell and Letherby, 1998; Sprague and Massoni, 2005) and therefore are more likely to seek them out for support (Barnes-Powell and Letherby, 1998). Institutions should ensure personal tutoring duties are distributed fairly and equitably across the organisation (Advance HE, 2025). Finding the correct balance (on an individual, department and institutional level) is an important element of maintaining temporal boundaries.

Independence and engagement boundaries

Student engagement has been less secure across the sector since the Covid-19 pandemic and the cost-of-living crisis (WonkHE, 2024a). Given that time is a priority for academics, it is perhaps unsurprising that you may become frustrated by apparent disengagement or levels of non-attendance among your student cohort, particularly in the face of their increasing academic and pastoral needs (Rhodes and Jinks, 2005; Stephen et al, 2008). In order to be an effective personal tutor, and maintain a balance between the different aspects of the academic role, student–tutor boundaries are essential (Grey and McIntosh, 2017). It is advised that ground rules, boundaries, guidelines and expectations for the relationship are set at your first meeting so that both parties may be held accountable (Stevenson, 2006; Swain, 2008; Ralston and Hoffshire, 2017; Yale, 2019). This can be done through 'contracting', a practice common in coaching (Foy, 2020; Gannon, 2025), where the ground rules of the relationship are explicitly discussed and even recorded in a contract, so that both parties know what to expect and what is expected from them. It is important to explore these boundaries in a group as well as in a one-to-one context given that students need to work well with one another in order to settle into student life and develop autonomy. Student engagement, management of expectations, and student autonomy is discussed in more detail in Chapter 7.

Boundaries are as important to the student as they are to you because they will need to be an active participant in their own education (Habermas, 1973 cited in Cook, 2017; Augustus et al, 2023). Tutoring exists to help students become independent and promote a shared understanding of independent learning which can be vital to supporting their success (Broad, 2006; Thomas et al, 2015; Grey and McIntosh, 2017). It is advisable that tutors do not suggest options to students but instead ask probing questions that facilitate engagement and ultimately help the individual make a transition from passivity to ownership (Gurbutt and Gurbutt, 2015). Egan and Reese's (2018) well-established *Skilled Helper Model* (Figure 4.1) can help you to help students manage their own problems and empower them to better help themselves. Their model is used frequently in coaching and counselling situations where the aim is to ensure that students are empowered to

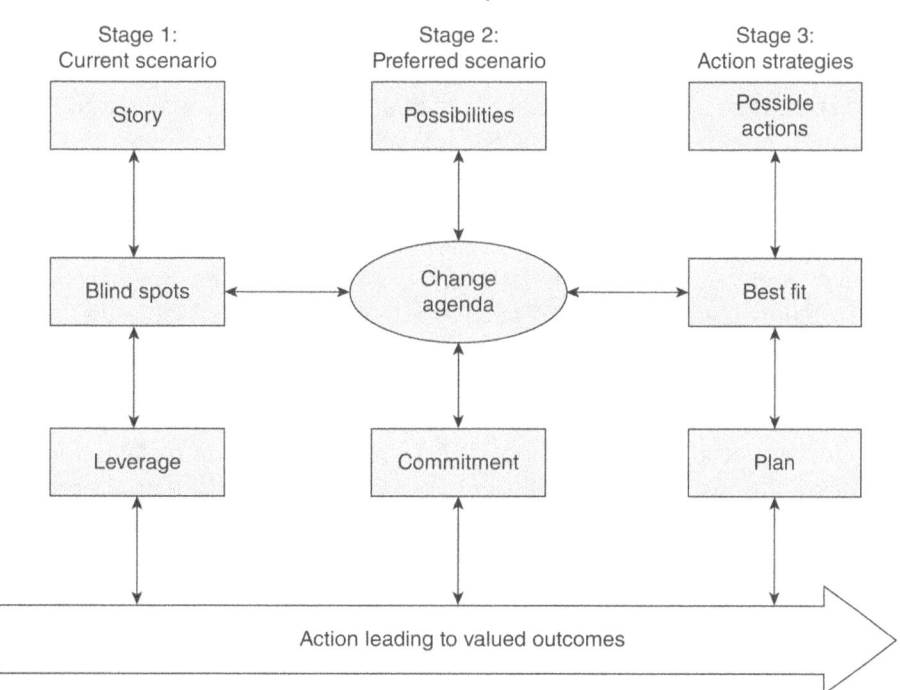

Figure 4.1 *Skilled Helper Model*

(Reproduced with permission, Egan and Reese, 2018)

manage their own problems more effectively and also explore any opportunities available to them. It can be a very useful and productive framework to use in a tutorial context. The model has three main stages: (1) current scenario, (2) preferred scenario and (3) action strategies. The first exploratory stage is to ensure that you are able to gather the facts about a given situation and reflect those back to the student in a non-judgemental way. This requires positive body language, active listening, acceptance and empathy as well as the ability to summarise, focus and ask questions. You should begin to challenge the student's viewpoint in a way which gets them to consider their situation from a variety of different perspectives. There are a number of reasons for this. The second stage is to consider some of the options that are available to them and to help them to commit to a preferred scenario. At this stage it might be helpful for you, as tutor, to consider a change agenda, helping the student to explore their feelings and to unpack the issues so that they are not too overwhelming. The third 'action strategies' stage involves encouraging the student to look at the ways forward and to commit to action. The intention is to motivate the student to take action and take realistic steps to improve their situation. We discussed alternative approaches that you can use in addition to this model in Chapter 2.

The rate at which students become independent may be influenced by their previous educational experiences. These can be negotiated and overcome via open conversation and supported by reflection early on in their course (Dobinson-Harrington, 2006; Bates and Kaye, 2014; Grey and McIntosh, 2017). The role you may play in discovering the aspirations of students and setting their expectations as part of their induction (Morgan, 2012b) is explained further in Chapter 5.

Tutor support is important in facilitating student engagement, not only with you as a tutor but with the institution, their peers and their course which, according to a significant body of evidence, leads to various benefits including higher motivation and commitment, improved mental health and greater levels of well-being (McIntosh, 2017; Thomas and Jones, 2017). While 'student engagement' has no fixed definition, it can be broadly themed into academic engagement, social engagement, and personal development. Examples of these include student representation, student consultation, student involvement in curriculum design and peer-learning initiatives. Such opportunities have increased in significance in recent years (Bovill, 2020b; Gravett et al, 2020; Matthews and Dollinger, 2023; Andreanoff et al, 2024) and are part of the partnership approach to education endorsed by students, academics and the HE sector in general (Little et al, 2009; Thomas and Jones, 2017). Various methods of engaging with students and measuring student engagement are covered further in Chapter 5. The ultimate aim is that students fulfil their role and obligations, as may be outlined in your institutional student charter, potentially including taking 'responsibility for managing their own learning: actively engaging in their course; ensuring they spend sufficient regular time in private study, and participating fully in group learning activities' (Department for Business, Innovation and Skills, 2011, p 11).

Student peer boundaries

While a good working relationship with a tutor is something students feel is important, their relationship with their peers is where they feel they gain most support (Wilcox et al, 2005; Cameron et al, 2015; Thomas et al, 2015; Lochtie and McConnell, 2024). Both types of relationship need to be present in order for a student to thrive (McIntosh, 2017; Varghese and Zijlstra-Shaw, 2021). Tutors can play a key role in establishing peer-learning communities which provide support and outline boundaries for students when working with each other (Calcagno et al, 2017; McIntosh, 2017; George and Rapley, 2022; Wright, 2022; Emsley-Jones et al, 2024). Peer interaction can be encouraged by engaging students with, and endorsing sections of, your student charter or student learning agreement, which typically refers to diversity, inclusion, respect and communication. Although not all institutions have these, those that do should use them to set clear mutual expectations concerning courtesy and professionalism while emphasising the need to treat fellow students equally and respectfully (Department for Business, Innovation and Skills, 2011). The development of these attributes is important in preparing students for the workplace, as well as combatting the challenges of group work tensions and peer to peer plagiarism. Rather than assuming that students know how to act towards each other, it should be acknowledged that they are likely to be at various stages of development in these areas. Student charters should be embedded into the institution as 'living documents' and should be referred to continually, not just when they are violated. These charters are open to ongoing review with active student involvement (including in induction) to encourage ownership (Dunbar-Morris, 2021). If your institution does not have a student charter, or similar document, consider conducting a group exercise at an early stage in the student journey which encourages students to work with each other to devise a set of statements to which they are all happy to subscribe. These statements should be broad and outline mutual expectations, roles and responsibilities. They should encourage students to work in partnership with their peers and also establish boundaries for working with you as the tutor. If this document is co-created, with the tutor as facilitator, then it becomes easier for students to understand and adhere to these boundaries. Group tutorials can play a significant role in supporting this activity and are discussed further in Chapter 6.

The difficulty of 'letting go' and when to do it

Inevitably, in some tutoring contexts, there is a limit to the involvement that tutors have in working with a student to provide the support that they need. The key is understanding what level of support can be realistically provided, your capacity to provide this support and knowing when this limit has been reached. At this point, 'letting go' and handing over to colleagues in specialist support services is necessary, especially when you feel you have exhausted all of your own supportive measures. The question is, how do you know when this is the case?

Critical thinking activity 1

» When did you last think that your own capacity to support students had been reached? Did you notice at the time that this had reached a limit? How did you know and what did you do about it?

Discussion

The answer you provide to the critical thinking activity will typically relate to the type of boundary you have reached. If it is a boundary of 'expertise', it could be that your level of knowledge, skill or experience is not sufficient to provide the student with further help and support. Your capacity to manage these issues can be improved and informed by guidance from central services, and with increasing experience over time, but this requires an honest conversation about whether you are comfortable enough to continue providing advice and guidance to the student. If the boundary relates to 'independence' it could be that you have given the student every opportunity, and significant support, to succeed but they have consistently either not acted upon that opportunity or not fulfilled their responsibilities to act on the advice that has been given. This might be due to inactivity, disengagement or even inability. When reviewing temporal boundaries, your limit could be harder to pinpoint. Here it is important to engage in regular conversations with your line manager, senior tutor, academic peers or a mentor and central services about the amount of time you are involved in tutoring, as a finite resource, and the boundaries between yourself and colleagues or central services as well as the teaching/tutoring/research boundaries within your role.

Some of the issues and challenges shown in the final column of Table 4.1 may negatively affect institutional performance indicators such as retention, success, attendance, punctuality, persistence and graduation rates. Indeed, there can be a tension between individual student issues and institutional influences. You may find yourself in the middle of these competing pressures. However tempting it is to try and tackle such issues yourself, the boundaries we have been discussing need respecting for the good of all parties, particularly students. These boundaries need to be clear and consistent and should be reviewed continually throughout your career, responding to your experience and interactions with students as their needs change. It is also important to remember that it can be beneficial to work as part of a tutorial team which provides consistent advice and support. This may be out of your control as an individual tutor but it is advisable that you encourage the sharing of best practice with colleagues wherever possible.

CASE STUDY

Amanda's one-to-one with Nico

The following dialogue is an excerpt taken from a one-to-one meeting between Amanda, a second year Sociology student, and her personal tutor, Nico.

NICO: *Hi Amanda. How are you?*

AMANDA: *Yeah, I'm okay.*

[Amanda is using closed body language and Nico notices that she appears tense and nervous.]

NICO: *Come in and have a seat. So, you wanted to have a meeting with me today. What's on your mind?*

AMANDA: *I've got two timed assessments next week and I'm feeling a bit overwhelmed. I don't think I'm able to get them both in. I'm so behind with my reading. I missed some lectures and I'm trying to catch up with them on the recording.*

NICO: *Okay, what assessments are these?*

AMANDA: *First I've got 'Thinking Sociologically' and I've got 'Sociology in a Global Context' a couple of days later.*

NICO: *You said you missed some lectures, what was the reason for that?*

AMANDA: *Well ... It was my mental health. I've been struggling again.*

NICO: *Okay. Did you go and see student services after our last meeting?*

AMANDA: *I did talk to someone in student support services, but I haven't been back.*

NICO: *Why haven't you been back?*

AMANDA: *I don't know ... I find it difficult to talk to people that I don't know very well. I'd prefer to talk to you.*

NICO: *Okay. I do want to support you but remember that I am not an expert in mental health, and the people in the student services are. They will be able to help you much better than I can. I can help you manage the impact of the mental issues on your studies, but I am unable to help you address the source of them. They have supported many students in the past and may know about a whole range of potential solutions that may not be obvious to me. I don't always have the time needed to talk through all these things either and I don't want to put you at a disadvantage.*

AMANDA: *Hmmm.*

NICO: *So, let's get you back in touch with student services. There is an online form you fill in and they will get in contact with you. Do you want to fill it in now? You should hear from them by the end of the week.*

AMANDA: *Okay. I can do it now.*

[Amanda gets out her laptop and fills in the contact form.]

NICO: *So, you've missed quite a few lectures and seminars this term. Remember that it is your responsibility to attend classes regularly and to let us know if there is anything that is preventing you from doing that. Do you think that your struggles with your mental health are an ongoing issue that may affect you in the future? Because if they are, we should consider contacting Disability Support, who can help to put in place adjustments for you that should make it less difficult for you to attend classes.*

AMANDA: *Hmmm. I don't know. I've had it since first year, so maybe?*

NICO: *Okay, do you want to have a think about it? I'll email you a link to the Disability Support website. Have a look through. The website tells you what kind of support they can offer you and also says how to get in contact with them.*

AMANDA: Okay, thanks. I'll have a look.

NICO: So, coming back to your timed assessments. How are you feeling about them?

AMANDA: I guess I'm okay with 'Thinking Sociologically' but it's the 'Sociology in a Global Context' one that I'm worried about because I did really badly in the essay. I didn't get a lot of feedback, so I don't really know why.

NICO: 'Thinking Sociologically' is Paul's unit isn't it? Have you asked him for further feedback?

AMANDA: I tried to after the seminar – I approached him two weeks in a row but he always rushes off. Would you be able to have a look at it for me instead?

NICO: I want to help but the feedback would be specific to that unit. Paul has a much better idea of the subject and what you were asked to discuss in the essay. It would be better if you emailed Paul to ask him for an appointment. Have you got his email?

AMANDA: Okay, I'll email him. I can find his address on the VLE.

NICO: Did you know the Study Skills Service has a whole range of online and in-person workshops to help students? They can help with time management and strategies for revision. Some of my other tutees have been and found the sessions really useful. Shall we have a look at their website to see if there is anything on in the next few days that may be useful for you? Look, they have a session on managing stress tomorrow, and one on how to prepare for timed assessments later on in the week.

AMANDA: That looks good.

NICO: Shall I email you the link to their booking page?

AMANDA: Yes, please.

NICO: Okay, good. I've got another student waiting for me outside. Do let me know if you decide to contact Disability Support. And good luck with your assessments.

Critical thinking activity 2

1. List which type of boundaries (contained within the chapter and in Table 4.1) are set or recognised by Nico and explain how he does this.
2. For each boundary, explain what benefits might be gained for Amanda and Nico.

Discussion

You will have your own thoughts about the manner in which Nico conducted the one-to-one meeting with Amanda. There are no fixed rules and regulations governing how tutorial meetings are conducted and it's important to develop your own style and acknowledge that this may change depending on the situation and the issues up for discussion. Also, body language (referenced in the transcript) can be a useful cue when listening and responding to a student during a tutorial. Your initial thoughts and reactions to what is discussed in these meetings are useful insights into your own tutorial approach. The topic of practice in one-to-one tutorials is covered in more detail in Chapter 6.

In terms of the boundary types established, we have identified the following examples.

Expertise and referral

> Nico: *Did you know the Study Skills Service has a whole range of online and in-person workshops to help students? They can help with time management and strategies for revision. Some of my other tutees have been and found the sessions really useful. Shall we have a look at their website to see if there is anything on in the next few days that may be useful for you?*

Nico has a good awareness of the support services available across the institution. Not only does he have the information to hand, but he also endorses the services by drawing on the experience of other students, making it a more positive option for Amanda.

> Nico: *Okay. I do want to support you but remember that I am not an expert in mental health, and the people in the student services are. They will be able to help you much better than I can. I can help you manage the impact of the mental issues on your studies, but I am unable to help you address the source of them.*

Again, Nico is aware of the limits of his expertise. He reassures Amanda that he's very much interested in providing her with support but that in order to discuss things further she should seek the help of a trained colleague.

Temporal

> Nico: *… I don't always have the time needed to talk through all these things either and I don't want to put you at a disadvantage.*

Nico is managing Amanda's expectations. Nico knows he has little time available, as he needs to respond to reviewers' comments on a journal article by the end of the week. He makes it clear to Amanda that he does not have the time required to talk through and unpack these issues. He makes sure that Amanda does not rely on his support alone and provides an opportunity for her to become more independent.

> Nico: *… I've got another student waiting for me outside.*

Nico sets healthy limits on the conversation to ensure that Amanda does not become over-reliant on lengthy conversations with him. He is attempting to divide his time equitably between Amanda and his other tutees.

Independence and engagement

> Nico: *So, you've missed quite a few lectures and seminars this term. Remember that it is your responsibility to attend classes regularly and to let us know if there is anything*

that is preventing you from doing that. Do you think that your struggles with your mental health are an ongoing issue that may affect you in the future? Because if they are, we should consider contacting Disability Support, who can help to put in place adjustments for you that should make it less difficult for you to attend classes.

Nico reminds Amanda of her own roles and responsibilities in the learning process. He sticks to the facts, has knowledge of the classes that she has missed, and lets her know there is help available to support her continued engagement with the course.

NICO: *... Have you asked him for further feedback? ... It would be better if you emailed Paul to ask him for an appointment. Have you got his email?*

Nico uses specific questions to assess Amanda's engagement with another lecturer. He uses these to determine whether or not she has sought feedback and encourages her to take further action.

We have highlighted some boundaries that were recognised and set between Nico and Amanda. The case study also contained examples of boundaries with academic peers, central services and between tutoring/research alongside examples of effective referral arrangements.

It is important to pay attention to the manner in which Nico approaches this conversation. How does he get these messages across to Amanda and is his approach grounded in the personal tutor core values of Chapter 3? In the context of the conversation as a whole, Nico approaches his tutorials supportively and exhibits the core values of approachability, compassion, being non-judgemental and embodying a partnership approach. It may be useful to consider the dialogue you might use in a similar situation as well as the tone and body language you would employ to deliver it.

One observation is that Nico talks more than Amanda. The use of open questions could have elicited more information from her. It is also important to avoid coming across as too patronising, especially if you are encouraging a student to commit to action. This is critical in the context of an adult learning environment where you are empowering and championing students to take ownership of their learning. The comment *Remember that it is your responsibility to attend classes regularly* could be rephrased as *Can you remind me what the student charter says about attendance?* The latter gives Amanda an opportunity to talk as well as checking if she actually remembers any initial conversations in class about the charter.

Another strategy is to encourage the student to identify and adhere to defined tutorial boundaries. This can be done with effective use of active listening and open questioning (considered in more depth in Chapter 6) but it does require a degree of confidence and commitment to practising this approach over time. This approach helps to reframe the situation and encourages the student not only to talk more in the meeting but also, more importantly, to understand better their role and responsibilities, which supports greater student autonomy and ownership. The overarching rationale for setting student boundaries is that for the student to truly engage they should be encouraged to take responsibility and be independent. A conversation about boundaries can also be used in the context of a small group tutorial where students can work together to discuss how to access support, advice and guidance. This often works well as part of a discussion about expectations, roles and responsibilities.

Critical thinking activity 3

Have a look at the below list of issues (*Table 4.2*) and decide whether you would signpost the student to another service within your institution, you would help the student yourself, or you feel it would not be appropriate for a student to receive help for this issue. Tick one of the three boxes: signpost, offer help or not appropriate, then give reasons for your choices. These reasons could be due to your university policy or your own expertise boundaries (see Chapter 4), for example.

Table 4.2 Signpost or not?

Issue	Signpost	Offer help	Not appropriate	Why?
Proofread an assignment draft				
Read an assignment draft				
Help with planning an essay				
Help with dissertation				
Help understand feedback				
Give assignment extension				
Help dispute/change a grade				
Listen to a personal issue				
Act as a counsellor				
Give careers advice				
Write a reference for job or further study				
Financial help/advice				
Give advice on university policies or procedures				

Summary

This chapter has demonstrated the importance of setting healthy boundaries, both for yourself and for your students. These boundaries promote well-being and protect both parties. The aim of setting these boundaries is to ensure that your students are aware of how to access the support they need and are also supported to become more responsible, autonomous and independent. The chapter identifies and defines the different types of boundaries that are most relevant to the personal tutoring process, alongside specific examples and rationale for adhering to these, including how to make effective referrals to centralised and specialist support services. The chapter also considers how boundaries with students, academic peers and central services can be set and reinforced by carefully managing interactions with them. Through an example of a one-to-one conversation with a student the chapter considers how this can be done in practice.

Critical reflections

1. In your personal tutor role, to what extent do you believe you, your students and your colleagues know and recognise the boundaries that should exist between one another?

2. Can you think of particular students (individuals and groups) who would benefit from having a clear conversation about boundaries? What types of boundaries would this conversation include? How will you go about doing this and will you need to make reference to any other institutional documents such as the student charter?

3. To what extent did you have the opportunity to discuss boundary setting (those boundaries examined in this chapter or others) as part of your induction, staff development programme or PG Cert HE course?

4. How much emphasis does your current institution (and your colleagues within it) place on setting boundaries and conducting referrals? What do you think could be done to improve this?

Personal tutor self-assessment system

As a reminder, the main boundary types are: expertise and referral, temporal and independence and engagement, as detailed in the following table.

PERSONAL TUTOR SELF-ASSESSMENT SYSTEM: Chapter 4 Setting boundaries

	Minimum standard 1 star	Beginner level 2 star	Intermediate level 3 star	Advanced level 4 star	Expert level 5 star
Individual	I clearly outline the various sources of support available to students, and set boundaries between myself and them, at the outset of their course. I keep to these expertise/referral, temporal and independence/engagement boundaries in my everyday practice.	I revisit these boundaries in group tutorials. Through one-to-ones and other support meetings, students have a clear idea of these key boundaries.	Through individual meetings, my students are progressively becoming more able to recognise the boundaries. My students benefit from clarity on a range of boundaries that help them to take responsibility and succeed.	My students are becoming responsible and independent as a result of these boundaries. I continually review the boundaries I keep in my own work and with students, colleagues and central departments for the benefit of all.	Effective boundary setting is embedded in all of my work and interactions with my students. As a result of this and other factors, my students take responsibility and are independent while I maintain a healthy balance in my work.
Institutional	My institution ensures that all students are given clear information on the various sources of support that are available and what is expected of them in terms of independent learning.	My institution provides clear guidance to staff on the necessary boundaries within academic roles, between staff and students and between student support services. Referrals are managed effectively.	Departments and/or support functions allocate and review resources relating to setting boundaries. Line managers discuss boundary setting and referrals with staff individually for the purposes of student and staff welfare.	Departments or support functions actively seek students' views in boundary setting and integrate these into resources. Academics are supported in maintaining a balance between all aspects of their role.	A range of different types of boundaries are set by departments or support functions which are informed by students themselves. As a result of this and other factors, students take responsibility and are independent.

5 Key activities: Identifying and supporting student populations

Chapter aims

This chapter helps you to:

- identify the various student populations you may encounter as a personal tutor and methods and good practice to support them.

This includes:

- clarifying the terms that may be used to describe 'at risk' students;
- identifying different student populations, understanding different risk factors and putting plans in place to support vulnerable students;
- exploring effective ways of working with students with additional needs including potential safeguarding considerations;
- understanding the tracking, monitoring and supporting of student progress in terms of rationale, methods (including dashboard-based learning/engagement analytics) and benefits.

Introduction

In this chapter and the next, we cover all of the key activities that a student is likely to benefit from, either directly or indirectly, if they are given effective tutorial support. We offer you a toolkit of actions to identify student needs, increase their motivation to learn and achieve or exceed their targets. Furthermore, to help each student to achieve these aims, we look at tracking and monitoring strategies that you can use to ensure that all of your students receive the necessary support from the wider institution.

Personal tutoring tools that cover all aspects of a student's experience are illustrated through several key personal tutoring activities, including tracking and monitoring students, identifying their support needs and providing activities which enable effective support for them as they progress through the key lifecycle stages which are identified in Chapter 6.

What is the purpose of the personal tutor key activities?

You will spend your time supporting students in a variety of ways. The main reason you assess the needs of your students along with tracking and monitoring them is to provide support so that each student has the best chance of succeeding on their course, and also to help them successfully progress on to their next step. To do this you will be implementing individual actions to increase students' motivation, supporting them to overcome or reduce as many of their barriers to learning as possible and developing their employability skills. The activities and strategies within this chapter and the next are designed to facilitate student success, student engagement, progression and 'learning gain'. Learning gain is 'the improvement in knowledge, skills, work-readiness and personal development made by students during their time spent in higher education' (Rogaten and Rienties, 2021, p 17). Related terms include 'value-added' and 'distance travelled'.

The tracking and monitoring of students

The close, regular, ongoing and systematic tracking and monitoring of student progress and performance is widely considered as a necessity in any successful student intervention or support system (McFarlane, 2016; Thomas et al, 2017; Wong and Li, 2020). Research suggests that students welcome this close attention, commonly referred to as personalised learning, and regular, proactive follow-up contact. A lack of contact and/or follow up can diminish a student's perception of the importance of the tutor–tutee relationship (Small, 2013; Ghenghesh, 2017; Yale, 2019). Though it is important to be aware of the limits and boundaries involved in effective tutorial relationships (see Chapter 4), a close monitoring of students is generally recommended (Naidoo and Jamieson, 2005). This is particularly the case for students who may be categorised as at risk or vulnerable (Calcagno et al, 2017).

What do we mean by at risk, non-traditional, disadvantaged and vulnerable students?

While the sector aims to address inequality so that all students, regardless of background, are supported to access, succeed in and progress from HE, outcomes for different student groups are not equal (Advance HE, 2021, 2024; Bolton and Lewis, 2023). In 1983, an article entitled *A Nation at Risk*, published by the National Commission on Excellence in Education, used the term 'at risk' and the term has since been used to refer to certain groups of HE students (Jones and Watson, 1990). Within the HE sector, the expression 'at risk' is sometimes connected to other terms or used interchangeably with them. We have made some subtle distinctions between these different, but potentially related, concepts below. It is critical to understand that while various terms are used to describe certain student characteristics, backgrounds and behaviours, they must not be used to label, homogenise or place limits on a student's ability. Instead, appreciating a student's context can help you to understand how to support them to succeed.

The term 'non-traditional students' generally refers to those students from low-participation neighbourhoods where, historically, fewer people have gone on to pursue HE opportunities. The term may also be used when referring to the changing profile of students as a result of demographic and sociocultural factors, related to widening participation (Small, 2013; Webb et al, 2017). Factors affecting, but not exclusive to, non-traditional students include disadvantage, for example, low income levels or an educational background which has restricted acquisition of knowledge, abilities and skills (Stephen et al, 2008; Reay et al, 2010; McIntosh, 2017; Webb et al, 2017; Bolton and Lewis, 2023; Office for Students, 2023b). These disadvantages may, in some cases, make them more vulnerable, impacting negatively on attendance, behaviour or completion of their course (McIntosh and Shaw, 2017). For example, the cost-of-living crisis has had a greater impact on students from disadvantaged backgrounds, and they are more likely to miss deadlines because of paid work (The Sutton Trust, 2023). This can increase the risk of non-completion or under-achievement against target grades (McIntosh and Shaw, 2017; Thomas et al, 2017).

There are other student groups, for example, Black students, students from traveller communities, those with disabilities, and mature students (those who are over 21 years of age), who may also experience barriers to success (OfS, 2023b). In 2023, the Office for Students (OfS) introduced the Equality of Opportunity Risk Register (EORR) which draws on research to outline 12 sector-wide risks to students' opportunity to access and succeed in HE. Each risk covers an area where certain student groups do not experience the same level of opportunity as other student groups, such as information and guidance, application success rate and insufficient academic or personal support (OfS, 2023b). The EORR was developed to help universities identify which of their students are most at risk in order to make arrangements to mitigate these risks. Such arrangements are enshrined in *Access and Participation Plans* (OfS, 2018), which HE providers in England have to submit as part of their registration (in the Office for Students' regulatory framework) in order to charge the highest level of tuition fees. Access and Participation Plans are published and publicly available on the OfS website.

What characteristics might mean a student is at risk or vulnerable?

How might you identify whether your students could be deemed at risk or vulnerable? Table 5.1 outlines some of the characteristics of at risk or vulnerable students. The characteristics are not exhaustive (for example, gender and religion, which are not covered, may be important factors) but they provide a reminder of the diversity of the student population. To enable you to think more broadly about where these influences may stem from, we have grouped them under the headings of student characteristics, home life and cultural/economic factors. It is important to keep in mind that a student may have more than one of these characteristics and that these intersect, meaning that, rather than seeing student characteristics or identities as mutually exclusive and separate, they can in fact interact and overlap, creating risks and circumstances that are unique and specific to that individual student. This intersectionality of student characteristics thus reiterates the need for individualised, tailored student support.

Table 5.1 Characteristics of at risk or vulnerable students

Student characteristics	**Home life**	**Cultural/economic factors**
A student who: • has a history or signs of alcohol and/or substance misuse (Shaw, 2014; Harrison, 2017) • has a disability, learning or mental health difficulty (McIntosh and Shaw, 2017; Hughes et al, 2018; Office for Students, 2023b) • is a part-time student (Thomas et al, 2017; Webb et al, 2017) • is a LGBTQ+ student (Office for Students, 2023b); • is a mature student (Thomas et al, 2017; Office for Students, 2023b) • has displayed offending behaviour and/or has had contact with the police or justice system (Harrison, 2017)	A student who: • has a history of abusive relationships, safeguarding issues or domestic violence within the family (Wootton, 2007; Watts, 2011) • is care experienced, estranged from their parents, whose parent was in the armed forces, or the first generation in their family to attend university (Thomas, 2006; Lochtie, 2015; Harrison, 2017; McIntosh and Shaw, 2017; Office for Students, 2023b); • has a history of homelessness or is living in unsafe housing (Harrison, 2017) • is pregnant, a student parent, responsible for dependents, or a young carer (McFarlane, 2016; Office for Students, 2023b) • is a commuter student or lives with a parent (Thomas and Jones, 2017; Office for Students, 2023b)	A student who: • is from a low-income household (OfS, 2023b). Eligibility for free school meals is often used as a proxy for low income. Other proxies include coming from an area of low young participation in HE (POLAR4) or high deprivation (IMD) • is ethnically minoritised (Thomas et al, 2017; Webb et al, 2017) • is an asylum seeker (McIntosh and Shaw, 2017) • is an international student, particularly if English is an additional language (Lamont, 2005) • has been previously identified as being at risk or vulnerable by a former educational institution or local authority

The way each of these characteristics is linked to the 12 specific risks of equality of opportunity for students (OfS, 2023b) is outlined in Table 5.2.

Table 5.2 Risks linked to student characteristics

Student characteristics	Related risk to equality of opportunity											
	Knowledge and skills	Information and guidance	Perception of HE	Application success rate	Limited choice of course	Insufficient academic support	Insufficient personal support	Mental health issues	Ongoing impacts of Covid-19	Cost pressures	Capacity issues	Progression from HE
Low income/FSM	✓	✓	✓	✓	✓	✓	✓	✓	✓	✓	✓	✓
First in family	✓	✓		✓		✓	✓			✓		✓
Disabled students	✓	✓		✓	✓	✓	✓	✓	✓	✓	✓	✓
Mental health condition						✓	✓	✓				✓
Mature	✓	✓	✓	✓	✓	✓	✓	✓		✓	✓	✓
Black		✓	✓	✓		✓	✓	✓			✓	✓
White	✓	✓	✓									
Asian					✓	✓	✓					
Mixed ethnicity	✓	✓	✓	✓		✓	✓	✓				✓
Other ethnicity	✓		✓	✓		✓	✓	✓				✓
Travelling communities	✓	✓				✓	✓					✓
Commuter						✓	✓			✓		
Service child	✓	✓			✓	✓	✓					
Young carers	✓	✓			✓	✓	✓			✓		✓

Table 5.2 (Cont.)

Student characteristics	Related risk to equality of opportunity											
	Knowledge and skills	Information and guidance	Perception of HE	Application success rate	Limited choice of course	Insufficient academic support	Insufficient personal support	Mental health issues	Ongoing impacts of Covid-19	Cost pressures	Capacity issues	Progression from HE
LGBTQ+					✓		✓	✓		✓		
SE background of 'never worked' or 'long-term unemployed'						✓	✓					✓
SE background of 'Lower supervisory and technical occupations'						✓	✓					✓
SE background of 'small employers and own account workers'												✓
SE background of 'intermediate occupations'							✓					✓
SE background of 'routine occupations' or 'semi-routine occupations'						✓	✓					✓
Christian							✓					
Spiritual							✓					
Muslim							✓			✓		✓

Key activities: Identifying and supporting • 87

Table 5.2 (Cont.)

Student characteristics	Related risk to equality of opportunity											
	Knowledge and skills	Information and guidance	Perception of HE	Application success rate	Limited choice of course	Insufficient academic support	Insufficient personal support	Mental health issues	Ongoing impacts of Covid-19	Cost pressures	Capacity issues	Progression from HE
Buddhist							✓					
Hindu							✓					
Jewish			✓				✓					
Sikh							✓					
Estranged		✓				✓	✓	✓		✓	✓	✓
Care experienced	✓	✓	✓	✓	✓	✓	✓	✓	✓	✓	✓	✓
Child in need	✓					✓	✓					
Parents					✓	✓						✓
Gender	✓ - M	✓ - F		✓ - F								✓ - F
Prisoners	✓			✓	✓	✓						
Vocational learners												✓

Source: Reproduced from the Office for Students. Contains public sector information licensed under the Open Government Licence v3.0.

Widening participation

The Dearing Report (Dearing, 1997) set out to increase participation in HE among, for example, students from low-income households and ethnically minoritised students. Data from HESA (2025) show that participation from those in low-participation neighbourhoods has been steadily rising. There has also been a small increase in students in receipt of the Disabled Students' Allowance (DSA) (HESA, 2025). Universities and colleges are required to submit Access and Participation Plans in order to commit to equal opportunities, with time-bound targets for improvements (OfS, 2023a). What does this mean for personal tutoring? As a personal tutor, it is important to be aware of the characteristics of the students you are supporting, some of which are mentioned in Table 5.2.

Campus, commuter and remote learning students

Commuter students, those who live at home and travel onto campus, represent around 25 per cent of the young students in the UK and these students are often those from poorer backgrounds (Donnelly and Gamsu, 2018). They may have lower outcomes than students studying on campus and can experience a reduced sense of belonging (Hallam, 2023).

Since the Covid-19 pandemic, more students have been undertaking remote or hybrid learning (Bangs and Gallacher, 2023). For tutors working with such students, more challenges may be experienced, for example, ensuring students are engaged during remote meetings. This can be particularly difficult if students do not wish to switch cameras on. Student retention can also be a problem for remote students, with graduation rates typically being lower than on campus students (Simpson, 2013; Sánchez-Elvira Paniagua and Simpson, 2018).

For remote learning and commuter students, a sense of mattering may be more important than a sense of belonging (Zawada, 2022), which could be difficult to achieve for students who do not live on campus or close by (Hallam, 2023). While as tutors we have limited influence on where a student lives, we can certainly contribute to their sense of mattering by taking an active interest in them. Getting to know your tutees individually can help them to feel that they matter to someone. You can do this by, for example, remembering details they have told you and asking them how they are getting on, or even just remembering their names and saying hello when you see them on campus.

Inclusive personal tutoring

Not all students feel equally supported at university. A study found that Black nursing students can feel unsupported by their personal tutors and that tutors at times lack a cultural understanding (McLetchie-Holder et al, 2025). It also found that personal tutors felt less confident in supporting students with a different cultural background than their own (McLetchie-Holder et al, 2025).

So how do we as tutors make sure that our practice is inclusive? It is important for personal tutors to increase their cultural awareness. Your institution may provide cultural competency training, but being open and curious about the experiences of students from different backgrounds will ensure you will be more inclusive in your practice.

There may be an issue around students' willingness (or lack of it) to access the support available. Roessger, Eisentrout and Hevel (2019) suggest that certain aspects of age or personality can affect readiness to seek support. Additionally, Yale (2020b) mentions that whether a student contacts their personal tutor can be a complex decision. This can be even more difficult for students from non-traditional backgrounds such as international students (Thomas, 2006), who may feel that they are 'bothering' their tutor (Raby, 2023).

To ensure our support of students is inclusive, it is key to treat students with compassion, to ensure they feel they matter (Advance HE, 2024), and with cultural competency (McLetchie-Holder et al, 2025). We can do this by acknowledging our students' individuality and making sure that we are aware if they have any particular needs. Some universities may have a system of identifying students with additional needs and may provide a document outlining the support required. As tutors we need to be aware if our students have any such support in place and make sure that it is being fulfilled.

We should also take care to use language which is inclusive around issues such as disability or gender, finding out from the students how they would like to be referred to. This would help tutors to build meaningful relationships with their tutees, again contributing to their sense of mattering.

Tailored support or student profiling?

While we advise against homogenising students, we do acknowledge that it is important to understand student contexts and to develop an awareness of why and how certain students might struggle while in HE. It may therefore be beneficial to tailor support or allocate specific tutoring expertise to individuals or groups according to the type or number of risk factors applicable (Smith, 2008; Lochtie, 2015). However, it is important to remember that every student needs to be understood and treated equitably as an individual rather than profiling them and simply supporting only according to a generalised set of characteristics (Priest and McPhee, 2000; May and Bridger, 2010; Gurbutt and Gurbutt, 2015; Calcagno et al, 2017). As discussed previously, acknowledging the intersectionality of student characteristics is an important way to ensure all characteristics are considered and support is tailored to individual students' needs. Likewise, just because students have one or more of the characteristics listed above does not necessarily mean this will have a negative impact on their progress. Conversely, you may have students who do not have any of these characteristics and yet are still at significant risk of dropping out. Exercising your own knowledge and intuition is critical here.

Most students do struggle at some point in their programme of study. Generally, students who possess any of the various characteristics listed above may have barriers to overcome (Kroshus et al, 2021) and find adapting and transition into university life more difficult than others or be hesitant to ask for assistance (Small, 2013; McIntosh and

Shaw, 2017; Office for Students, 2023b; McLetchie-Holder et al, 2025). They may be disengaged from mainstream forms of support, face specific practical challenges which impact on their academic and social engagement or initially lack the tools and environment required to succeed (Whittaker, 2008; McIntosh and Shaw, 2017; Thomas and Jones, 2017; Office for Students, 2023b). Calcagno et al (2017) suggest identifying at risk students during the 'getting to you know you' stage of tutoring while building a relationship with the student, and it is generally seen as good practice. These decisions inform at risk meetings where further exploration can occur and support be provided if required (as discussed in the next section). In some institutions, particular tutors are assigned to work with students who are at risk.

The tools to keep your students on track to succeed

This section aims to provide a good practice model for student tracking and monitoring. You may not recognise some of the phrases used in Table 5.3 – for example, 'staff comments about students', 'cause for concern or congratulations' – as these differ depending on the institution you work for. However, even though the phrases may differ, the meaning behind them is usually the same, whichever student you work with or institution you work for. Table 5.3 outlines some of the key activities you can use to ensure students succeed.

Table 5.3 Tracking and monitoring activities

Method	Explanation
At risk meetings	• Formal meetings where you discuss the progress of each of the students in your cohort in turn. • Discussion focuses on each student's progress in relation to SMART targets. • Discussion takes place with other staff and support staff who work with those students, such as the senior tutor.
At risk categorisation	• Where you identify the likelihood that students may not pass the course or achieve their target grade. • You will take a holistic view of each student's progress and profile. • Remember, the role of the tutor can include improving intellectual and academic ability as well as nurturing the well-being of your students. These factors can influence the student's at risk category (discussed in detail later in this chapter).

Table 5.3 (Cont.)

Method	*Explanation*
At risk documentation	• Methods by which you record the reasons for your students' at risk categories. • At risk documents should be seen as 'live', in other words they should be added to and updated accordingly over the academic year. • The method for recording is not as important as actually going through the process of identifying the at risk category and support needs of every student with the relevant lecturers, support staff and managers. • It is good practice for you to notify all staff who work with a student on a regular basis of the student's at risk category, reasons for this and supportive interventions. As this is considered 'personal information', the UK GDPR applies, and you should follow its principles when sharing data. Updating on the at risk categories will help to establish a more informed and co-ordinated approach to each student's individual needs.
One-to-ones with students	• Arranged and structured conversations that allow you to discuss the progress the student is making. • Where SMART targets are agreed along with actions for improvement and dates when these will be reviewed.
Course progress feedback	• This can be discussed with the student within the classroom or in a one-to-one situation. • How well (or not) students are doing on their course will affect their at risk category.
Staff comments about students	• The majority of institutions now have a dashboard-based analytics system for monitoring individual student progress. • Usually these systems allow lecturers and support staff to make comments (positive or developmental) about every student's progress. • This information is usually visible to all staff (and students in some institutions) and is vital to indicate the at risk category and supportive actions.
Cause for concern or cause for congratulations	• Dashboard tracking and monitoring systems usually allow staff to share when students are causing real concern or when they have really excelled. • These things need to be recognised and sometimes discussed with the students and will partly inform their at risk category and the supportive actions you will take.

Critical thinking activity 1

1. In relation to the tracking and monitoring activities in Table 5.3:
    a. Which of these are commonly used in your institution?
    b. Which of these have you used in your practice as a personal tutor?
2. Rank the seven activities listed in Table 5.3 in order of what you feel has the greatest impact on your ability to track and monitor whether all of your students are on track to succeed (1 = greatest impact).
3. The seven activities listed are only *some* examples of tracking and monitoring activities. What others can you think of?

Feedback to the student

To be truly effective, all tracking and monitoring activities must inform timely and effective feedback to the student. To achieve this, depending on the time you are given within the institution, the aim is to have regular discussions with every student in your cohort to convey how they are progressing against their SMART targets. Discussions can take place at any time, for example, in the seminar room or corridor. However, usually the most effective method is through an arranged one-to-one.

For student feedback to be effective it must:

- be a two-way conversation in which, where appropriate, you employ many of the core skills discussed in Chapter 3, for example, active listening and questioning, challenging, reflecting back and summarising;
- involve the student doing the majority of the thinking and talking. Ineffective feedback is where you do the majority of the talking and the student is disengaged. You should be trying to get the students to think and reflect about their own progress and develop agreed targets with you.

Critical thinking activity 2

» Think of the most useful face-to-face feedback you have had which you acted upon and which helped you to improve. List the factors which made that feedback so effective.

How risk is assigned to a student

When you start to work with your tutees in group tutorials and one-to-ones, you will be creating a picture in your mind of the type and level of support each will need in order to be successful on their course. Many personal tutors also teach their tutees, which can help build up an idea of the needs of individual students. Regularly speaking to colleagues and using the institution's dashboard student tracking and monitoring system are of equal importance to inform your view of each student's progress. So that you and everyone who works with individual students are clear about the support they need, it is useful to assign an at risk category to each of them if your institutional dashboard does not already do this automatically.

The at risk category helps you to have a clear understanding of your tutees and to decide the actions needed to support each student effectively. By sharing these categories with your colleagues, such as the senior tutor or student administration, your department will have a clear overview of the needs of the cohort, and who is in need of extra support. As the academic year progresses and each student's situation changes, so should their at risk status and the level and type of support you provide. It is good practice to review each student at regular intervals to ensure that you are tracking and monitoring that each is on course to succeed, and you should particularly look out for any sudden changes in behaviour patterns, such as a sudden drop in attendance or marks. Table 5.4 outlines some at risk factors and at risk categories by which students can be categorised.

Critical thinking activity 3

1. Table 5.4 provides risk factors and general at risk categories Thinking about your institution, complete the table with phrases or statistics that characterise the at risk category for each risk factor. We have given some examples in italics.
2. Pick a few of your tutees and for each risk factor, indicate which risk category they fall into. Then assign an overall risk category to that student.

Discussion

The reason we have asked you to provide your own specific criteria is because each institution is different and therefore will use different criteria to determine what factors put a particular student at a particular level of risk. For example, one institution may consider that a student who has below 85 per cent attendance is at high risk, but another may only consider that student to be at medium risk. Also, it is important to note that institutions may have created their own at risk categories with associated criteria and indeed they may use a different term for 'at risk'. Additionally, some institutions are moving away from using the language of risk to inform their student support systems. Therefore, it will be useful for you to ascertain, if you do not know already, what terminology is used in your own institution and what definitions are provided.

Another aspect that you should consider is how these categories are used. Are they used to simply reflect whether students will pass or fail their course or should they incorporate a more holistic view (for example, including background characteristics)? We believe a holistic view of the student is preferable, because personal and academic issues are often intertwined and therefore personal issues are strongly linked to a student's success. However, senior managers may only want to use it to reflect whether students will pass or fail their course, and you may find it useful to reflect on why this might be.

A final point to consider is, to what extent should you share the categories with the student? Although institutions may use this categorisation primarily for their own purposes,

Table 5.4 Risk factors and at risk categories

At risk category	Criteria				
	Student progress against SMART targets, including target grades	Attendance and punctuality	Engagement in class/tutorials	Submission records	Background characteristics
Outstanding	The student is making exceptional progress above their SMART targets and target grade.	100 per cent			
No risk					
Medium risk					
High risk					

arguably it is useful for students to be aware of their progress, and any factors that may be impeding this, so that they can gain a realistic view of their routes to progression.

At risk meetings

Once an at risk category has been assigned to each of your students, it is important to regularly review the reasons for the at risk category and the actions being taken to support every student. Some institutions have regular at risk meetings to discuss the risks associated with each student. These meetings are most effective when they are:

- undertaken on a regular cycle;
- run as formal meetings in which anecdotal comments, gossip and any 'moans' are kept to an absolute minimum;
- attended by staff who work closely with the students in question, including lecturers, support staff and managers where appropriate.

If at risk meetings are not common practice at your institution, then you could adopt an alternative strategy and regularly hold informal discussions with your colleagues about students who are deemed *most* at risk. The purpose of these discussions should be to evaluate the impact of current supportive actions and to agree future actions.

Within formal at risk meetings, your role as personal tutor is to lead the conversation and discuss each student in turn to review the reasons for their at risk category. You should discuss what actions have been, and need to be, taken to support that student to be successful (in other words, to ensure that they are supported to keep on track and realise their potential), with dates when these actions will be reviewed. It is important to remember that this method of tracking and monitoring is not solely focused on students who may be at risk of failing or withdrawing from their course; it should be equally focused on students who may be at risk of not doing as well as they could. The former helps to improve retention and success rates whereas the latter helps to improve the experience of students who need to be continually stretched and challenged. Together, they improve the overall student experience.

The name and format given to at risk meetings will differ between institutions and some may not have them at all. If this is the case, it is not your role to formally implement this system. Experience suggests that this is a good practice model that achieves positive results both for the students and the institution. Again, it must be emphasised that these systems are only indicative of the most appropriate types of tutorial support that may be offered to students and must not be used to place subjective judgements or limits on their ability or potential.

Critical thinking activity 4

» Table 5.5 is an example of a live at risk monitoring document. This is an overview of students with the at risk category for each, which includes reasons for the category and support actions taken. It is completed by you as personal tutor and is an example of at risk documentation as mentioned in Table 5.3. Read the document and write down what actions you would take to support these students.

Table 5.5 Example at risk monitoring document (actions omitted)

Student name	At risk category	Reasons for the category	Actions
Zhou Zhong	High risk	Zhou is repeating the year, due to failing a number of her units previously. She has had poor attendance (45 per cent) and has failed to submit two pieces of coursework. You have had a few positive learning conversations (see Table 5.6) with Zhou and are aware that she has some financial problems and that she has not yet been able to pay her tuition fees.	
Nils Alberg	Outstanding	Nils has very good attendance (100 per cent) and has also submitted all assignments. His attainment has been steady around the 2:1 class, with some firsts. Nils wants to achieve higher than this to ensure a first-class degree classification.	
Ibrahim al-Afzal	Medium risk	Ibrahim entered the year with a very good previous study record. He submitted extenuating circumstances for the assessments in the first semester of this year, and you are aware he was in touch with student support services at the time. He did not submit extenuating circumstances for the most recent assessment period, but he has low marks. Ibrahim told you previously he intends to go on to postgraduate study, but based on his current results you know he might not be accepted on his chosen postgraduate programme. His attendance is currently 67 per cent.	
Omowale Ogunleye	High risk	Omowale has returned to study after she suspended her studies due to mental health issues. She engaged well last term and did well in her assignments. Her attendance fell towards the end of the term and she has not submitted her end of term assessments. You receive an email from her mother who is worried because Omowale has not been in touch.	

Discussion

When documenting actions to support students, it is important to:

- keep previous actions on the at risk document as you progress through the academic year. This helps to show any progress and also gives a clear overview of the support given to each student;

- ensure that your actions to support the student include, for example, one-to-ones and SMART targets. Supportive actions should not be, for example, transferring or withdrawing the student from the course. These would be the final result, not the supportive actions taken;

- share this information with as many colleagues who will be supporting that student within your institution as possible, for example, academic colleagues, support staff and managers. Ensure that anything sensitive or confidential is not mentioned within a document like this and that the principles of UK GDPR are adhered to.

Critical thinking activity 5

» *Using the students you identified in critical thinking activity 3, complete an at risk monitoring document that includes all of your students. State the at risk category, reasons for assigning students that status, actions taken so far to support each student and future actions you will take.*

Tools to re-engage students

The specific tools to help you re-engage your students are explained in Table 5.6.

Table 5.6 Tools to re-engage students

Tool	Aim	Explanation	When to use
Positive learning conversation (PLC)	To uncover underlying reasons for poor attendance, engagement or completion of work and thus re-engage the student and effect a behavioural change.	An individual meeting between the personal tutor and student to discuss issues with attendance, engagement or completion of work. It could be one, a combination or all three of these. Use the key principles of an effective one-to-one with a student from Chapter 6 but with the added dimension of purposefully trying to effect a positive behavioural change. The SMART targets set should reflect this. You may wish to request a manager to be present if appropriate.	With a student whose standards of attendance, engagement or completion of work has fallen below the institution's expected standards. A useful guideline is to use after two or three 'causes for concern' from lecturers. Use before formal disciplinary stages at manager level.

Table 5.6 (Cont.)

Tool	Aim	Explanation	When to use
PLC review	To review whether the targets set in the PLC have been achieved.	If PLC review targets are repeatedly not met, the student can be referred to the formal disciplinary process at manager level. Again, you may wish to request a manager to be present if appropriate.	Shortly after the PLC, depending on the issue. A useful guideline is one to two weeks after the PLC.
Student progress report or review	To effect a change in engagement or attainment for a student whose progress needs monitoring.	A report, incorporating learning and engagement analytics combined with the views of (personal and module) tutors each semester reviewed by staff as part of the assessment process.	In isolation or can work well alongside a PLC or when a formal disciplinary meeting has taken place and where showing improvements from the report have been set as a condition of continuing on the course.
Informal mediation process	Restore justice/repair relationships/ heal hurt feelings between fellow students or between students and lecturers.	A meeting of students (or students and staff) between whom there has been disagreement/gossiping. You are present in a personal tutoring capacity and are joined by other colleagues. Rules of the meeting include: • only one person to talk at a time; • each person to be able to state their points; • all views respected; • no raising of voices; • keeping as calm as possible.	After a conflict situation between fellow students or students and lecturers.

The case for a positive approach to re-engagement

If a student appears to be disengaged from, or disinterested in, their course, it is important to try to dig down to the underlying reasons for this and to provide positive reinforcement to students (some of whom may have never experienced this before). Wallace (2013, p 95) states: 'What looks like simply a lack of respect may be a signal that something more complex needs addressing in terms of the learner's needs'. Reading and interpreting student behaviour and seeing it as a way of communicating in order to understand what it is telling us (Wallace, 2013) is key. Although Wallace is talking about further education students, we can also apply this principle to HE students.

It is important to emphasise that this goes hand in hand with the aim of encouraging the student to become independent, take ownership and responsibility. Positive strategies, which include conversations with the student to address these issues, can initiate behavioural change and can reduce the number of incidents in a more effective way than simple, punitive measures. You should still be robust when addressing issues of disengagement and have tight rules and clear procedures but know that ultimately it is a student's choice to join the course and, depending on your attendance policy, to attend and engage in class. The aim of these tools and strategies is not for us to control student behaviour but for students to eventually take ownership and control it themselves.

Despite all these efforts, even a highly effective personal tutor will inevitably sometimes have tutees that will fail and drop out. This can be one of the most challenging and unpleasant parts of the tutoring role as you may be the member of staff that has to explain to a student that they will not be able to complete their studies. All you can do is provide the best support you can, utilising the knowledge available to you and within the boundaries discussed in Chapter 4. You can do all you can to offer the student a fair opportunity to succeed but you cannot complete the course for them and must also afford them the freedom to fail. If and when they do, however, you have a responsibility to offer to support them on their next steps as best you can, again being mindful of the boundaries already discussed. Before a student gets to the stage of programme termination they might benefit from informed advice about course suspension or change (discussed in the next chapter). Often, there are trained student support colleagues within an institution who can speak with students about the options available to them.

Working with students who have additional support needs

There is plenty of information already out there on the topic of additional support needs (ASNs) themselves, in terms of the definitions, approaches, issues and support needs related to specific learning difficulties and disabilities. This section is specifically concerned with your role as a personal tutor regarding your students who have support needs and your relationship with other staff within the institution when it comes to monitoring these issues. UK-based HE institutions are required by law to make reasonable adjustments for students with disabilities in relation to learning, teaching and assessment and to make teaching and learning truly inclusive; these adjustments should be made without the need for 'evidence' (Advance HE, 2024). Some universities are now embedding their reasonable adjustments into everyday practice in order to make HE a more welcoming place for those with disabilities (Hamer, 2025). This means that all staff, including personal tutors, will need to have an awareness of incorporating inclusivity into any activities. We will consider the role of the personal tutor in this (Wisker et al, 2007; Riddell and Weedon, 2014; Kendall, 2017).

First, a quick note on terminology. Students can be referred to as having a disability, a health condition, including mental health conditions, a specific learning difficulty or ASNs. As you can see from the title of this section, we are using the last of these but without the acronym ASN. The staff employed to work directly with these students may also have different titles. One of the most common names for the relevant group of staff or department is 'student support services', which is the term we use. Other common terms are 'disability services' or 'disability advisors'.

Critical thinking activity 6

You have a student, David, who has an additional support need. We have not specified the particular support need on purpose since we would encourage you to think about your role as personal tutor in terms of facilitating and providing appropriate support for students with additional support needs generally rather than specific actions related to a particular need, which can have a wide range of individual differences within them.

1. List what you think are the key actions to support David generally.
2. For each action, state whether it should be carried out by you as personal tutor, other members of staff or a combination of both.
3. Make notes that explain and discuss how you decided on your answers to question 2 and how important each action is.
4. Compare your answers to the suggestions in Table 5.7.

Table 5.7 Additional support actions, roles and explanations

Action	Who to carry out?	Explanation and discussion
With David, complete a referral to student support services for assessment.	Any member of staff working with David	This may have already happened at an early stage of the year and David may have declared his need at enrolment, meaning an additional referral from you is not necessary. You may have other students who you feel might benefit from additional support but who have not had any referral, and who you'll need to refer.
Talk to David in his first one-to-one meeting about support needs and whether he feels they are being met.	Personal tutor	This is an important part of your initial one-to-one and subsequent one-to-one meetings. It needs handling sensitively of course in that a student may not want undue attention being drawn to the additional support need. Also, it may have been declared but is confidential between the student and relevant staff. David's support needs may also be flagged in the institutional dashboard or progression monitoring system.
Adapt my approach in one-to-ones and group tutorial for David.	Personal tutor	Like other academics, your own approach to a student such as David in face-to-face support and learning situations may need adapting (as informed by an individual support plan).
Use information about David's additional support need to inform at risk meetings, documentation and actions.	Personal tutor	Continuing with the holistic view, these issues need to inform at risk discussions and actions. Of course, David may be judged to be 'no risk' or 'low risk' if there is no negative impact on his chances of success and appropriate support is in place.
Communicate with the relevant student support services staff member.	Personal tutor and other staff	Clear communication and conversations are paramount. Other academic staff should also be in regular communication with the relevant additional support staff, but as the primary support, much of this responsibility will rest with you.
Raise awareness of the support need to the department and academic staff.	Professional support staff; possibly the personal tutor	You can have a role in raising awareness of support needs and issues, particularly if you feel there is a need for this in the curriculum area. However, it is not your primary role on a formal level and professional services staff also need to be proactive in this. Again, the principles of GDPR and confidentiality apply here and David may have set limits on the number of people he wants to be informed about his additional support needs.

Table 5.7 (Cont.)

Action	Who to carry out?	Explanation and discussion
Advise other academic staff about how they need to adapt their teaching and approach to David.	Professional support staff; possibly the personal tutor	While you can have a role in this, the relevant student support services member of staff is key here and this information should be on a shared individual support plan for a student such as David and, ideally, uploaded to the dashboard tracking and monitoring system.
Work with in-class support for David.	All academic staff including the personal tutor	If allocated, these are members of staff you need to work with in group tutorials (and possibly one-to-ones).
Ensure additional support information informs any PLCs and/or disciplinary meetings that David may have. Ensure a relevant professional student support services member of staff is present in disciplinary meetings.	Personal tutor; relevant managers	This information should inform disciplinary meetings and it is good practice for a member of the professional student support services team to be present as another advocate for the student in an appropriate way. The latter is not directly your role and the managers should initiate this; however, you can be useful in reminding those organising the meeting that this should happen.
Undergo training in David's specific support need.	Possibly the personal tutor and other academic staff	While many institutions will have specialist staff who are the 'experts', it is useful for personal tutors to undergo training in additional support needs and learning difficulties. It is not a prerequisite of working with a student who has a particular need, but in order to provide holistic support you may request this or research and talk to others informally.
Allocate support staff.	Student services manager	It is not your role, but if you feel there is a need you can discuss the requirement for resourcing with your line manager or directly with the student services manager.

Discussion

To fulfil the aim of providing effective and holistic support to students, ASNs have to be taken into account. You may be the first staff member to whom a student discloses details of their need or disability, but you are not the only source of support and student services have a key role to play. If a student discloses their support needs to you, it is important to ascertain whether they have registered with student support services. If the student has not disclosed their need or disability, you should give the student information on how to register with student support services and discuss the pros and cons of disclosure if the student is reluctant to register. Thus, additional support issues are something you will have much involvement with while at the same time remembering expertise and temporal boundaries. You are not expected to be an expert in all of these needs, but you will inevitably gain more knowledge of these issues as you undertake the role and you may want to pursue an area of particular interest for your own development. A clear referral process, both internal and external, is key.

Safeguarding

Cast your mind back to the beginning of the book. There we listed all of the different roles you have to play, thinking of them in terms of alternative job titles. Among them was therapist or counsellor. Once again, we need to remember the expertise and referral boundary. You are not a therapist or counsellor but a personal tutor. However, any social issues relating to a particular student will almost certainly impact upon the things you are given the task of ensuring: effective learning and assessment; 'stretch and challenge' and the retention of students in the institution. Moreover, you are often the individual with whom students build the most trusting relationship, meaning that they may often talk to you about such issues rather than speaking to other individuals either within or external to the institution.

You will no doubt be familiar with the term 'safeguarding'. 'To safeguard' has a generic definition of 'protect from harm or damage with an appropriate measure' (Oxford Dictionaries, n.d., online). While there is a statutory duty for further education colleges and schools to safeguard and protect children in their care, the same is not true for HE institutions. Although there has been intense debate around whether universities have in fact a statutory duty of care to students, this has not been tested in the courts (Department for Education, 2023) and the law is still evolving (Dickinson, 2023). They are already subject to a legal duty to take steps to ensure reasonably foreseeable harm does not occur by way of careless acts or omissions by the institution (AMOSSHE, 2023), particularly in relation to a vulnerable adult (often referred to as an 'adult at risk'). Vulnerable is defined as 'in need of special care, support, or protection because of age, disability, risk of abuse or neglect' (NHS, 2023), though it should be noted that any adult can become vulnerable, according to circumstance. This tells us that it is the duty of all staff and the institution to safeguard vulnerable adults; but in the day-to-day language of the educational institution it is often used as an umbrella term for those students who have had, or are still undergoing, safeguarding issues. A typical statement when discussing a student may be 'she has a safeguarding file'. Among the issues involved could be domestic violence, abuse, sexual exploitation or neglect. Institutions also have a duty towards children or young people who come into contact with their students or staff. Therefore, a safeguarding case may arise if a student discloses something to you, and that student is a parent or carer for children. In a scenario where a student discloses information to you which suggests that they, or children in their care, may be vulnerable to harm, it is usually a case of referring the information to the relevant member of staff at your institution – for example, the 'safeguarding officers' – while also ensuring that the student feels supported and listened to at all times. Where safeguarding information is already held on a student within your cohort, this information should inform your approach from the beginning of the academic year, but it can be received in-year. The processes at your institution should ensure that you are a member of staff with whom relevant safeguarding information is shared.

Dashboards and learning/engagement analytics

As part of their academic support benchmarking tool, the National Union of Students (NUS) suggest having some 'systems in place to alert staff to sudden drops in performance or attendance' and that this should be a minimum requirement (2015, p 1). The use of learning and engagement analytics is becoming the norm in the majority of educational institutions because they can help identify those who may be at risk of withdrawal (McCluckie, 2014; Webb et al, 2017). These systems capture data from a range of 'touchpoints' and store this information in a data warehouse. This enables institutions to identify patterns and trends, inform their planning and decision-making, create predictive models and identify students who need, or are predicted to need, assistance and interventions. An early warning system may trigger when, for example, a student drops below 80 per cent attendance in the first few weeks of the semester, thus offering an opportunity for bespoke, targeted and timely interventions (McCluckie, 2014). Figure 5.1 displays information on the data that may be gathered and the student support mechanisms they may inform. The results of analyses are often presented in dashboards for easy consumption. There are numerous companies in the marketplace

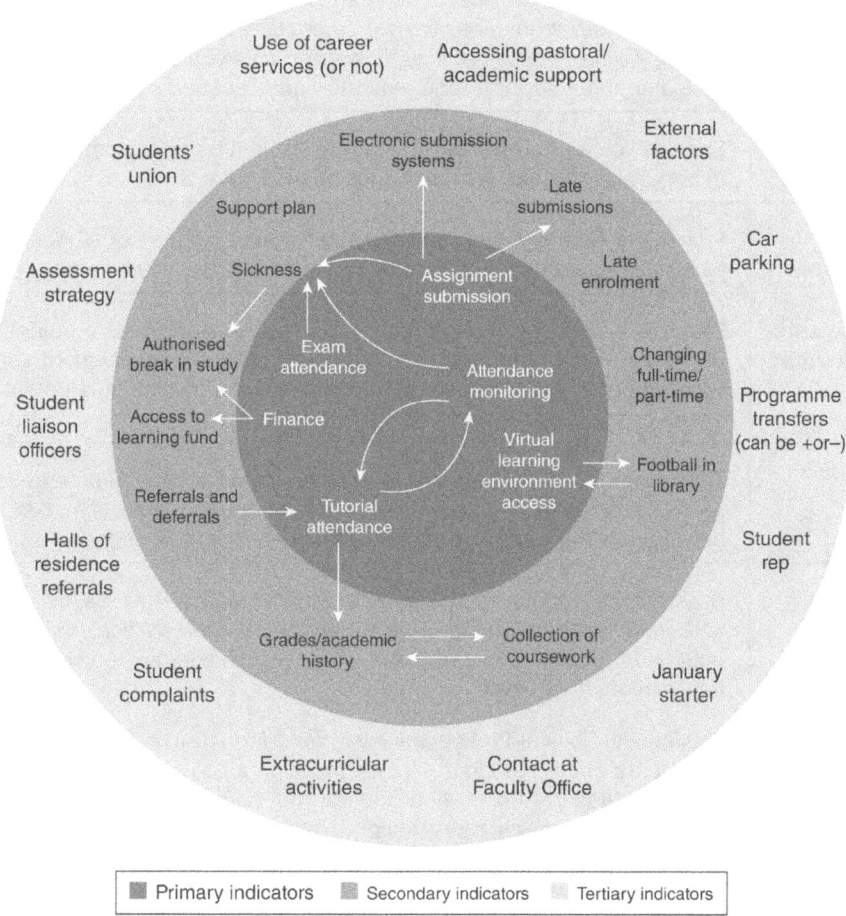

Figure 5.1 *Engagement analytics diagram*

(Reproduced and adapted with permission, Mutton [2013])

that offer systems which, broadly, do a similar job. In this section we are not going to name different systems or list their characteristics. However, we feel it is important to illustrate some of the most useful features for achieving the best outcomes for students.

Overall, the most important element of these electronic dashboards is that they are a 'one stop shop' for all information about every student. Information about individual students or groups should be updated by all tutors and support staff and be visible in real-time. These attributes are what make these systems so useful to your personal tutor role and key activities. Table 5.8 details useful features of dashboard systems relating to learning and engagement analytics.

Table 5.8 Useful features of dashboard-based learning and engagement analytics

Feature	Why it is useful
Additional support information	Students with additional support needs should have their support requirements available instantly, enabling more informed lesson planning and decision-making by academics, personal tutors and support staff.
At risk categories	Allows all staff to instantly see all students' at risk categories, usually by adopting a flagging or traffic light system. This enables quicker decisions to be made about support requirements and allocation of resources.
Attendance data	Enables you and other staff to identify any issues or any patterns which will inform student meetings and inform SMART targets.
Centralised grades system	Provides a clear overview about the academic progress of students. This is particularly useful in one-to-ones to inform SMART target setting.
Staff comments about students	Provides instant feedback from any member of staff about a student, particularly his or her progress against attendance, engagement and completion of work standards. This qualitative information is useful in one-to-ones.
Student meetings	These meetings with students are useful for documenting progress against SMART targets. It also allows you to document and share discussions you have had (with students) with all colleagues to inform support.
Safeguarding information	Due to confidentiality it is unlikely to include any specific issues, rather, it acts as a 'flagging up' that a safeguarding file for a particular student is held and that staff can see the designated safeguarding officer for more information, if required. This section is vital for keeping every student safe. The previous 'staff comments about students' feature provides a good overview of the progress of every student, which, when twinned with safeguarding information clearly informs the at risk category, supportive actions and student meetings.
Target degree outcome or classification	Enables you to set and review effective SMART targets in order to help ensure students achieve their potential and/or stretch and challenge them to achieve more.

Good practice tips when using dashboards and learning/engagement analytics

- Ensure you use clear language that students can understand and aim to avoid misinterpretation. This includes being clear about why you are putting information on the system. For example, if you include a comment that the student is having a difficult time then seek the student's permission to note this down and clarify that you are putting this on the system because you want other personal tutors and support staff to be sensitive around the student at this time.
- Use SMART targets where applicable.
- Ensure updating of information about students is done in a timely manner, particularly in relation to the features shown in Table 5.8.
- Where comments can be made about a student on your dashboard, try to not be *overly* critical of the student. In other words, try to turn a negative point into a positive action that could be taken by the student. For example, try not to say, 'Simone does not take part in seminars'; instead, say, 'We have agreed a target for Simone to contribute regularly to seminars'. This provides clear instruction on how improvements can be made.

It is prudent to be cautious about relying solely upon data, automated analysis or computer-generated information to drive your personal tutoring practice. For example, while some research indicates a positive correlation between attendance and academic achievement, it is debatable whether this relationship is causal (Moores et al, 2019), and in which way this causality runs. Students may achieve less due to low attendance, but equally students may become less engaged with their course due to low achievement. Likewise, student attendance may not necessarily equate to student learning and non-attendance does not necessarily indicate that learning is not taking place (Davis, 2011; Gurbutt and Gurbutt, 2015). Consider when assessing what support a student requires. Some students may quickly learn how to play whatever system you might create; for example, we have experienced instances of students remaining logged on to appear active in a virtual learning environment, or sharing QR codes to mark themselves present at a lecture or seminar. Again, face-to-face communication and knowledge, as well as using intuition, is critical here. This attendance data can be extremely insightful but they require your interpretation to add significant value.

If data are analysed and contextualised in a careful, structured and considered way (in conjunction with strategic coordination between students, staff and senior management) it can be extremely valuable (Witt et al, 2016). As a personal tutor, it is important that you can identify patterns and accurately infer meaning from a variety of information sources. When considering this information it is essential that you take into account the wider context (which may vary considerably from one student, programme, department or institution to another) because this can both inform and improve your professional practice. When recording information, either in a dashboard system or elsewhere in a tutorial record or notebook, it is important to strike a balance and include the right level of detail to capture what was discussed and observed. Too much time spent behind the scenes recording information in great depth and detail can impact negatively on your ability to work with students face-to-face. Admittedly, in complicated situations, recording more detail might be necessary. As discussed previously, it is this contextual information that can be critical to providing the right support for students. Systems work well when they facilitate greater interaction with students rather than reducing the time you have available to do this properly. It may be worth discussing approaches to recording tutorials with other tutors in your team to ensure consistency of practice.

Summary

In this chapter, we have looked in detail at the characteristics of students that may increase their chance of risk and vulnerability. We have discussed that it is important to consider the intersectionality of these characteristics to ensure we provide tailored support for the unique needs of students, rather than profiling them on certain characteristics. We have outlined good practice in supporting students and the role personal tutors have in supporting students with ASNs. We have looked at the tracking and monitoring of students, and how this is one of the key activities of a personal tutor to improve students' success. Such tracking should not only be focused on students who are at risk of failing or withdrawing from their course, but also on students who may be at risk of not achieving their target degree classification or assessment outcomes. Many factors will influence the effectiveness of your tracking and monitoring. One of them is the relationship you have with your colleagues. When you are developing actions for students who are underperforming, not all staff will have the same view. Some may think that a firmer approach is needed, while others may think a softer approach will work best. Agreeing a way forward is not always a 'straight line' and this subjectivity is something you must learn to manage through your influencing skills. Remember, however, that everyone has the right to a view but not everyone's view will be right. It is your responsibility to allow these individual perceptions to inform your holistic interpretation of each student's performance and support needs, while ensuring that the actions that you and others take always have students' success and well-being at the centre of them.

Critical reflections

1. Analyse the emphasis that your institution places on tracking and monitoring student progress (if you have taught at more than one institution, compare and contrast the two institutions' approaches, using examples). What are the positive points about the methods used and what things could be improved?
2. Evaluate:
    a. how you feel dashboard-based analytics improve the tracking and monitoring of student progress compared to using spreadsheets;
    b. how this may influence the impact of the personal tutor role.

3. Using Figure 5.1 as a guide (whether you have a dashboard analytics system or not):

   a. identify your strengths and points for development in the tracking and monitoring of your students;

   b. set yourself two development targets to work on over the next six weeks. On completion, critically review your progress.

   c. What are your views on the boundaries between tailored support and profiling students? Under what circumstances, and with what information, do you offer additional support to students?

Personal tutor self-assessment system

As a reminder, some key activities for the personal tutor are:

- tracking and monitoring your students;
- identifying the needs of your tutees on an individual and group level;
- working with students who have ASNs.

PERSONAL TUTOR SELF-ASSESSMENT SYSTEM: Chapter 5 Key activities: Identifying and supporting student populations					
	Minimum standard 1 star	Beginner level 2 star	Intermediate level 3 star	Advanced level 4 star	Expert level 5 star
Individual	I ensure that I consider the potential needs of various student populations before tutoring commences. I understand and can use any dashboard analytics systems that my institution utilises.	I regularly reflect on the needs of my tutee cohorts, based upon any information I have. I build these reflections into my future planning and discuss them with my head of department/line manager during appraisal meetings.	I regularly assess the needs, engagement and development of my students, recording any observations made on any dashboard systems my institution utilises.	Feedback from my students regarding the key activities is consistently very positive. Feedback from colleagues shows they regard them as having a strong impact on student progress and outcomes.	I have detailed plans in place to ensure I identify the needs of my students at an early stage and I monitor these needs as they evolve throughout their studies. I continually and thoroughly analyse the data provided by the dashboard system to seek new ways to improve my practice. I discuss consistency of practice with my fellow tutors.

Institutional	My institution ensures that any information held about students, which may affect or support them, is made available to tutors (in line with GDPR) and this is regularly utilised.	The strategy for supporting specific student populations is effectively communicated to all new staff and updates for existing staff are frequent. Where dashboard analytics systems are used there is basic uniformity in their application to record student interactions.	The identification and support of specific student populations are routinely discussed in all academic staff's appraisal meetings. Tutors and student support services regularly utilise analytics to inform practice.	The use of dashboard-based analytics is embedded into all relevant departments of the institution. Analysis of the data they produce informs programme and department-level student support planning.	Relevant data on key performance indicators are used to systematically review the institution's student support strategy. This analysis feeds into a rigorous departmental self-assessment system and the outcome is SMART quality improvement plans. Staff training and development includes discussion on how to use dashboard and analytics systems and promotes continuity of practice.

6 Key activities: Effectively supporting all stages of the student lifecycle

Chapter aims

This chapter helps you to:

- identify the importance of transitions in HE and how they relate to the personal tutor role;
- understand the following typical stages in the student lifecycle, your role within them and their impact upon students:
  - pre-arrival;
  - induction and first year;
  - internal progression (getting students back on track, course changes or suspension of studies);
  - external progression (preparation for graduation and beyond).

It will explore these stages through the application of the key tutoring activities, helping you to:

- understand the purpose of one-to-ones with students and strategies for conducting them effectively;
- identify the reasons for, benefits of, and best practice in group tutorial planning and teaching;
- reflect upon what an effective tutorial curriculum might look like at your institution.

Introduction

Chapter 5 looked at some of the key activities of the personal tutor in the context of the various student populations you may encounter in your role. This chapter explores further key activities within the context of supporting students through the recognised stages of their journey. As an educator, one of the greatest pleasures you may enjoy is seeing how an individual progresses from applicant to graduate, overcoming various challenges along the way.

The stages of the student lifecycle can be broken down as shown in Figure 6.1. As you can see, the student lifecycle starts before students arrive at university. Ideally, a personal tutor would make contact with their tutees during this early stage. In reality such early contact may not be possible due to the logistics of student enrolment and tutee allocation but we recommend this is conducted as soon as possible.

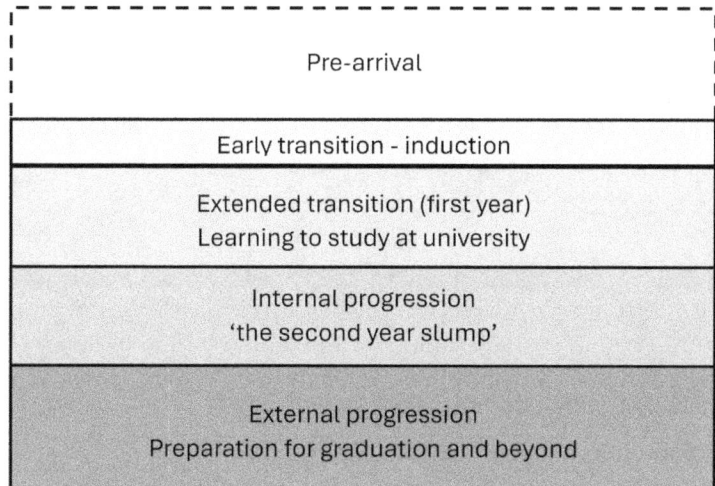

Figure 6.1 Stages in the student lifecycle

It is crucial that students are supported in their engagement with learning throughout their time at university, from first contact to when they become alumni (Morgan, 2022). *The Student Experience Transitions model* (Morgan, 2022) sets out the lifecycle stages each student undergoes as shown in Figure 6.2. This model emphasises the importance of supporting students through each transition, and not just when they first arrive at university. Reorientation and reintroduction, which for a three year full-time degree would happen at the beginning of the second and third year, and preparation for life after study ('outduction'), are equally important.

This chapter guides you through these stages and the transitions that students typically experience as they progress through them, informed by transition theory (Schlossberg, 2011), transition pedagogy (Kift, 2015a), and *The Student Experience Transitions model* (Morgan, 2022). The role of the tutor in supporting students during each phase is explored, including one-to-one and group tutorials as part of a tutorial curriculum, tailored to the needs of students at each stage of the lifecycle. When thinking of these stages it

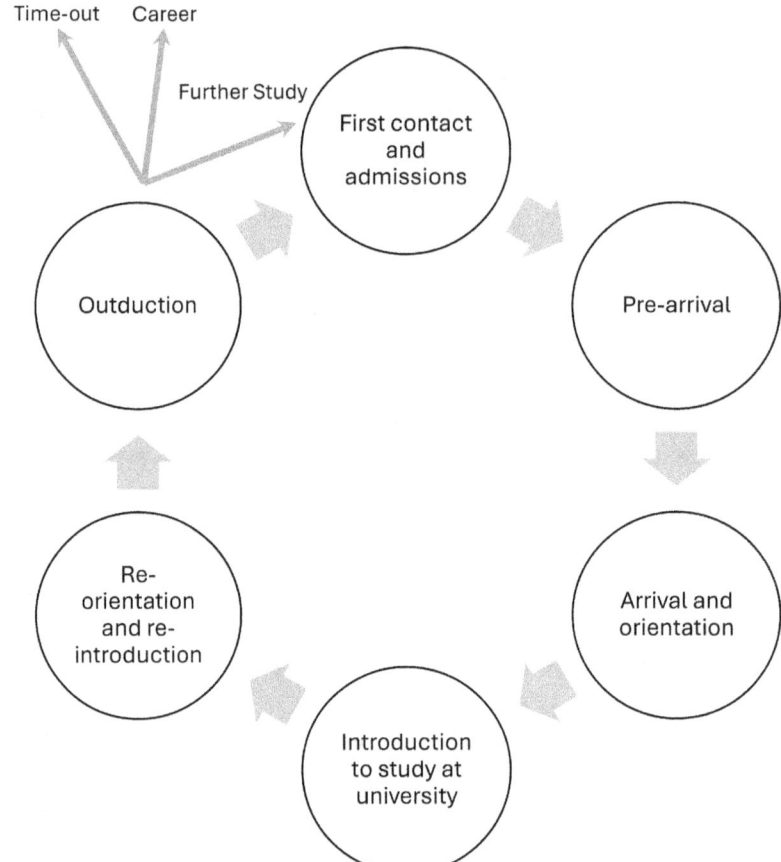

Figure 6.2 *The Student Experience Transitions model*
(Reproduced with permission from Morgan, 2022, p 159)

is important to keep in mind that these are general descriptions rather than homogenous pathways that all students follow and transitions are ongoing rather than discrete stages (Gravett and Winstone, 2021).

Transitioning to university life

The process of transition that students undergo before and at the start of their course can cause psychological distress, anxiety, depression, sleep disturbance, stress, loneliness and a reduction in self-esteem and well-being (Hicks and Heastie, 2008; Palmer et al, 2009; Conley et al, 2020; Kroshus et al, 2021). The first 12 months of HE is widely recognised as the highest point of attrition in post-secondary education (Meehan and Howells, 2019) with around one-in-11 starters in 2019 leaving HE altogether (Hillman, 2024). While the first eight to ten weeks are clearly the most difficult period of transition, research on students' psychological functioning and well-being shows that students are still adjusting in the second year (Conley et al, 2020). This has led some to call for an extended period of transition (Yale, 2020a). Students can feel overwhelmed by new responsibilities and expectations that can leave them feeling confused, panicked, lost or isolated (Cage et al, 2021). Attrition in the early part of the course is usually caused by a lack of social and/or academic integration and often linked to difficulties in making friends or homesickness (Boddy, 2020). New students need support to deal not only with the academic culture shock of adapting to HE (Gravett and Winstone, 2021; Thompson et al, 2021) but also with other material factors such as the emotional shock of moving away from the familiar home environment to a very different life at university (Thompson et al, 2021). Students often experience loneliness during the transition to university (Jaud et al, 2023) and are at greater risk of developing mental ill health during this time (Conley et al, 2020). For students juggling a multitude of commitments outside of university, such as part-time work, family and caring responsibilities, these factors can impact considerably on their ability to cope with student life. It is often students from widening participation backgrounds (including those with low-income circumstances, with caring responsibilities, and those from minoritised backgrounds) who have these additional demands on their time. These students may also find the transition to HE difficult because their minority status can make them feel isolated (McLetchie-Holder et al, 2025). Rates of non-continuation are, for example, higher for Black, disabled, or mature students, and students from disadvantaged backgrounds (Hillman, 2024). Adequate arrangements need to be put in place to support them to manage these conflicting commitments. While the individual student is responsible for making this work, they require support in order to do so.

Effective transitional support

Schlossberg's *Transition Theory* and model, a vehicle for analysing human adaptation, suggests that the support available at the time of transition is critical to an individual's sense of well-being (Schlossberg, 1981, 2011). Such support can be given prior to students arriving in the form of communications consisting of comprehensive and easily accessible information via email, social media and events (Calcagno et al, 2017). This can inform expectations, develop academic skills and foster early engagement with peers, current students and staff (Thomas, 2012). Once students arrive, immediate programme involvement and induction adds purpose, direction and structure, which makes students less vulnerable to drift (Walker, 2010; Spiridon et al, 2020). As was discussed in Chapter 2, transition pedagogy should support students to adapt their previous learning strategies into HE throughout the student lifecycle. This should be followed by supporting and facilitating their transition into later years and future employment (Kift, 2009). First-year curriculum design should have interconnected organising principles embedded into it, including enabling effective transition/engagement, developing academic/personal skills and generally supporting any subject, attendance or independent study-related issues (Wilcox et al, 2005; Yorke and Longden, 2008; Kift, 2009; Fergy et al, 2011). It is important to bear in mind that students are consistently in transition, given that every year of study involves a new set of considerations and expectations. These should be consistently negotiated. It is beneficial to apply Kift's six principles of transition pedagogy that were discussed in Chapter 2 when designing student success interventions.

The social dimension

Dealing with a new social environment is one of the key challenges in the transition to HE (Thompson et al, 2021) and the initial transitional phase can be a lonely time for students (Jaud et al, 2023). During this time, students have an urgent need to find a safe place, belong, identify with others and negotiate their new identities as university students (Wilcox et al, 2005). There is increasing awareness across the sector of the importance of 'mattering' and a sense of belonging for the student experience and its impact on student well-being and retention (Vytniorgu, 2022). 'Mattering' refers to feeling that you are important and valued (Flett et al, 2019; Gravett et al, 2021; Morgan and O'Hara, 2023; Thijm, 2023), which has an important impact on students' self-efficacy (Morgan and O'Hara, 2023) and sense of belonging (Thijm, 2023). By building meaningful individual relationships with tutees, personal tutors have a positive impact on students' feelings of mattering (Thijm, 2023), which in turn increases a student's sense of belonging.

Having a connection with peers and academic staff helps foster a sense of belonging in students (Meehan and Howells, 2019; Vytniorgu, 2022; Drew, 2023), and social integration is as influential as academic skills in ensuring successful transition (Stephen et al, 2008; Richardson et al, 2012). Providing students with support through transition and an induction centred around helping students to settle in, connect to peers and get to know each other, can help increase students' sense of belonging at an institution (Meehan and Howells, 2019; Blake et al, 2022; McLetchie-Holder et al, 2025) and reduce levels of loneliness in the first year (Thomas et al, 2020). The first week of university requires specific attention as it is a key time for students to form relationships and gain a sense of group and cohort identity (Hartwell and Farbrother, 2006). The impact of effective early transition can play a key role in transforming students in terms of their skills, active learning and engagement, and can therefore help determine and support future persistence and success (Foy and Keane, 2018; Spiridon et al, 2020).

It is important to note that a student's background can have a significant impact on how that sense of belonging develops (Gopalan et al, 2022; Gilani, 2024). Research shows that minoritised students have a lower sense of belonging compared to students from majority backgrounds (Shaheed and Kiang, 2021; Gopalan et al, 2022; Gilani, 2024), and that students may not want to belong if they feel they have to make too many sacrifices or change who they are (Gilani, 2024). Focusing instead on the strengths and advantages students from underrepresented backgrounds bring and supporting them to recognise and use these strengths, can help to build a sense of belonging for these students (Gilani, 2024).

The role of the tutor in transition

The personal tutor has an important role in students' transition to university because they provide crucial support to help them make the transition (Drew, 2023) and because they embody the relationship that students have with the institution (Wootton, 2006). A good tutor–tutee relationship can therefore increase students' sense of belonging (Meehan and Howells, 2019; Yale, 2019; Grey and Osborne, 2020) which is particularly important for students from backgrounds underrepresented in HE (Thomas, 2006). It also helps with academic and social integration (Barefoot, 2000), and dealing with the stresses of the first year (Meehan and Howells, 2019; Yale, 2019, 2020a; Grey and Osborne, 2020). In other words, a good relationship with a personal tutor helps students integrate and feel settled. Early encounters with a tutee are crucial, as it sets the tone for the ongoing relationship (Yale, 2019) and influences future interactions (Yale, 2020b). A favourable first impression of you formed by a face-to-face meeting with your tutees during the first week of study is of significant importance and value to them. Effective personal tutoring involves getting to know, building trust and a relationship with your tutees, and serving as a first point of contact very early on during their induction (Calcagno et al, 2017; Yale, 2019). If your tutees do not meet you, or find you intimidating, uncaring or cold, they may feel rejected, try to find support elsewhere, and even reconsider the value and financial implications of their decision to go to university (Yale, 2019).

To be effective as a personal tutor, it is important to understand the worry and anxiety new students feel in relation to the social aspects of transition to university (Alberts, 2021) and convey to them that this feeling is perfectly normal and they are not alone.

Your main focus when tutoring new students should be connecting and settling them into the institution while also helping them adjust to university-level study – essentially facilitating both academic and social integration (Thomas, 2006; Calcagno et al, 2017). While students may feel worried or apprehensive about starting university, they will also feel excitement about meeting new people, learning more about their chosen subject, and perhaps moving to a new city. Reaffirming these feelings of excitement are also an important part of these first meetings. Students may have varying expectations of tutoring and support based on previous experiences, and therefore a first encounter should include the setting of expectations, and explicitly articulating the role and value of personal tutoring (Yale, 2020a, 2020b). In order to provide robust academic support, it is necessary to encourage students to reflect upon their needs, motivations and aspirations for studying at university, while also familiarising them with the range of student support services available and the role personal tutors play as part of those services (Calcagno et al, 2017). It is important to support your students, at a very early stage, to develop their awareness, curiosity and academic skills. At the same time it is necessary to encourage them to explore healthy study habits as well as gain assessment literacy (including reflecting on feedback and planning improvements). All of these things can help them develop a higher academic self-efficacy and increase their motivation (Calcagno et al, 2017; Yale, 2019). Academic well-being can also be promoted through educational socialisation, including peer-learning initiatives such as Peer Assisted Study Sessions (PASS) or student representation, which links academic and social integration together (McIntosh, 2017; Lochtie and McConnell, 2024). If you have an understanding and appreciation of the challenges that students may face, for example, living away from home for the first time, striving for financial independence and navigating a new environment, you are in a better position to assist them with social integration (Lee and Robinson, 2006). It is also important to champion extra-curricular activities (such as student clubs and societies) as these can be instrumental in establishing a renewed sense of belonging and connectedness with the institution. As part of this, you can encourage them to engage in these activities for their own well-being and benefit (Calcagno et al, 2017; Grey and McIntosh, 2017). Finally, if students feel that you understand their context then they are more likely to engage with you and follow your advice.

It is widely agreed that induction and transitional support, particularly for specific populations, should continue past the first few weeks after arrival. This is because students benefit significantly from information given at the point of need and this includes reinforcing information about the support they can access when they truly need it. This support should be 'live' and ongoing, not just buried in a handbook or an induction talk (Owen, 2002). It is recommended that your institution develop a curriculum or framework for personal tutoring which provides a structured programme of activities for tutors to use to support transitions and encourage student development (Calcagno et al, 2017). An example framework for a three year full-time undergraduate degree is displayed later in the chapter in Table 6.2. Support for students as they go through the different stages of their lifecycle, including reorientation and reintroduction, can be delivered via a range of key tutoring activities including one-to-one and group tutorials. These frameworks must be informed by the student lifecycle and be based on the delivery of 'just-in-time' information.

Key tutoring activities

One-to-ones with students

Students value one-to-one time with their tutors and this can be an effective way to support and empower them in their learning (Wisker et al, 2007; Alberts, 2021). Students expect to have one-to-ones with their personal tutor (Drew, 2023) and would like to see their tutors more frequently and routinely but, as discussed in Chapter 4, this becomes more challenging as the profile of the student body changes and student numbers rise (Thomas et al, 2017; Yale, 2019; Grey and Osborne, 2020). Indeed, the quality of the interactions is far more important than the frequency of interactions (Yale, 2019), and both students and tutors have called for more structured and focused support for their one-to-ones to reflect the complexity of their relationship (McIntosh et al, 2022). It is important that meetings have an explicit purpose and structure to ensure students and tutors do not resort to guesswork to figure out what personal tutoring is for (Thomas et al, 2017). You could, for example, formulate intended learning outcomes for each tutorial.

While many tutors believe students would benefit from taking responsibility for making appointments, students have called for tutors to be proactive and to schedule tutorials in advance (Alberts, 2022b). Here there is a danger that those who need support the most may not seek it and slip through the net (Malik, 2000; Owen, 2002; Neville, 2007; Wisker et al, 2007). It is therefore important that tutorial support is proactive and seen as an integral part of all students' education rather than a safety net or as part of a deficit model (Stenton, 2017).

CASE STUDY

One-to-one meeting between Rosa and Nina

The following dialogue is taken from an arranged one-to-one meeting between Nina, a third year Hospitality and Tourism Management student, and her personal tutor Rosa.

ROSA: *Right, come in Nina. Take a seat.*

NINA: *Thanks.*

ROSA: *Right, so we've got our termly catch up. How are you getting on with your studies?*

NINA: *Er ... Okay, I think. I'm not really sure. It's been quite a lot of work, and I've found it quite hard to get my assessments in on time.*

ROSA: *So, did you get them in?*

NINA: *Yes, I did. But I don't know how well I did, because I didn't have so much time for each of them.*

ROSA: *Okay, so you've had problems with your time management.*

NINA: *Er. I guess ... I've just had a lot on with my coursework for Tourism Crisis Management and then Global Brand Management too. It was hard to fit it all in with my shifts at work and going to the lectures. And I've been having some problems in my flat too.*

ROSA: *Okay, I think you need to go on the time management course the student support services run. I'll send you the link.*

NINA: *Er ... Okay.*

ROSA: *Have you got any other problems?*

NINA: *Er..., no. I'm fine.*

ROSA: *I can't remember what other units you are taking. Can you remind me?*

NINA: *I've also got Tourism Trends & Futures.*

ROSA: *Oh yes. Did you get your assignments in for that?*

NINA: *It was a bit late, but yes.*

ROSA: *Let me just make some notes of this on our system.*

NINA: *Okay.*

ROSA: *Oh, I can see on the system that you have missed quite a lot of classes over the past weeks. What's going on?*

NINA: *Well, I decided to go home for a bit because I was having some problems with my flatmates.*

ROSA: *Did you let the admin team know?*

NINA: *No, I didn't. Sorry.*

ROSA: *You really should let them know next time, so that we know what is going on. You have to tell us if you have a problem. So, when we have our next termly catch up, I'd like you to have done the time management course with the student support services and have your attendance back on track. Okay?*

NINA: *Okay.*

ROSA: *Okay, great. I've got another meeting to get to now. So I'll let you know when I have time for our one-to-one next term. Okay?*

NINA: *Yes ... fine.*

Critical thinking activity 1

» How would you evaluate this meeting? Note down three points about the meeting which you feel would make useful areas for development for Rosa.

CASE STUDY

One-to-one meeting between Rosa and Nina – take two

ROSA: *Hi Nina! Come in Nina and take a seat. It's nice to see you.*

NINA: *Thanks.*

ROSA: *Thanks for coming along today for our termly catch up. I'm interested to find out how things are going and make some plans with you for the term ahead. So, how are you?*

NINA: *I'm okay. I've been enjoying the course, but I have had quite a lot of work over the past weeks. I struggled to get all my assessments in on time. I did get them in in the end.*

ROSA: *Well, well done for getting them all in. It sounds like you've had a hard time this term.*

NINA: *Yes ... It's been difficult.*

ROSA: *Do you want to tell me what has been difficult for you?*

NINA: *I've had to cover some extra shifts at work. I didn't want to say no because I can't afford to lose the job. I've been going back home quite a lot too because I've had some problems with my flatmates.*

ROSA: *Do you want to tell me about them?*

NINA: *Erm. Okay. I moved into this shared flat with a friend and with some friend of hers that I don't know very well. I don't really get on with them, and there's often a weird vibe in the house. I'd rather be at my parents'. Especially when I'm trying to study as it can be hard to concentrate.*

[Rosa and Nina continue to discuss these issues. They both agree some small things Nina can do to help her situation and let her focus on her studies. They agree to revise these at their next one-to-one.]

ROSA: *Okay, so let's have a look at your marks for the assessments then. So, I see you got your essay in for Tourism Crisis Management. Well done. Have you had a look at your feedback?*

NINA: *Yes, it was generally positive but I need to work on the structuring of my work. I find it really difficult.*

ROSA: *Finding the right structure can be hard! There are some really good sessions in the library on how to structure essays. Have you heard of them before?*

NINA: *No …*

ROSA: *Let me send you a link to their website. It will tell you how to sign up.*

NINA: *Great.*

ROSA: *And I see you got 58 per cent in the timed assessment for Global Brand Management. How do you feel about that?*

NINA: *Er … I guess I'm feeling a bit disappointed. I felt it was all a bit rushed because I also had the essay for Tourism Crisis Management.*

ROSA: *Okay. What do you think you could have done differently to stop you feeling rushed?*

NINA: *Er … maybe I should have started earlier?*

ROSA: *That is one way. But it also helps to plan out all your deadlines and the time you have available.*

[Rosa and Nina continue to discuss time management strategies, and Rosa asks Nina which one she would like to try.]

ROSA: *Okay. So, you are going to have a look at the library sessions on structuring essays. And to help with your time management for next term you are going to plan out all your work shifts and deadlines at the start of term.*

NINA: *Yes.*

ROSA: *Ok, so I'd like to see how you are getting on with that when we have our next one-to-one meeting on the 21 February. Does that sound okay to you?*

NINA: *Yes, that's fine.*

ROSA: *You've been doing really well. And with these strategies you should feel less rushed and overwhelmed. If you continue to push yourself, you can do even better.*

NINA: *Thanks. I hope so!*

Critical thinking activity 2

» Examine whether your three points from Critical thinking activity 1 have been addressed.

Dos and don'ts for one-to-ones

Critical thinking activity 3

» Concentrating on the dos from Table 6.1, tick those that you use regularly. Look through the dos that you don't yet use, and think about how you can use these in your one-to-ones from now on.

Table 6.1 Suggested dos and don'ts for one-to-ones

Dos	Don'ts
Prepare for them, for example, by reading notes from previous one-to-ones, at risk meeting documents, 'staff comments about students' and speaking to other tutors and support staff about progress.	Be unprepared, because poor preparation or no preparation at all may lead to issues being missed, thereby reducing the impact of the meeting.
Appear pleased to see the students and have a sincere and calm approach (even if you are busy and have competing priorities; Dobinson-Harrington, 2006).	Let it appear to the students that you are just 'ticking off' your one-to-ones as an administrative duty you must fulfil.
Explain at the start of the meeting what things you would like to cover, but ensure you are clear that students can discuss anything that they have on their mind.	Go straight into reviewing the targets without some opportunity for discussion about how the students are feeling about their studies and any factors which might be affecting their progress.
Use more open questions to allow students and yourself to explore their thoughts and feelings.	Use more closed questions, because this will elicit only brief answers which do not help to build rapport or understand and explore issues deeply.
Record details of the conversation using the dashboard system for future reference.	Focus more on the recording of the conversation than on the quality and depth of the discussion.

Table 6.1 (Cont.)

Dos	Don'ts
Sit near and facing the student. Facing them slightly at an angle is preferable.	• Have a table between you. • Sit in a way that blocks access to the door. • Be too close so as to invade their personal space.
Display active listening, as well as body language and tone of voice that show you are genuinely interested. Also challenge, reframe, reflect back and summarise where appropriate.	Appear unengaged in the conversation.
Start with and praise the positive things that students have, or feel they have, tried or achieved.	Ignore their perspective or be too general.
Be honest about any areas that students need to improve.	Start with or ignore areas for development.
Be clear about the consequences of not improving.	Fail to explain the consequences of not improving.
Encourage the students to reflect and have a clear, open and honest discussion about progress against previous SMART targets (these could be, for example, academic, attendance, punctuality, engagement or personal targets).	Briefly mention previous SMART targets and offer no opportunity for discussion around these.
Allow the discussion to develop SMART targets that are stretching but are agreed between you and the students.	Set targets for the students which you have not discussed or agreed, because this will reduce the level of ownership that they feel for them.
Use solution-focused coaching techniques (see Chapter 2) where appropriate.	
Make clear your desire to help resolve any problems where it is possible.	
Ensure that the agreed targets are SMART and that the meaning of SMART targets are explained to the student.	
Finish on a positive and ask the student to summarise the agreed targets before the end of the meeting.	
Ensure dates for the review of these targets are agreed before the meeting finishes.	

A final thought on one-to-ones

As with teaching and curriculum planning, there is no secret formula for a perfect one-to-one. As an academic and personal tutor, you will have many conflicting demands on your time. Therefore, try to avoid spending too much time on detailed planning or recording. The 'dos and don'ts' in Table 6.1 is a useful checklist for your one-to-ones. As every student and educational institution is different, your one-to-ones will be different too. You will need to be able to adapt to the needs and context of every student as well as the resources available, and to keep in mind the boundaries discussed in Chapter 4. Carrying out effective one-to-ones with students is a skill that can be learned through practice and reflection, and as you get better the impact on your students' progress and outcomes will improve.

Group tutorial planning and teaching

Group tutorial models are increasingly being used in response to resourcing issues in HE. Nevertheless, the benefits of group tutoring go beyond cost saving and include facilitating helpful student–student and tutor–student social integration (Wilcox et al, 2005; Whittaker, 2008; Stevenson, 2009). Small group tutorials can be central to effective transition and useful in formalising social relationships and networks (Braine and Parnell, 2011; Richardson et al, 2012; Thomas, 2012; Parkin et al, 2022). Getting to know other students can help foster a sense of belonging, develop common experiences, support stress management and aid the development of peer-learning communities (Fergy et al, 2011; Richardson et al, 2012; Calcagno et al, 2017; Roldán-Merino et al, 2019). There are many issues regarding student transition that can be tackled via the group tutorial process, such as where to go to seek help and support, which normalises certain healthy student behaviours without singling out individual students. Group tutorials can also make support more accessible. Students have reported that the most positive aspects of group tutorials include getting to know their tutor. Students felt that they were more likely to approach tutors whom they had got to know in a group setting first, especially if they encountered problems later (Calcagno et al, 2017). Students themselves also believe that group tutorials should be part of personal tutoring (Alberts, 2022a; Drew, 2023).

There are very few common definitions of group tutorials but a helpful way of thinking about them is as offering a 'secondary curriculum' for personal development including supporting active and independent learning, building study skills and enhancing graduate attributes (Barrie, 2007; Wootton, 2007; Calcagno et al, 2017). Tutorials are central to the delivery of an integrated curriculum, not separate from it, and should be seen as such. As students may not readily engage with group tutorials (Calabrese et al, 2022), it is important to make the purpose or intended learning outcomes of the group tutorial sessions clear to the students when they start and to explain the relevance to their course, career pathway (if they know it) and wider lives. Group tutorials provide another opportunity for you to co-ordinate the student journey, with the aim of enhancing the student experience and helping to improve student outcomes, such as retention, progression and performance, as well as National Student Survey (NSS) satisfaction scores.

We recommend that, where possible, group tutorials are:

- **timetabled** for both tutors and students (Braine and Parnell, 2011; Thomas et al, 2017; Stuart et al, 2021);
- **compulsory** for every first-year student (Calabrese et al, 2022);
- **credited** as students have an instrumental approach to their time so will commit to an activity more if credits are awarded for the time spent (Woods, 2023);
- **mainstream**, appearing to the student as a seamless part of the curriculum (Earwaker, 1992; Calcagno et al, 2017).

Critical thinking activity 4

» *Of course, you, as an individual tutor, may not be able to directly influence some of the above considerations. There is no one correct way of doing things and the purpose and model for delivery can differ between institutions. Note down your answers to the following questions.*

» *To what extent do you agree with each of the four previous recommendations and why?*

» *Does making group tutorials compulsory for students increase their importance or make them an obligation that will lead to reluctant compliance? Why, or why not?*

» *Does adding credits to tutorials (with assessed reflection) add importance or detract from other subjects? Why, or why not?*

Discussion

You can hopefully see the benefits of making group tutorials timetabled, compulsory, credited and mainstream. You may find your group tutorials begin to feel more closely comparable to regular curriculum-based seminars.

The principles of good teaching are largely the same whether you are delivering core curriculum content or a group tutorial.

The key differences are as follows:

- Group tutorials tend to be shorter; therefore, this should be taken into account in your planning, particularly the learning outcomes, activities and assessment methods.
- There is more opportunity to be flexible to the immediate needs of the group, for example, allowing students to influence the content based upon the challenges they face at that time.

- There can be greater flexibility, meaning you may want to consider some different learning activities or room layout, for example:
  - have the room with the chairs in a circle and no tables. This can allow for open discussion. Be sensitive to those students who do not want to contribute. If they normally contribute but do not want to, this could be an indicator of an issue that you may want to approach later in a one-to-one discussion;
  - if group tutorials are used to provide or discuss feedback on assessments it is useful to provide an opportunity for them to reflect on the work they have done or the feedback from their module tutor (although this may have been done already in class). Ways to do this include:
    - individual reflection – allow students time to reread their work and ask them to write down three things they did well and three things they need to do better next time;
    - peer reflection – pair students up and ask them to read each other's work and then discuss with their partner three things they did well and three things they could do better next time. This needs to be managed carefully in terms of the sensitivity of students analysing each other's work and usually works best when it is not done with their friends.

Group tutorial contextualisation

Group tutorial delivery (as well as the tracking and monitoring of students and one-to-ones) works best when it is embedded within the institution's strategy for learning, along with being tailored to the subject area the students are studying. Tailoring the content to be specific to particular industries or career pathways helps to improve the relevance and enjoyment for the student as well as the impact on their career prospects. In some instances, schools or departments may choose to run a schedule of group tutorials that is embedded in, or closely aligned to, the curriculum of the programme.

Differentiation

You may be familiar with the concepts of differentiation and inclusive learning and be employing some of these techniques already. These may include modification of:

- the dialogue and support you give to each student;
- the tasks you set them;
- the pace students can work at individually;
- the way you group the students;
- the resources you use;
- the outcomes you expect or find acceptable.

It is important to differentiate the content within group tutorials for two main reasons. To ensure:

1. it is accessible and relevant to the student populations you are working with;
2. that, as students progress, the content and activities offer appropriate variety and depth, especially when there is a chance they may cover the same or a similar topic again.

Course suspension or change

At an early age, young people in the UK have to make fairly big choices affecting their future. In comparison to some other countries there is a greater specificity of subject. As a result, many students consider changing their course or institution at some point during their studies, with many stating they would apply to a different course or institution if they had the choice again (Department for Education, 2017). This may be because they entered HE without clear goals, their personal or employment circumstances changed or for a host of other reasons, academic or otherwise (Department for Education, 2017). Dropping out or changing course can have significant financial and career implications for students and the rules governing these decisions are very complicated (Malcolm, 2013). A more flexible approach to study for both providers and students has been called for and this is something institutions will need to adjust to (Brennan, 2021), particularly with the introduction of the Lifelong Learning Entitlement in England, which allows students to transfer between courses and providers (Department for Education, 2024).

Students should have the option of taking a break from their studies and/or transferring to a different course or institution and be aware of the associated consequences (Department for Education, 2017). Your institution will have a set of academic policies or regulations that refer to course suspension or change which may be complicated (there may be specific deadlines with various financial implications or specific procedures to adhere to). Students are likely to call upon trusted advisors, such as personal tutors, for guidance on these matters (Bowden, 2008; Malcolm, 2013). While you do not need to know your academic regulations in their entirety, you should know how to access them, have a reasonable understanding of them and utilise them to inform your students, as and when this is required. Similarly, as an effective tutor, you do not need to be an expert in student finance but you should know where you can refer students to for support at an institutional or national level. Often, the senior tutor or the person or department responsible for tutor training at an institutional level will have resources available to help you navigate the help on offer.

On occasion, the best course of action for an individual student may not be the ideal option for their institution. Universities are judged on their performance using specific metrics to assess student continuation, experience and completion and this is discussed in more detail in Chapter 9. For example, a high-achieving student may want to withdraw because of a lucrative job offer or a struggling student may want to cut their losses rather than gamble further money on fees. In these cases all an effective tutor can do is try to ensure that the student makes a fully informed choice. This choice must be informed by the relevant support functions of the university offering appropriate support in line with any relevant boundaries or policies.

Critical thinking activity 5

» Look at the case study dialogue from a one-to-one meeting between Patrick and his personal tutor Linda, which is taking place in week 2. Identify helpful behaviours that enable Patrick to form a decision about the best way forward for him.

CASE STUDY

Linda's one-to-one with Patrick

LINDA: *How's the course going so far?*

PATRICK: *Alright …*

LINDA: *Tell me two things you most enjoy about it.*

PATRICK: *Erm … dunno really … looking forward to the trip.*

LINDA: *But anything you've done so far that you've enjoyed?*

PATRICK: *(shrugs)*

LINDA: *How about two things you find hard or have not enjoyed then?*

PATRICK: *There's so much writing … and lots of units and topics to cover …*

LINDA: *Okay … it does take hard work to get a degree and academic writing is a significant part of that … what modules are you taking?*

PATRICK: *Health and Well-being, Chemistry and … Anatomy and Physiology.*

LINDA: *How do you feel about those classes?*

PATRICK: *Not much … not really enjoying the course to be honest.*

LINDA: *Okay, let's go back a step … what do you do at home when you're not at university?*

PATRICK: *Not a lot … work at Sportsworld, watch TV, look after my little brother and kick-boxing club once a week.*

LINDA: *I noticed your face lit up when you mentioned the club … what's so good about that?*

PATRICK: *It's just … I really enjoy the challenge, the competition and I'm not bad at it. The bloke who runs it gets me to teach the kids there some of the techniques.*

LINDA: *And you like that teaching part as well as the competition and the keeping fit?*

PATRICK: *Yeah, all of it really.*

LINDA: *Interesting. So if you had to list all the things you do outside university and had to say which you enjoy most, what would your top two be?*

PATRICK: *Kick-boxing and ... looking after my brother ... well most of the time [smiles].*

LINDA: *I know what you mean [smiles]. Do you do much reading or writing at home?*

PATRICK: *Not really ...*

LINDA: *What do your parents do?*

PATRICK: *My dad's a lab technician.*

LIZ: *And is that where the idea to do science came from?*

PATRICK: *Yes.*

LINDA: *Right, okay. If you had to say how much out of ten you enjoy practical and sporting subjects what would you say?*

PATRICK: *Probably nine ...*

LINDA: *Wow ... right, okay. Now do the same for factual, scientific or theory subjects ... what would you say?*

PATRICK: *It depends ...*

LINDA: *On what?*

PATRICK: *If the topic is something I'm interested in then I don't mind doing some theory ...*

LINDA: *Ah, okay ... can you give me an example?*

PATRICK: *Well, this guy at the club told me all about fitness.*

LINDA: *Right, well that's really interesting ... You're right, it's not always a clear divide between theory and practical ... often there's a mix. What do you think about Sports Science for example?*

PATRICK: *Sounds good ... that's what attracted me to the course in the first place.*

LINDA: *On the Human Biology course there is the opportunity for you to partially concentrate on sports science. Your Health and Well-being module in the spring will introduce you to this and you can then specialise in Year 2 as part of the Nutrition and Metabolism for Sport and Exercise module. In Year 3 students can take Biomedical Implications of*

Exercise, Activity and Health, Advanced Nutrition for Sport and Sport Toxicology. Does that sound interesting?

PATRICK: *A lot more, it's just the other stuff I'm not really into.*

LINDA: *Well it is a Human Biology course so you will have to take other modules as well. Did you think about the Sports and Exercise Science course?*

PATRICK: *Yeah but my parents said Biology was more academic than Sport.*

LINDA: *Well there are various merits and challenges involved in studying on each course and the potential career each one of them might lead to.*

PATRICK: *What modules make up Sport and Exercise?*

LINDA: *Well ... Research and Academic Skills – so there would still be plenty of writing! Anatomy and Physiology as you would in Human Biology but with a different focus. You can do Coaching and Skill Acquisi ... [Patrick interrupts]*

PATRICK: *That's what I really like to do. Coaching sport, elite sport but maybe kids' sport too?*

LINDA: *It's not really my area of expertise but the Strength and Conditioning pathway in the Sport Rehabilitation programme would seem to support that. Look, I'm not going to tell you what to do, it is your decision but you need to make an informed decision. What do you think you might need to know to make the choice?*

PATRICK: *Should I talk to my parents? Is there a tutor on that programme I could speak to?*

LINDA: *Yes and yes. Definitely speak to your parents. They know you far better than I do and will, I'm sure, have your best interests at heart.*

PATRICK: *Yeah, they support me ... as long as I work hard!*

LINDA: *Good. I'm emailing my colleague Helen and copying you in now. She'll be able to tell you about that course, any admissions criteria and the sports science elements of Human Biology too. Look at the academic regulations here – when would you have to make a change?*

PATRICK: *It says the end of next week.*

LINDA: *I strongly recommend you go and see Helen now – even if she is teaching her office hours are written on the door. Have you spoken to careers at all?*

PATRICK: *Erm, they were in the induction talk weren't they?*

LINDA: *Yeah, I've sent you the link to sign up to meet with them too.*

PATRICK: *Thanks – do I really have to decide all this now?*

LINDA: *Well, look at this section of the regulations ... 5.2.*

PATRICK: *If the two courses are linked, I could potentially move at the end of the year.*

LINDA: *Potentially, so you don't have to do anything rash ... but it is more difficult to catch up on the second year of that course if you haven't taken all of the first-year content. The best thing you can do is fully inform yourself now. Talk to your parents, careers, Helen, your classmates, anyone else?*

PATRICK: *Sports Science students?*

LINDA: *Exactly. Then draw up a list of pros and cons? You may find that you're on the right course after all but it's good to check. There's a PASS, Peer Assisted Study Scheme, on that course too. Why not ask whether you can join them for one session to meet some of the other students and find out more about the course content?*

PATRICK: *Yeah ... okay, I can do that. Can I let you know how it goes?*

LINDA: *Absolutely, shall we schedule a video call?*

Discussion

Some helpful behaviours that we can take from Linda's approach are:

- use of open questions, for example, asking the student to list the most enjoyable and least enjoyable aspects of the course rather than closed questions such as 'are you enjoying your course?' which is likely to elicit a simple 'yes' or 'no';
- trying a different tack when information is not forthcoming, for example, appealing to life outside university in order to gain a picture of interests;
- using scaling, in other words where you get the student to mark a statement out of ten;
- linking thoughts or actions to feelings;
- trying to uncover underlying reasons for the student's choice of course;
- emphasising the positives and reassure, thus creating a supportive environment making honest discussion more likely;
- not fixing the student's issue or swaying them with your opinion; just offering them the benefit of your knowledge and experience so they can make an informed choice for themselves.

Towards the end of the academic year, the module selection for the following year is usually introduced and explained in group tutorials or core module classes. Your role as a tutor may be to advise students about the options available to them, drawing upon their experience and attainment this year and linking this to their planned career destinations. The focus of personal tutoring for year 2 and 3 students is enhancing employability, professional skills and preparing for graduation (Calcagno et al, 2017). Although much of the research on attrition focuses on the first year, students in the second year report getting less enjoyment out of their course, and more students consider dropping out (Webb and Cotton, 2019). In the second year, greater academic demands are placed on students and assignments are increasingly likely to affect the degree classification, thus increasing pressure on students (Birbeck et al, 2021). It is also during the year 2 stage that other factors such as employment, health issues, financial problems, family challenges and relationship difficulties can have significant impact (Jevons and Lindsay, 2018) and students may find it difficult to balance their external life with university demands (Birbeck et al, 2021). This comes at a time when university support, including from personal tutors, is often reduced. It is useful to see this stage as a series of ongoing transitions, during which the support from a personal tutor is crucial. As an effective tutor you can advise students regarding these challenges, suggest they utilise all support available to them, help them remain focused and ensure they are aware of any extension or interruption procedures. As discussed above, expectations do change as a student progresses on their course and so regular conversations with students, in group and one-to-one settings, can help ease any ongoing transitional issues that they are experiencing.

External progression

Personal tutoring activities towards the end of a degree programme focus increasingly on support for completing dissertations and transitioning out of university. This includes information about whether students are acquiring and evidencing graduate attributes which will enhance their employment prospects (Calcagno et al, 2017). Your role is therefore to make the link between academic learning and professional careers, including serving as a professional role model, by showing you continually reflect on your own practice, for example (Small, 2013). Working closely with the careers and employability service can help here. You will also be asked to write references for tutees going on to graduate employment or further studies.

A curriculum for tutorials

The content that you cover in tutorials is usually flexible (depending on your institution) and must be able to meet the needs of your students. Since all institutions are different and the students within them are divided by subject area and level, the following suggested tutorial content in Table 6.2 (adapted from Calcagno et al, 2017) covers themes that can be adapted and differentiated, as appropriate. Some institutions may favour individual tutorials for certain aspects while others may favour group tutorials so the delivery method may have some flexibility. You may already have tutorial content set; however, the following information acts as a useful guide.

Key activities: Effectively supporting all stages • 133

Table 6.2 A suggested personal tutoring curriculum

Journey point	Theme	Aims	Outcomes By the end of this stage students will	Activities	Link to professional frameworks
Pre-arrival	**Getting to Know You**	Building relationships. Easing the transition to university. Identifying 'at risk' students.	Know who their tutor is and how to contact them. Outline broad goals for their time at university. Identify issues and areas of concern about moving to university.	(Video) messaging with tutor via email, social media or virtual learning environment. Complete pre-entry survey.	**UKAT:** R1 R2 R4 R6 P1 **PSF:** V1 V2 K2 K4 A4
Year 1, semester 1, first 4 weeks	**Getting Connected**	Becoming more informed. Building relationships. Social integration. Settling in.	Have familiarised themselves with: • the institution • the campus • their timetable • the location of programme information • tutorial policies, purposes and values • student voice and representation	Ice-breakers and team building. Each student is given a passport with details of student support services details and have to visit each to get a stamp before their next tutorial. Note taking. Library skills.	**UKAT:** R1 R2 R4 R7 I6 **PSF:** V1 V2 K2 K4 A2 A4

Table 6.2 (Cont.)

Journey point	Theme	Aims	Outcomes By the end of this stage students will	Activities	Link to professional frameworks
Year 1, semester 1, week 5 onwards	**Preparing for Success**	Establishing the rhythm of the student year. Supporting tutees to be prepared for their assessments. Study skills assessment.	Be familiar with communication processes, complaints procedures, information systems, absence and attendance processes. Know how to submit coursework. Understand how to prepare effectively for exams.	Planning and writing assignments. Using references and avoiding plagiarism. Revision guidance and exam technique. Reminder of relevant student support services. Study skills self-assessment.	**UKAT:** R4 R5 R7 P1 I1 I2 I3 I5 I6 **PSF:** V1 V2 K1 K2 K4 A2 A4

Table 6.2 (Cont.)

Journey point	Theme	Aims	Outcomes By the end of this stage students will	Activities	Link to professional frameworks
Year 1, semester 2	**Making the most of University**	Working effectively. Action planning and using feedback. Establishing effective independent learning. Engaging with extra-curricular opportunities to develop graduate attributes.	Reflect on feedback on assessed work and use to plan for improvements. Know how to be independent, take responsibility and manage their time effectively. Understand the range of extra-curricular opportunities for developing graduate attributes available within the university.	Using feedback for personal development – reflective learning and action planning. Time management, independent learning and organisation activities. Exploring sources of information on extra-curricular opportunities. SMART action planning.	**UKAT** R3 R4 R6 **PSF:** V1 V2 K1 K2 A2 A4
Year 2, semester 1	**Refreshing, Reflecting and Developing**	Review of tutorial content covered at year 1. Review paid work/study/life balance. Further action planning.	Fully reflect on academic performance, social integration at year 1 to inform future action plans. Ensure relevant support is in place for level 5.	Return to previous assessment feedback and connect learning to upcoming assessments. Action plan for year 2 including ongoing review.	**UKAT:** R3 R4 R5 R6 I2 I5 **PSF:** V1 V2 K1 K2 A2 A4

Table 6.2 (Cont.)

Journey point	Theme	Aims	Outcomes By the end of this stage students will	Activities	Link to professional frameworks
Year 2, semester 2 (including any time spent on work placement)	**Enhancing your Future**	Employability. Developing graduate attributes. Linking module and pathway selection to careers.	Understand the importance of engaging with extra-curricular opportunities which develop graduate attributes. Have developed a CV and covering letter. Understand the process of finding and applying for jobs or future study. Engage with the careers service.	CV and job application exercise. Career choice exploration and/or presentation. Module and pathway selection guidance.	**UKAT:** R3 R4 R5 R6 R7 I5 I6 **PSF:** V1 V2 A4
Year 3, semester 1	**Becoming a Professional**	Reflecting on any work placements. Planning for the future. Selling yourself/your skills.	Have a plan for what they intend to do after graduation, with clearly identified actions for implementation. Have a professional online profile and an effective CV. Have provided information to their tutor to facilitate the production of effective references.	Employability audit – to identify students who would benefit from interventions. Mock interview and assessment day exercises with the careers service. Reflection activities on work placements and what they mean for graduation. Set SMART targets for post-graduation.	**UKAT:** R3 R4 R5 R6 R7 I2 I6 **PSF:** V1 V2 K2 A4

Table 6.2 (Cont.)

Journey point	Theme	Aims	Outcomes By the end of this stage students will	Activities	Link to professional frameworks
Year 3, semester 2	**Moving On**	Transitioning out of university. Staying connected. Providing feedback.	Understand the graduation process. Appreciate the importance of providing feedback on their student experience.	Explaining graduation and opportunities for remaining connected to the institution as Alumni.	**UKAT:** R1 R3 R4 R6 R7 I6 **PSF:** V1 V2 K2 A2 A4

You can use the information much as you would a course curriculum from which you can develop your own tutorial scheme of work. It is also necessary to recognise the natural overlap between the sections and the importance of revisiting topics or themes, just as you would do in the core curriculum.

In Chapter 3, we discussed UKAT's professional framework for personal tutoring (UKAT, 2023). This framework sets out good practice in personal tutoring, and can therefore inform content of group tutorials. The framework has a conceptual, relational, professional, and informational component and each has its own core competencies, which outline the range of knowledge and skills needed to be an effective personal tutor. These competencies are too lengthy to state here, but they can be found in their entirety on the UKAT website (ukat.ac.uk). The final column of Table 6.2 states the relevant competency for each theme.

The curriculum outlined above is an ideal schedule of activities to undertake with tutees. Institutions will differ in the number of contact points between tutor and tutees in each year. Nevertheless, the curriculum gives an idea of the areas of focus for students at different levels.

Critical thinking activity 6

1. Using Table 6.2, identify any topics you think need adding and any you think are less important for your students.
2. Expand upon the content in the fifth column to develop student activities for each theme.
3. Using these student activities, with a particular individual or group in mind, plan a tutorial session on any topic from Table 6.2, which is fully contextualised within the (or a) subject area the individual or group is studying.

Summary

The personal tutor role can feel all-encompassing, as part of a busy academic workload of teaching, research, and admin. Students need support specific to the stage of the lifecycle they are in. Early in your career or in a new role you may not know what support they may need and how you might help. This chapter has, hopefully, assisted by informing you:

- what the key stages in the student lifecycle are;
- what key tutoring activities personal tutors can use to support students through these stages and transitions;
- what an effective tutoring curriculum might look like.

Moreover, you should now have a chance to reflect on the terminology in order to further understand and enquire about how things work in your institution.

If you want to be effective in the role and have ambitions to progress, you need to be a constructive enquirer of those around you including those in more senior roles. You'll need the appropriate knowledge and language to do this. There will be more on the higher-level support skills in the next three chapters where we also discuss the bigger picture enquiries needed when you are aiming to be highly effective.

Critical reflections

1. How much knowledge do you have of the stages in the student lifecycle from your induction or PG Cert HE?
2. Can you recognise a curriculum of personal tutoring in your institution that guides students through the various stages? How much does the example curriculum provided reflect the practice of your institution?
3. What is your view on the relative importance of one-to-one meetings compared to group tutorials in enabling students to succeed? Do you think your colleagues, and more widely your institution, have a similar view?
4. From your experience of group tutorials, explain how much of your time is spent on managing the students and how much is spent on developing and supporting them, including pastoral activities. Which factors influenced how you divide your time?

Personal tutor self-assessment system

As a reminder, some key activities for the personal tutor are:

- supporting students through the challenges of their initial transition to HE;
- one-to-ones with students;
- group tutorial planning and teaching;
- supporting students through the stages of internal progression on their course;
- advising students regarding potential suspensions, course changes and terminations;
- supporting students' external progression by preparing them for the next step in their education or career.

PERSONAL TUTOR SELF-ASSESSMENT SYSTEM: Chapter 6 Key activities: Effectively supporting all stages of the student lifecycle					
	Minimum standard **1 star**	**Beginner level** **2 star**	**Intermediate level** **3 star**	**Advanced level** **4 star**	**Expert level** **5 star**
Individual	I am aware of the key stages of the student lifecycle from pre-arrival support to graduation. I ensure that key activities, including individual and group tutorials, which support transition through these stages are fully thought through and planned before they begin. My students are aware of the transition support available and how they relate to them.	I regularly reflect to identify strengths and areas for development related to the key activities. I build these into my transition planning and discuss them with my head of department during appraisal meetings. This informs the support I provide for relevant students at an individual and group level.	I regularly ask for student feedback on how effective my individual and group tutorials are at supporting student transitions. I hold formal end-of-year reviews with relevant colleagues to identify strengths and areas for development.	My actions to support student transition put the student first and provide holistic and comprehensive support. Feedback from my students regarding individual and group tutorials is consistently very positive.	I identify and implement methods to measure the impact of individual and group tutorials on my students' progress and outcomes. I reflect and constructively question key activities with managers and others involved to review and improve them regularly. This is a significant factor in improving some key performance indicators.

Key activities: Effectively supporting all stages • 141

| Institutional | My institution has an awareness of student transition into higher education and has the key activities embedded into its strategy for supporting it. Staff are aware of the key activities. | The strategy for supporting students through transitions is effectively communicated to all new staff and updates for existing staff are frequent. Recommended content and structure for one-to-ones and group tutorials are widely disseminated. | Sufficient hours for tutoring (one-to-one and group) are allocated in the timetable to send a clear message to tutors and students that the institution values the role/activity. Clear guidelines on the roles and responsibilities of both tutors and tutees are discussed at the outset. | The key activities (including individual and group tutorials) are routinely discussed in all delivery staff's appraisal meetings. All staff clearly know their roles in supporting transition and carry these out effectively. | The key activities are regularly reviewed involving all relevant student-facing staff and a selection of students. As a result, staff feel invested in them. There is a highly consistent approach to the key activities across my institution. |

7 Key concepts for effective personal tutoring

Chapter aims

This chapter helps you to:

- Further understand key concepts involved in personal tutoring including:
  - managing expectations;
  - effective relationship building;
  - student engagement and motivation.

Although it is challenging to identify every concept relevant to personal tutoring, from experience, we have determined a few key concepts which we believe are most important to personal tutoring, due to the amount of coverage in personal tutoring literature and our experience of leading personal tutoring over a number of years. Some of these concepts have been discussed elsewhere; however, in this chapter we investigate them in more depth and outline how they are essential in promoting student success.

Introduction

In this chapter, the key concepts of managing expectations, effective relationship building and student engagement and motivation are outlined. For each of the three concepts, there will be a definition from the literature, an outline of how the concept relates to personal tutoring and how and when the personal tutor can influence students by using the key tenets of the concept. We believe that use of these concepts in personal tutoring can have a positive effect on student success, which we will define below.

What is student success?

Following the sector's adoption of blended learning approaches, there is a need to acknowledge personal tutoring as being a core factor in student experience and success (McIntosh and Thomas, 2022). Therefore, as personal tutors, you need to be aware of what is meant by student success and how you can help promote it.

Student success is difficult to define. It differs across international contexts and is shaped and impacted by so many factors, not least by the participation of large numbers of students in HE, their own diverse and personalised context and the educational journeys which have brought them to tertiary education in the first place. In 2014, the Higher Education Academy in the UK (now Advance HE) wrote that:

> *Success means different things to different students. It is a complex challenge for all of us in the sector to help students achieve that success, but it is essential that we do so: helping students to transform their lives through higher education is what we are here to do. But the diversity of the student body and its expectations means that trying to pin down a watertight definition of 'student success' is a reductive exercise. At a practical level, however, institutional Strategic Plans and learning and teaching (L&T) strategies are the embodiment of how to achieve student success.*
>
> (Advance HE, 2024)

Success could be viewed in terms of academic achievement; after all, students probably choose to go to university to gain a qualification. However, policymakers now recognise that success includes developing confidence, critical thinking and readiness for employment (Campbell and Nutt, 2008). Success has also historically been linked to retention and progression rather than attainment (Yorke and Longden, 2008), and Holland et al (2020) argue that attainment should be viewed as holistic rather than limited to grades. Therefore, it is clear that success relates to more than simply academic attainment. Chan and Rose (2023) conclude that student success should be viewed holistically, and they outline three domains of success: personal, social and academic.

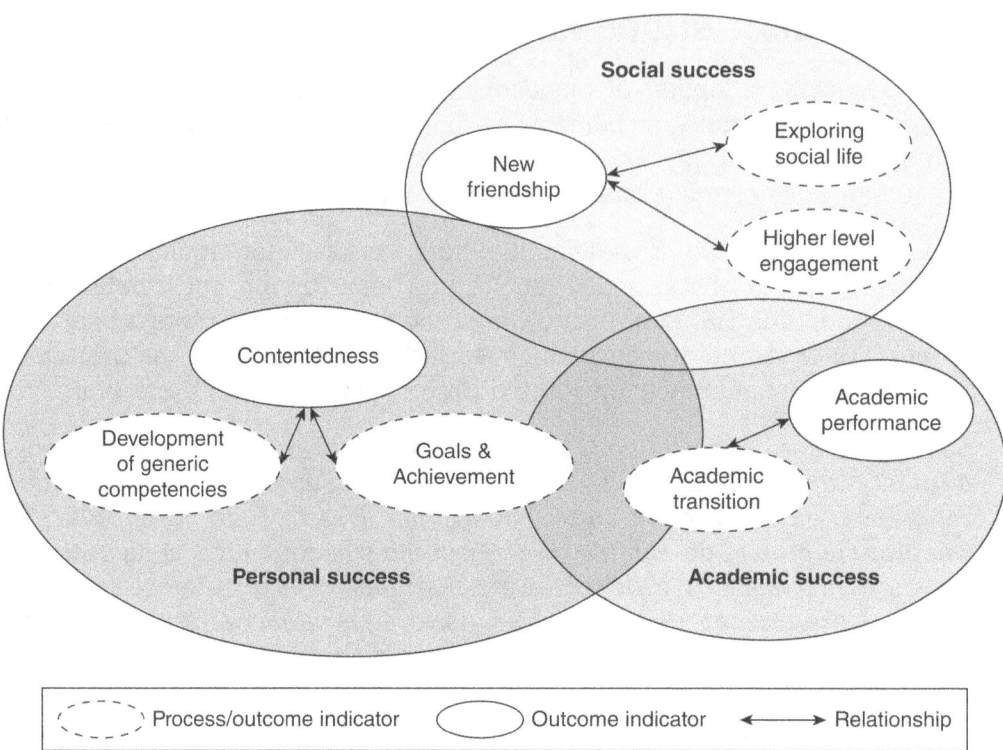

Figure 7.1 Concept of success
(Reproduced with permission from Chan and Rose, 2023)

As seen in Figure 7.1, these areas overlap, with each domain affecting the others, and personal tutors are therefore well placed to help students achieve success in all of them, as they will often speak to tutees about them all. These three domains also feature in Thomas' work (Thomas, 2012; Thomas et al, 2017). In the 2012 What Works report, success is defined as students achieving their desired academic outcomes, but also involves their ability to engage meaningfully with the academic environment, develop supportive peer relationships, interact effectively with staff, build confidence and identity, and experience HE in a way which aligns with their interests and future goals.

Tutors should also be careful to differentiate between student success and institutional success, as sometimes the best advice for a student may be to drop out of university, negatively affecting retention rates (Troxel et al, 2021). It could be concluded that student success is not only about their academic achievement but could also be in terms of reaching their potential, whether that is reflected in results or not.

According to Troxel et al (2021), personal tutors are well-placed to support students both in and out of the classroom, helping them in their development and therefore contributing to their success. There are many ways personal tutors can help support student success, and we look at how the core concepts we identified can achieve this in the following sections.

Managing expectations

One of the challenges of personal tutor–student relationships is the expectations both parties hold about each other (Van Nieuwerburgh, 2017). If tutees are not obtaining what they expect from a relationship with their tutor, this can lead to disappointment and frustration (Raby, 2023). Similarly, tutors may not always be aware of what students are expecting from them.

In the past, *psychological contract theory* was used to help understand relationships between employers and employees. However, several authors (Bordia et al, 2010; Koskina, 2013; O'Toole and Prince, 2015) have since used it to look at relationships between students and their research supervisors. O'Toole and Prince (2015) defined a psychological contract as, '… the subjective beliefs concerning rights and responsibilities that an individual holds with regard to an exchange agreement between themselves and an organisation, which 'solidifies' into a mental model' (p 161). It originally stems from *social exchange theory* (Blau, 1964), which entails both parties sticking to the rules of the exchange, in other words, what they expect from each other. This develops into obligations and expectations of each other (Bordia et al, 2010). Yale (2020c) used this theory to examine students' expectations of their relationships with personal tutors in HE, and this study can help tutors to understand students' attitudes and behaviours. As she points out in the study, the psychological contract students have with their personal tutor is not simply about the policies institutions have in place around personal tutoring but goes beyond this as students arrive with their own expectations of that relationship in mind. These expectations could be shaped by a previous relationship with a personal tutor at school, college or a previous university, and may be very different from the provision of personal tutoring in their new institution. This is especially true of first-year students or those transferring from another HE provider.

Raby (2023) investigated this in her study of the personal tutoring relationships between Chinese students and their tutors and found that students' expectations were vastly different from the provision of the university. Students expected their tutors to be able to proofread drafts of their assignments, for example, and expressed disappointment when tutors did not provide this. They also expected tutors to answer messages at all times of day or night and preferred personal tutors who would respond quickly to messages. Students also held expectations around how close their relationship with a personal tutor should be, and preferred to have a close, friendly relationship. On the other hand, some students had no expectations of the relationship before they arrived at university, as they understood that it would be different from their home experience. Although this study was focused specifically on Chinese students, it could also be true of students of other nationalities, or indeed home students. It is therefore important, as personal tutors, that you manage the expectations your students might have before they arrive.

Student expectations may be around the following areas:

- Study/academic support
- Personal support

- Frequency/speed of contact
- Aspirations of closeness

See Table 7.1 for further information on these areas.

Table 7.1 Students expectations of personal tutors

Type of support	Explanation
Study/academic support	Students may expect help with their assignments, e.g. viewing drafts, help with essay planning, help with dissertation, understanding feedback, giving extensions on coursework. Students may expect tutors to help dispute or change their grades. The amount of support expected in this area could differ significantly between students.
Personal support	Expectations could be around listening to students' issues and challenges, or they may even expect their tutor to act as a counsellor (George and Rapley, 2022). They could expect help with careers advice and writing references for job applications or further study (Gray and Shanmugam, 2022). They may expect financial help and advice (McFarlane, 2016).
Contact	Students may expect to receive instant responses to their emails or messages, sometimes out of working hours. Some students may expect their tutors to be more proactive in reaching out to contact them (Millmore et al, 2022).
Aspirations of closeness	Students could expect to have a close, friendly relationship with their personal tutors. Conversely, they may expect more of a transactional relationship and only wish to contact their tutor when they have a particular need such as a form to be signed or when they need general information.

Part of managing these expectations is signposting where there is a boundary in terms of our own expertise, time or it is not appropriate for a personal tutor to offer help in a certain area. This could involve directing students to library services for help with assignments, or well-being for assistance with mental health issues, for example.

Another part of managing expectations is sharing responsibilities with your students, as the onus is not completely on you to instigate a positive relationship; rather, it should be a two-way relationship. Through shared responsibility, tutors can develop positive relationships with students, and the more you move towards sharing responsibility with students, the more you embrace a partnership approach (Bovill, 2020a).

You may, for example, expect your students to notify you of any extenuating circumstances or learning differences which they expect the university to take into account. Students may assume that personal tutors will be informed of such declarations; however, sometimes systems are slow to communicate information, meaning that tutors do not always find out important information straight away. You could make clear to your students at the start which actions are their responsibility and which they could reasonably expect you to do for them.

In your initial meetings with students (either group or individual), you could collaborate with them to draw up a document or contract (Foy, 2020), outlining the responsibilities you expect each other to have in terms of the tutor–student relationship.

Personal tutors can use the concept of managing expectations to enhance their relationships with tutees, leading to a positive impact on student success. It is necessary to manage these expectations so that students do not experience disappointment or frustration. Firstly, giving clear information around the role of the personal tutor to students upon their arrival and reiterating this at various points throughout the academic year to avoid freshers' overload (Yale, 2020a) can help tutors and students to understand what is expected. It is also a good idea to ensure that personal tutors are clear about their roles, so that they can communicate this effectively to their students.

There are a few suggestions below on how this information could be shared to students:

- A welcome week session on personal tutoring (repeated later during the year).
- A checklist of what personal tutors can and cannot do for students.
- A website area or section of VLE site with clear information around personal tutoring.
- Regular information given at group tutorial sessions.
- Email signatures of personal tutors containing information around expected response times and office hours.
- Make personal tutors' contact information prominent on student-facing records.
- Create posters or leaflets around personal tutoring and its function.

Effective relationship building

We discussed in Chapter 2 how personal tutoring is situated as relational pedagogy, with positive relationships between staff and students at the centre of teaching (Bovill, 2020a). As personal tutors, it is vitally important to develop effective relationships with our tutees. In a world which is becoming more automated, human connections can be particularly important for both tutors and students. In fact, this human connection with a supportive academic is often the factor which will make a difference to a struggling student (WonkHE, 2024a).

Felten and Lambert (2020, p 61) outline five factors in promoting meaningful relationships:

- Value students: view them holistically and value the assets they bring to the institution.

- Value the efforts staff make towards building relationships: reward those who value relationships with students, cultivating a workforce which places importance on building relationships.
- Value high-quality teaching: promote effective educational practices and relational pedagogy.
- Value webs of human interactions: offer plenty of opportunities for students to make connections.
- Value engagement over prestige: acknowledge that meaningful relationships can enable social mobility and leadership.

The first point talks about valuing the whole student and the assets that they bring rather than focusing on the problems they may have, which is linked to solution-focused coaching, discussed in Chapter 2. As tutors, we should be looking for the positive aspects we can see in our tutees and encouraging them to appreciate and develop these. We are often tempted to focus on points for improvement, but reflection should also involve appreciating the positives and successes.

Learner analytics can help us to understand and get to know our students (Lowes, 2020). They can provide us with useful background information and insight, which can then be enhanced by our face-to-face contact. We looked at using this information in Chapter 5 on supporting different student populations.

Effective listening is an important core skill of the personal tutor mentioned in Chapters 3 and 6 and in many of the approaches of academic advising suggested by NACADA (Drake et al, 2013). One of these approaches is the proactive advising approach (Varney, 2013), in which Nutt (2000) states that it is vital that advisors develop the skills of effective listening, questioning and referral in order to conduct effective one-to-ones with students. McGill et al (2020) conducted research with personal tutors in three different countries and found that they should possess 'patience and empathy, listening skills and the ability to oscillate from tiny details to the bigger picture' (p 7). From both seminal and more recent literature, we can see that the skill of active listening remains highly important for personal tutors.

The Higher Education Mental Health Implementation Taskforce have outlined principles of Compassionate Communication with the support of the Academic Registrars' Council (ARC), setting out five principles for HE providers, which are promoting a culture of kindness, mindful and timely communication, inclusivity and reflection and continuous improvement (ARC, 2025, p 4). By embedding these principles into communication, personal tutors can enhance a sense of mattering and belonging in their tutees.

Critical thinking activity 1

Reflect for a moment on your own listening skills. Do you find yourself wandering off in your mind when someone is speaking to you? Do you feel that you are waiting for someone to finish speaking so that you can say something? Do you find it difficult to focus and remember what people are saying? If so, you may need to think about how to improve your listening skills.

We will consider some suggestions on how to improve listening skills. Have a look at Table 7.2 of suggestions below and rank them in order of importance to you for your improvement. Also note the ones which you already do. Pay particular attention to the last point on the table and think about how you can incorporate your listening skills into written communications.

Table 7.2 Improving listening skills

Suggestion	Explanation
Notice non-verbal communication	Is your student showing signs of anxiety during their communication with you? They may demonstrate this by avoiding eye contact or fidgeting. You may also spot signs of anxiety in their voice, e.g. struggling to express themselves or sounding shaky.
Keep an open, non-judgemental mindset	Try not to express any surprise or shock at what the student is saying to you. Do not judge, even if you feel they have done/said something which does not fit with your moral compass.
Focus	Actively focus your mind on what the student is saying and try to understand how they might be feeling.
Summarise back	When they have finished speaking, give a brief summary to show that you have heard and understood what they have said.
Respect	Respect the student by not interrupting and looking interested in what they are saying. You can show interest by nodding or smiling at appropriate points or interjecting with short words or phrases such as 'yes', 'I see'.
Maintain eye contact	Look at your student while they are speaking to you, but don't overdo it by staring too intently.
Do not be afraid of silence	It is not always good to jump in straight away when someone has finished speaking. A reflective pause can help students to think about what they have said and see that you are considering their thoughts carefully.
Ask questions	Ask your student to give further details (if they feel comfortable) or to clarify anything you didn't quite understand fully. You could also ask them how something made them feel and try to understand their emotions.
Consider your written communication	Bauer and Figl (2008) conducted a study to discover whether active listening could translate into text conversations such as instant messaging or emails. They found that following active listening principles can also be applied to text conversations. As personal tutors, we could think about how we respond to messages and show understanding through our written communication. Something as simple as a 'thumbs up' to a message could encourage positive communication.

Active listening is a good way to show your students you care. In the next critical thinking activity, you will consider other ways of showing care and empathy.

Critical thinking activity 2

In Chapter 2, we looked at how personal tutoring is situated within relational pedagogy, and the importance of showing students that we care. This activity therefore examines how else you can build positive, meaningful relationships with your students.

- What other ways can you think of to show your students you care?
- How can you ensure you view the student as a whole person?
- What does proactivity mean to you? How do you demonstrate this to your students?

Table 7.3 may help you to answer the above questions. Read the suggestions and see which ones you already use (if so, consider how you feel it went) and which ones you plan to try. These suggestions all relate to how you may demonstrate a caring, holistic approach with your students.

Table 7.3 Building positive relationships with your students

Suggestions	Explanation
Ask interested questions about your students	You could ask them about their hobbies, likes/dislikes, etc., but nothing too personal at the start if they do not volunteer personal information.
Remember details	e.g. if your student told you they have an important event coming up, ask them how it went afterwards.
Remember their names and say 'hello' when you see them on campus	It seems fairly obvious but can be challenging if you have a large number of tutees.
Send regular emails/messages to your students and invite them for one-to-ones	Make sure your students know that you have time set aside and they are not disturbing you.
Understand their background	Learner analytics may be helpful but try to get to know your students by encouraging them to share their backgrounds with you.
Ask them about their aspirations	Ask students questions about their future aspirations so you can help them to accomplish their goals.
Be prepared to share information about yourself	This can sometimes help students to open up about themselves.
Give your students time	This can be challenging but do not make your students feel as if you are rushing them.
Challenge	Another core skill of the personal tutor is being able to challenge students. Challenging them to reach their potential is a good way to show you care.

Student engagement and motivation

Student engagement has been defined by Trowler (2010) as:

> *concerned with the interaction between the time, effort and other relevant resources invested by both students and their institutions intended to optimise the student experience and enhance the learning outcomes and development of students and the performance, and reputation of the institution* (p 3).

Of course, some students will have more time and capacity to engage than others, for example, those students who need to work may have limited time to engage extensively. To understand student engagement, we also need to acknowledge the links engagement has with a sense of belonging to the university (Brown, 2022), and that personal tutoring can support this sense of belonging (Yale, 2019).

How can you increase student engagement in personal tutoring? Perhaps at your institution personal tutoring is timetabled and could count towards a student's attendance data. As we saw in Chapter 6, to establish personal tutoring as a core activity, timetabling and an effective curriculum can enhance engagement (McIntosh et al, 2022; Wright, 2022). In Chapter 2, we explored coaching and mentoring approaches to personal tutoring, which have been used to good effect in terms of student engagement (Woods and Lefever, 2022). These case studies have shown that whether carried out in groups or individual meetings, engagement in personal tutoring seems to be enhanced by being a timetabled part of the curriculum.

So what motivates our students to engage in personal tutoring? As already mentioned, if personal tutoring is timetabled then students may be more motivated to attend. However, it could be more beneficial for students if they actually *want* to engage in personal tutoring and view it as a valuable part of their education. Creating an interesting curriculum which students find useful could encourage engagement. Co-creation would be beneficial for this: if students have input into creating the personal tutoring curriculum, they may be more inclined to attend. There may also be students who want to engage but are prevented by time constraints or other issues. For these students, personal tutors may need to be flexible in the support they offer, for example, by offering to speak to students at different times of day which may better suit their schedules.

Critical thinking activity 3

1. To what extent do you feel students are engaged in personal tutoring? Why or why not?
2. What do you think could be done to increase student engagement and motivation?
3. What have you tried that works/does not work? Why do you think this was the case?

Creating meaningful interactions with students can help students to become more motivated and engaged in personal tutoring. In other words, attending one-to-one or group tutorials could be seen by students as beneficial if they regard them as meaningful activities. Here are a few suggestions for making one-to-one conversations meaningful:

- have set topics to discuss at different points in the year (i.e. a tutoring curriculum);
- prepare a list of questions to ask students;
- ask students to prepare some reflection before their appointment;
- ask students to complete an action plan during or shortly after each meeting.

For group tutorials, it could be beneficial to follow a curriculum of subjects with set learning outcomes which would be useful for all students, for example, study skills or professional development. See Chapter 6 for more information on a curriculum for group tutorials.

Summary

This chapter has considered three key concepts we believe will have a positive effect on student success. It is recommended that you consider how you and your institution make use of these and what you could do to improve effectiveness.

Critical reflections

1. In your personal tutor role, to what extent do you believe you are encouraging student success?
2. Can you recognise those students who require more motivation and engagement to succeed? Do you have an action plan on how you can encourage those students?
3. Do you believe you build positive relationships with your students? If not, how can you improve your interactions? Do you encourage your students to be independent?
4. To what extent does your institution manage student expectations of the personal tutoring relationship? If this could be improved, how do you think you may be able to help your institution to do this?

Personal tutor self-assessment system

See the following table.

Key concepts for effective personal tutoring • 153

PERSONAL TUTOR SELF-ASSESSMENT SYSTEM: Chapter 7 Effective student interactions, engagement and relationships

	Minimum standard 1 star	Beginner level 2 star	Intermediate level 3 star	Advanced level 4 star	Expert level 5 star
Individual	I provide engaging sessions for my students. I effectively interact with my students and aim to develop a relationship with them.	I continually work to improve the engagement of my students in the sessions I provide. I can see that my interactions with students are developing into a positive relationship.	My students benefit from the engaging sessions I provide. My students are clear that I am willing to interact and develop a positive relationship with them. They understand that I am helping them to be successful.	My students are becoming successful in reaching their potential. Based upon feedback, my students and I experience a positive, beneficial relationship.	Effective engagement with students is embedded in all of my work with them. As a result of my interactions, students are successful in reaching their potential.
Institutional	My institution ensures that personal tutors are equipped with materials to provide engaging sessions for students. They encourage tutors to develop a positive relationship with their students.	My institution provides clear guidance to staff on how to improve engagement and positive interactions.	My institution reviews resources to ensure they are appropriate and engaging. They encourage tutors to seek student views on their relationships and engagement.	My institution actively seeks and considers students' views on their personal tutoring relationships and engagement.	My institution co-creates resources with students to promote effective engagement. My institution rewards staff who prioritise relationships.

8 Reflective practice and professional development

Chapter aims

This chapter helps you to:

- identify the difference between reflection and reflective practice;
- understand why reflective practice is important for your personal tutor role;
- consider the benefits of, and potential barriers to, effective reflective practice for your personal tutor role and the institution you work for;
- explore a number of reflective practice models and apply these to typical personal tutoring scenarios;
- understand the professional development opportunities available to you as a personal tutor.
- identify your training needs;
- consider how to develop your professional identity;
- identify how you can receive support in your personal tutoring practice and how you can support others.

Critical thinking activity 1

» *In preparation for this chapter, it is important to consider the significance of reflection, reflective practice and professional development, and how this contributes to the approach of the institution you are part of and your beliefs and attitudes as a personal tutor. Copy and complete Figure 8.1, filling in the empty boxes by stating your current approach to reflective practice and professional development. You could include benefits, barriers to carrying it out, relevance or importance to your personal tutor role and the tutoring approach endorsed by your institution. You could also include the professional development opportunities afforded to you as a personal tutor within and outside of your university. Try to make your statements as specific as possible because this will provide you with a reference point and help you in understanding and implementing reflective practice and managing your professional development in the future.*

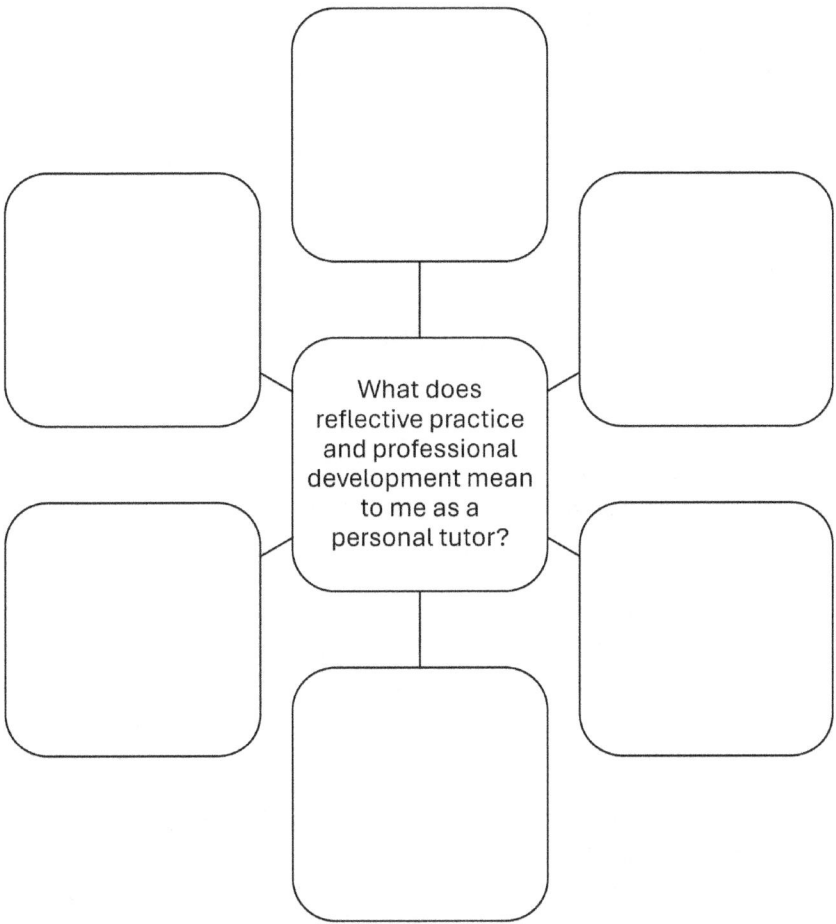

Figure 8.1 *What does reflective practice and professional development mean to me as a personal tutor?*

What do we mean by reflection and reflective practice?

Reflection and reflective practice are important tools to enable professionals to learn from their own experiences. Although they are very similar and complement each other as part of a continuous learning cycle, there are subtle differences between them (Figure 8.2).

156 • *Effective Personal Tutoring and Academic Advising in Higher Education*

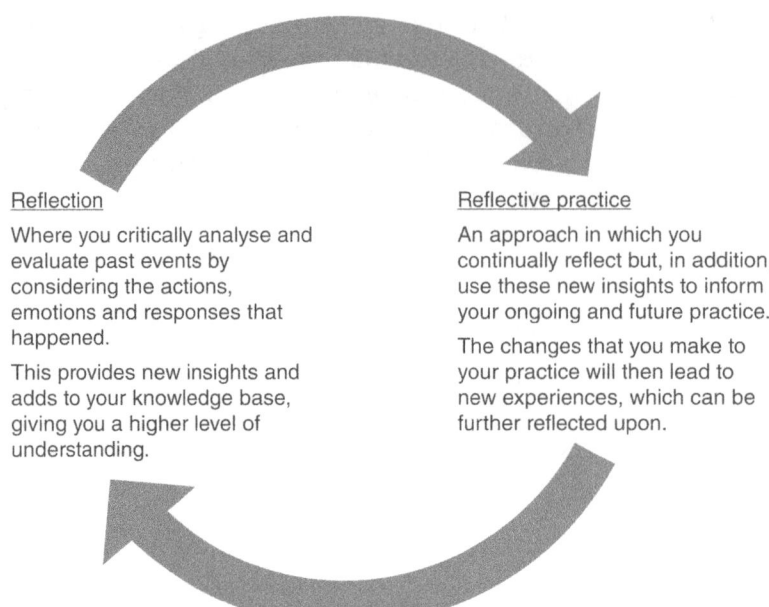

Figure 8.2 *Reflection and reflective practice*

As mentioned at the start of the book, whether you are a new or an established academic, finding time in the 'whirlwind' of teaching and personal tutoring can be a challenge due to the numerous demands placed on you by your students and the institution you work for. How often have you stopped what you are doing for a *useful* and *significant* period of time and reflected upon your experiences in an organised way to make sense of them? Valuable thinking or reflection opportunities provide you with the chance to contemplate the aspects of your practice which you would like to change or develop; for example, whether something could work better the next time you try it. Time for reflection should be built into working practices, either on your own or with your mentor. Reflective practice can also help you to understand how personal tutoring contributes to your own development as an academic. With so many institutions focusing on student continuation, completion and success, the role of the personal tutor is becoming more central to achieving student-centred strategy. As a consequence, the training and professional development needs of personal tutors is becoming increasingly significant, with a firm focus on developing skills and professional practice networks. Regular reflection can help you to develop tutoring skills, identify areas of interest and support training and professional development needs. Reflection also enables you to work through particular tutoring issues and also helps to recognise patterns of student behaviour, as well as identify themes for discussion with other tutors and colleagues. Finally, reflection on your tutoring role should also inform your overall academic career progression and, in that respect, the tutoring role should be an integral part of the academic performance review process. This is discussed later in the chapter.

Improving your teaching through reflective practice is widely considered as vital for both new and established academics and it is no different when it comes to your personal tutoring role, which is also central to teaching and learning. Fundamentally, reflection involves thinking deeply about an experience in order to understand it and make sense of it. However, reflection alone is not sufficient to stimulate effective learning and improve your personal tutor practice. Even if you regularly reflect on your practice, ten years' experience as a personal tutor may consist of ten years doing the same thing in the same way. The key principle is to regularly act on your reflections, informed by your practice and the perspective of others, which will ensure effective learning and continuous professional development.

Throughout your academic career you are likely to encounter a significant number of theoretical frameworks, definitions and models related to this topic, some of which are explored in the section of this chapter on models of reflective practice. This chapter aims to contextualise reflective practice for your personal tutor role.

Reflective practice and the personal tutor role

A large proportion of your time as a personal tutor involves supporting students individually and to do this effectively requires a great deal of focus, emotional energy, adaptability, decision-making and, most of all, skill. If you are new to personal tutoring you may consider approaching another academic colleague to act as your mentor. Mentoring by a trusted colleague can help you to critically evaluate your practice and is valuable at any stage of your professional development as a tutor. Mentoring is integral to the reflective process. It helps you discuss skills and specific issues and can also help you to decide how to act upon the advice you are given. Mentoring can help to highlight areas of best practice and can also assist you to evaluate the stage you are at in your tutoring role, as well as explore avenues for further development. Formal academic mentoring schemes may already exist within your institution but mentoring can also take place informally and can usually be set up in consultation with your line manager. In Chapter 3, we discussed the UKAT professional recognition scheme (2023) which could help you to evaluate your practice as a personal tutor. It involves writing a reflective account of your personal tutoring practice, and could therefore help you to consider your practice in this area.

Tutoring is a vital part of academic practice and, in line with other teaching and learning activities, tutors must hone the necessary skills and experience to support this activity. To this end, reflecting on and discussing your practice, as well as participating in other professional development activities, will help you to decide how best to invest your time. In terms of your personal tutor role, the following key points highlight what reflective practice is and is not, as well as the expected benefits and challenges of undertaking this activity regularly.

It is:

- a time to think clearly, be honest and consider the facts of your chosen area of reflection;
- an activity which can be undertaken individually or with another person (for example, a mentor or trusted colleague);
- a process which should be undertaken regularly, for example, once a week or after a significant event;

- a skill which can be learned and honed;
- an activity which should be undertaken alongside other professional development activities, such as peer observation, training and work shadowing;
- about applying critical analysis to your reflection, such as:
  - what actually happened (good and bad);
  - what everyone's feelings were at the time;
  - what else you could have done or done differently;
  - what you might choose to do differently next time.

It is not:

- something you need less as your experience as a personal tutor increases;
- a waste of your planning and development time;
- an easy thing to do because critically analysing yourself can mean asking tough, probing questions.
- purely negative or overly self-critical.

The benefits of reflection are as follows.

- It can improve your ability to view events clearly and more objectively.
- It can help you to respond more positively to difficult issues or problems.
- If carried out with a trusted colleague or mentor, it enables you to 'offload' any difficult or emotional issues in a structured, positive and supportive way (sometimes referred to as 'supervision' within other fields).
- It can reduce stress and feelings of anxiety.
- It can reduce feelings of isolation and combat a culture of individualism, particularly when undertaken with a trusted colleague and mentor.
- It can help you to identify your personal strengths and relative limitations and to gain new professional insights.
- It can improve your confidence, professional judgement and practice as a personal tutor.
- It creates a positive, continuous professional development cycle when undertaken regularly.

The challenges of reflection are as follows.

- It can be difficult to find the time to engage with.
- You may lack the experience and/or knowledge to make sense of some issues. This could lead to you following the reflective models more 'mechanically' and

not reflecting critically or deeply enough to fully understand the real issue(s). Undertaking reflection with your mentor or an experienced, trusted colleague would help to mitigate this.

- As it requires a critical and honest approach, you could find that you view your areas for improvement as failures, instead of an opportunity to learn and develop. Therefore resilience and a positive attitude is needed.
- You may fear that if you discuss your moments of reflection (such as examples of poor judgement) openly with colleagues, you may be jeopardising or damaging your reputation.
- The educational institution's culture and processes may not actively support you and other personal tutors to be honest and open in your moments of reflection.

Models of reflective practice

Models of reflective practice encourage a structured process to guide your thinking, learning and your application of new knowledge. There are a number of models and theories that you can choose from; however, it is important to recognise that there are various specific models that are used within an HE setting. The model that you choose should help you to reflect constructively on your personal tutoring practice. In this section we will consider a range of models from Kolb, Gibbs, Johns and Brookfield. However, there are more models and theories of reflective practice to research and consider using, such as Dewey (1933), Schön (1983), Atkins and Murphy (1994), Rolfe et al (2001) and Moon (2004). Our experience has shown that it can be useful and appropriate to use one model of reflective practice as a basis, but use elements from other models if they best fit your particular situation. Therefore, it is important to try a number of models and, through trial and error, find which best suits your needs as a personal tutor and even, possibly, create your own personal reflective practice model.

The Experiential Learning Cycle: Kolb

Kolb's publications, notably his book *Experiential Learning: Experience as The Source of Learning and Development* (1984) and the development of his Experiential Learning Cycle theory, have been seminal in developing our understanding of human learning behaviour. In essence, the model advocates 'learning from experience' and is typically represented by a four-stage cycle. Kolb viewed learning as an integrated process, with each stage being mutually supportive of, and feeding into, the next. It is possible to enter the cycle at any point and follow through the sequence; however, Kolb believed that 'effective learning' only occurs when you are able to execute all four stages of the model, suggesting that no one stage of the cycle is an effective learning process in isolation (Figure 8.3).

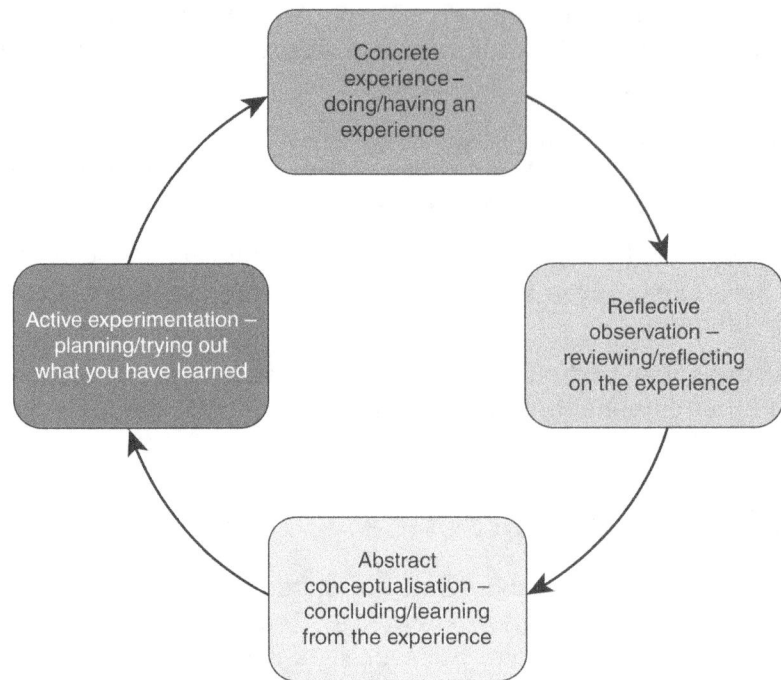

Figure 8.3 Kolb's Experiential Learning Cycle
(Adapted, 1984)

Concrete experience

The concrete experience is the 'doing' element which stems from your actual experience of personal tutor practice.

Reflective observation

The reflective observation component of the model derives from your analysis and judgements of events relating to delivery and support activities that you engage in as a personal tutor. You are likely to naturally reflect on your experiences, particularly if you are new to the personal tutor role and possibly less confident in your knowledge and ability. It is very common for practitioners who are new to the personal tutor role to work with a student on a one-to-one basis or in a group tutorial and consider, intuitively, that it did not go very well. This 'common sense reflection' a phrase coined by Jennifer Moon (Moon, 2004, p 82), is a useful starting point, but how do you really know what was good and bad, and why?

Donald Schön (1983) made the important distinction between the two reflective states: *reflection-in-action* and *reflection-on-action*. Both of these are critical to the personal tutoring role and relate to both the concrete practice and reflective observation elements of Kolb's model. *Reflection-in-action* relates to a setting where your reflection can still benefit the situation rather than deciding how you would act in the future after the moment has passed. This type of reflective tool is extremely helpful in deciding how to act at the time an event occurs. Accordingly, as a tutor, you can decide what might work best for that given situation, drawing on your knowledge and experience. *Reflection-on-action*, however, considers how your practice might develop after the event has passed. Both states are important to the overall development of tutoring practice and can help develop the flexibility to think on your feet.

Essentially, you need to articulate these thoughts or reflections in a clear and systematic way so that you can remember what you thought in order to build on that experience. Examples of ways to capture and crystallise your thoughts could be through keeping a journal of your reflections after one-to-ones and group tutorials or after any significant event at work (see Brookfield's suggestions for reflective journals later in this section). Other useful information which will feed into and add to this holistic reflection might be formal observations of your practice by your mentor, peer observation, appraisals and student feedback.

Abstract conceptualisation

In addition to your reflections on your experience you should be informed by wider reading and educational theory, particularly in relation to the four theoretical constructs – transition pedagogy, relational pedagogy, learning-centred advising, and coaching and mentoring approaches – outlined in Chapter 2. These will act as a useful starting point for your personal tutoring practice. To inform your reflections, you could also read books, research journal articles or HE blogs and websites, attend a training session or speak to a colleague or mentor who you feel may have sufficient experience in that area. In essence, this section allows you to bring together the theory and analysis from the reflective observation stage, which will allow you to form conclusions about your personal tutoring practice and inform your professional development.

Active experimentation

The conclusions you formed from the abstract conceptualisation stage will form the basis by which you can plan the changes to your practice and turn your reflections into reflective practice. This is where the cycle starts again; active experimentation is where you put into action the desired changes you want in your role as a personal tutor in order to create another concrete experience and thereby create a continuous professional development cycle.

The Reflective Cycle: Gibbs

Gibbs' (1998) *Reflective Cycle model* provides useful questions to guide your reflections. It encourages a clear description of the situation, analysis and evaluation of feelings, the event, your experience, as well as examining how you might change your practice in the future. As a personal tutor, you will work with students on a one-to-one basis regularly, and an effective way of capturing learning from ad hoc experiences during these one-to-ones and group tutorials is to review completed reflections together to identify any patterns or trends in your practice which may not be immediately obvious. If you choose this model for your reflections, it is advisable to follow the six stages, with each one informing the next. The analysis section is where you will need to use discursive, analytical writing. The other sections require mainly statements of description, statements of value (whether something was challenging or rewarding) and statements of summation or statements of justification (why something was done) (Figure 8.4).

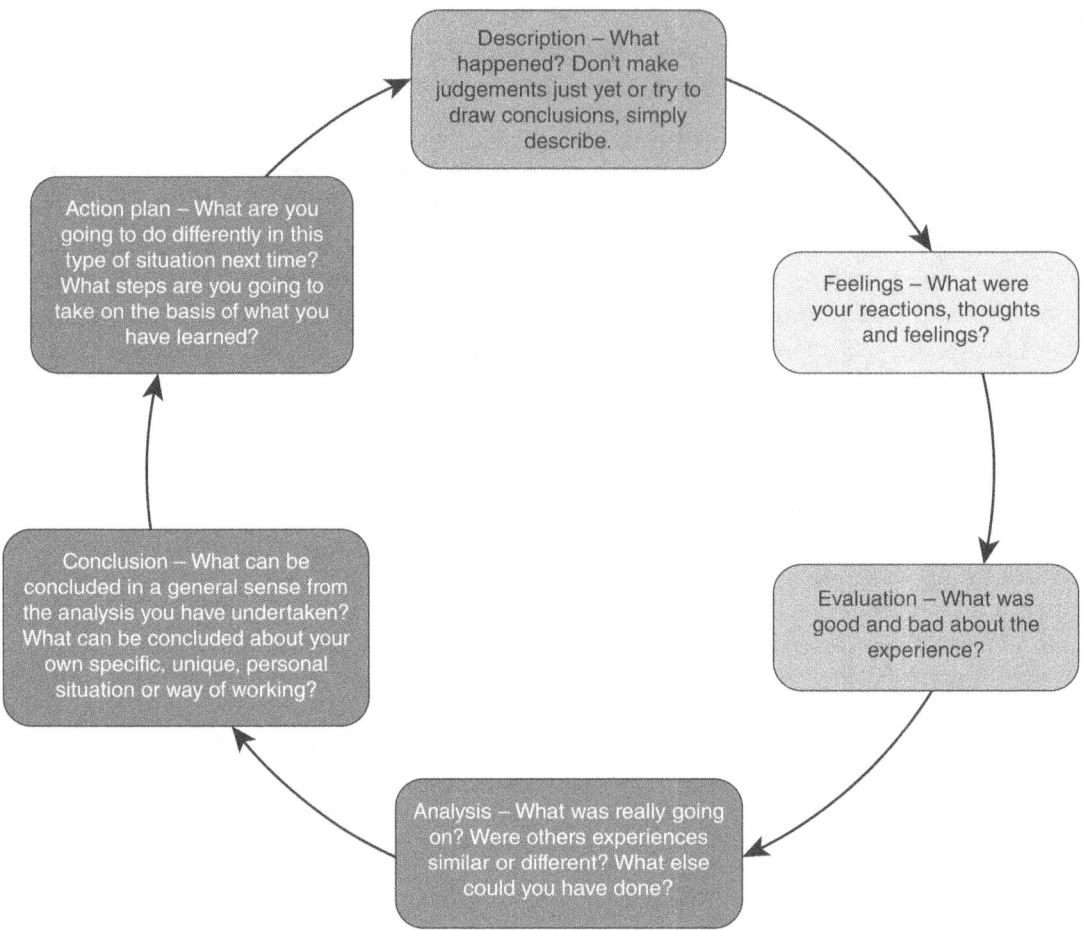

Figure 8.4 Gibbs' Reflective Cycle (Adapted, 1998)

Model of Structured Reflection: Johns

Johns' (1995) *Model of Structured Reflection*, similar to Gibbs' model, provides useful questions to stimulate and structure your thoughts. This model can be used individually; but the model also supports the idea of undertaking reflective practice with an experienced colleague and refers to this as 'guided reflection'. Talking to your colleagues about what happens when you work with students can sometimes, sadly, become a rare experience. Even though, for the majority of people, reflective practice itself is an intensely personal process, valuable discussions with a colleague or mentor can help shed new light on your experiences as a personal tutor, and even though you may not find a solution, it can be reassuring and sometimes motivating to realise that your experiences are often shared by others.

As discussed in earlier chapters, effective personal tutors develop a high level of rapport with students while maintaining clear professional boundaries, and as a result they tend to find out a lot more about their students than some of their fellow colleagues.

Furthermore, it may be that you will find out a lot more about your students through your personal tutoring role, when working with them in one-to-ones, than through your teaching role. The things that you find out can affect your emotions. This is why peer reflective practice is a very useful tool for your personal tutoring role. Another person's point of view removes some of the subjectivity from the reflection, which can be more effective in making sense of, and dealing with, difficult issues.

Even though Johns' model is not portrayed as cyclical, it is advisable to treat it as such and begin each reflective practice session at the description phase. The questions have not been designed to be asked in a particular order, although there is a progression within the questions. Also, you do not have to use all of the questions in every reflective practice session, and, if appropriate, you can use any question more than once.

Johns' Model of Structured Reflection (1995): adapted

Stage 1: Description

- Write a description of the experience.
- What are the key issues within this description that I need to pay attention to?

Stage 2: Reflection

- What was I trying to achieve?
- Why did I act as I did?
- What are the consequences of my actions for the following:
  - the students;
  - myself;
  - the people I work with?
- How did I feel about this experience when it was happening?
- How did the student/colleague feel about it?
- How do I know how the student/colleague felt about it?

Stage 3: Influencing factors

- What internal factors influenced my decision-making and actions?
- What external factors influenced my decision-making and actions?
- What sources of knowledge influenced or should have influenced my decision-making and actions?

Stage 4: Alternative strategies

- Could I have dealt with the situation better?
- What other choices did I have?
- What would be the consequences of these other choices?

Stage 5: Learning

- How can I make sense of this experience in light of past experience and future practice?
- How do I feel about this experience now?
- Have I taken effective action to support myself and others as a result of this experience?

Four critically reflective lenses: Brookfield

Even though Brookfield relates his thinking on reflective practice to the traditional teaching role, some of his suggestions are equally relevant to the personal tutor role, and in places we have adapted them to fit this.

In order to succeed in becoming critically reflective, Brookfield (1995, pp 29–30) asserts that teachers must view themselves through four critically reflective lenses, which are:

1. Our autobiographies as learners and teachers: using our own unique personal self-reflection and collecting the insights and meanings for teaching.
2. Our students' eyes: making an assessment of oneself through the students' lens by seeking their input and seeing classrooms and learning from their perspectives.
3. Our colleagues' experiences: by peer review of teaching from colleagues' experiences, observations and feedback.
4. Theoretical literature: by frequently referring to the theoretical literature that may provide an alternative, interpretive framework for a situation.

Often, academics are required to undertake some of the four aspects of Brookfield's model as part of their PG Cert HE and other aspects are likely to be built into the processes of the institution that you work within such as the performance review process. A key aspect, which you may not have been asked to carry out as a personal tutor, is keeping a reflective journal – in Brookfield's terms a 'Teaching Log' (stage one of his model), in our terms a 'personal tutor log'.

Brookfield (1995) argues that it is useful for teachers to keep a weekly record of the events that have impressed themselves most vividly on their consciousness, particularly focusing on events that were positive, stressful or challenging. He argues that one of the principal benefits for teachers of becoming critically reflective is to ground them emotionally, and this is certainly useful within the personal tutor role due to the multitude of issues you can be faced with. In order to make this personal tutor log a feasible task, try filling in the journal weekly for 15 to 20 minutes. Brookfield (1995) recommends some of the following questions and suggests that you should jot down any brief responses that seem appropriate.

- What was (were) the moment(s) this week when I felt most connected, engaged or affirmed as a personal tutor – the moment(s) I said to myself, 'This is what being a personal tutor is really about'?

- What was (were) the moment(s) this week when I felt most disconnected, disengaged or bored as a personal tutor – the moment(s) I said to myself, 'I'm just going through the motions here'?
- What was the situation that caused me the greatest anxiety or distress – the kind of situation that I kept replaying in my mind as I was dropping off to sleep, or that caused me to say to myself, 'I don't want to go through this again for a while'?
- What was the event that most took me by surprise – an event where I saw or did something that shook me up, caught me off guard, knocked me off my stride, gave me a jolt, or made me unexpectedly happy?
- Of everything I did this week in my personal tutor role, what would I do differently if I had the chance to do it again?
- What do I feel proudest of in my personal tutoring activities this week and why?

Despite the fact that our personal tutoring experiences run the risk of being dismissed as 'merely anecdotal', Brookfield, while conceding that 'all experience is inherently idiosyncratic', asserts that our autobiographies are 'one of the most important sources of insight into teaching to which we have access' (1995, p 31).

Regularly updating a personal tutor log is a good way to begin to make reflective practice more of a routine and less of a one-off when the need arises, and it will produce benefits for your ongoing professional development as a personal tutor. Your institution may have a dashboard or electronic personal tutor system where you can formally record these reflections in the format of tutor notes or an electronic tutor log. These are usually intended to keep records about tutoring conversations and record specific information about a student's progression. Nevertheless, it is advisable to keep a separate personal tutor log for your own professional development and, indeed, this is good practice. As discussed previously, journaling for personal tutoring is a very important and personal exercise that not only helps you to keep a dated record of details of specific personal tutoring sessions, perhaps in bullet point form, but also helps capture reflections from conversations with students, colleagues and even your mentor. A tutoring log can also help you record notes from any training that you participate in, any reading you complete and other professional development activities that you might undertake for your broader professional development. Notes which contain details about specific students should be kept confidential by using student numbers rather than names and always ensure that your notes are kept securely.

Critical thinking activity 2

From your experience of working with students so far, think of one personal tutoring scenario which you feel did not go to plan and wished the outcome could have been better (for you and/or the student). Using your preferred reflective practice model, answer the following questions.

1. Are there multiple issues for reflection from this single scenario? If so, list them.
2. What is the key issue for critical reflection?

3. Focusing on the key issue, note down your thoughts for each stage of your reflective practice model and how you could use this new knowledge to make improvements in your practice.

Reflective scenarios

All moments of reflection are different and have varying levels of complexity. Therefore, they require differing levels of analysis and evaluation and also require you to focus on different aspects of your reflective practice model. On occasion, new academics and personal tutors may feel that some aspects require more urgent consideration. Academics new to the reflective process can be tempted to engage with the action plan part of their model more quickly and readily than the other preceding stages. This should be avoided to ensure there is greater consistency between your analysis and course of action. Irrespective of your starting point, you need to engage in the process, recognising that you need to be open, honest and authentic throughout to really benefit while realising that critical reflection will on occasion create uncomfortable professional awareness but ultimately will lead you towards becoming an effective personal tutor.

The following scenario illustrates a potential situation that you could encounter within your personal tutor role. After the explanation of the scenario there is a list of points that contain some further questions and thoughts which could inform the stages of your reflective practice.

Scenario 1: group tutorial

During a group tutorial on the topic of gender and sexuality, a small group of students make inappropriate comments regarding sexuality to two other students which you overhear. You firmly address the individuals in question, but the comments between the two groups become more heated and offensive as the discussion continues. Eventually, arguments break out between different groups. You regain order, but the session is about to finish and the arguments appear to continue in the corridor.

Group tutorial potential reflection considerations

- From your knowledge of the group and in the planning stages for this session, were there any potential issues that you could have pre-empted and taken action to overcome? Could you have, for example, shared the university policy around protected characteristics?
- Did you establish clear boundaries and discuss expectations before starting the session either at the start of the academic year or within the previous group tutorial? Have you educated the students on relevant equality, diversity and inclusion (EDI) policies or student charters that your university promotes?
- Did you reiterate or even need to reiterate the consequences for any poor behaviour within the classroom?
- Were the learning activities and content suitable for this level of students?

- Was the approach to student behaviour fair and appropriate in light of the comments made? Did the approach follow the institution's guidelines and procedures concerning student behaviour?
- Should you have kept some or all of the students involved behind afterwards to address the situation?
- What are other colleagues' feelings about these students and this incident?
- Has this type of issue or any other issue happened before between these groups of students?
- What is the overall profile of the students involved? Are there students with particular issues within the group tutorial?

Critical thinking activity 3

Having read the example personal tutoring scenario, consider the following two scenarios within your current educational institution and with your students. Then, imagining that you are the personal tutor in each scenario, answer the following questions.

1. Are there multiple issues for reflection? If so, list all of the potential issues in a similar way to the worked example (see the considerations from the previous scenario).
2. What is the key issue for critical reflection? Is there a distinction to be made here between reflecting, *in-action* and *on-action*?

Possible reflection considerations are provided in the discussion section that follows the scenarios. However, try to complete the activity before reading these.

Scenario 2

You are supporting Maria, a very academically capable student, through one-to-one meetings. She wants to achieve high marks in her academic assignments so she can graduate with a first. However, after a recent poor exam result her motivation and confidence have dropped dramatically and she has started to miss many of the SMART targets you had both agreed upon. She regularly comes to see you for advice as her personal tutor and, even though you have many other things to do, you try to find time to help her.

Scenario 3

One of your students, Marcin, has apparently been disengaged during class and is falling behind with handing in his coursework. On numerous occasions you have tried to have positive learning conversations with him, but he refuses to talk about these issues, which you find frustrating and, even though you do not want to, you cannot help showing it. You eventually get him to talk about the issues and he opens up that he has been feeling tense and anxious lately.

Discussion

Scenario 2: reflection considerations

- Were the initial SMART targets too ambitious or about right?

- It is important to remember that Maria's academic ability will not have faltered significantly in such a short space of time and to make her aware of this. It is important that you put this particular exam mark in context and help Maria to see this as part of the broader learning and development process.

- Other than the recent poor exam result, were there any other factors that have contributed to the dip in her performance?

- Due to the short space of time that Maria needs to turn things around, what are some small key things that you can discuss with her so that she has the best chance of achieving her aim? If it is a confidence/motivation issue, what are some small steps she can take to regain this? When a student is facing a confidence/motivation issue, finding ways to achieve 'quick wins' is a useful way to create momentum towards a goal and make it feel more achievable. Goal setting with a student can be hugely motivational and help them to quickly realise the benefits of learning from the assessment process by responding appropriately to feedback.

- What do her other tutors say about her past and current performance? When you have identified a way forward with Maria, it would be sensible to reassess the previous SMART targets to see if they are still suitable.

Scenario 3: reflection considerations

- How long has Marcin been visibly disengaged in class? Is it a recent issue or more of a long-term pattern?

- What are the *immediate*, *visible* reasons for Marcin's poor behaviour and dip in performance? (For example, tired from working too much or staying up or being out too late, issues with fellow students or friends.)

- What do Marcin's other tutors say about his engagement and performance in class?

- What additional support needs does Marcin have now he has disclosed his anxiety issues? Is the institution providing/can the university provide support for this? How can you initiate a referral to some of these central, specialist, student support services?

- Some personal tutoring situations are frustrating but it is important not to let these frustrations prevent you from supporting the student to improve.

- Disengagement in class, especially when it affects the learning of others, is not acceptable. The university should provide support and procedures for you and your colleagues to address this.

- It is unlikely that you will see an immediate improvement until Marcin firstly recognises that he is disengaged and takes ownership of his actions, which should be one of your primary goals.
- In order to support Marcin and address this issue you need to refer him for additional support from your well-being team or other trained professionals.

Professional development

While reflective practice forms a key part of the academic professional development process, there are other important activities that you can engage in as a tutor which will not only inform the reflective process but also help you to develop key skills relating to personal tutoring. This section aims to discuss some of these activities and provide you with some key pointers for your consideration.

Peer observation

Peer observation should be seen as a developmental process but is still not common practice in HE personal tutoring. Nevertheless, the feedback from peer observation, particularly if this is done by a trusted mentor, can be really beneficial, especially when used to inform your own development. If you have high expectations of your students, you need to have high expectations of yourself and observation gives you an opportunity to judge how you are progressing. These positive aspects of observation are more likely to happen if your institutional culture embraces a constructive approach to tutoring. It is always possible, however, to set up informal peer observations if no formal scheme exists.

Peer observation is highly effective for the personal tutor role and these also apply to the broader mentor/mentee relationship, as discussed previously. The reasons for this are:

- it is supportive and developmental;
- it provides coaching and mentoring opportunities for you and your peers;
- the giving and receiving of feedback develops the skills you are using with students by enabling you to use them with colleagues too;
- you are likely to have an established and positive relationship with the other person. Among the key benefits of this is good-quality feedback. If there is mutual trust and respect, both sides have permission to offer critical feedback because they want to help one another;
- the support of peers is very important when faced with a variety of challenging student issues;
- the observer (someone in the same role) arguably brings more specific knowledge and understanding;
- it promotes sharing of good practice between people who are performing the same role.

Personal tutor training

Many institutions offer some form of personal tutor training, although the breadth and depth of this differs between organisations. Training for tutors within institutions may take on many forms and is often transactional rather than developmental. The Professional Standards Framework for Teaching and Supporting Learning in HE (Advance HE, 2023), PG Cert HE and the UKAT professional recognition scheme provide a set of standards around teaching and tutoring practice. You will also find a professional development curriculum on the UKAT website: ukat.ac.uk/curriculum. We suggest that you also take the time to survey your institution to find out what is currently on offer and make enquiries as to how you can inform and support this academic training. It is unlikely, however, that any formal training will prepare you completely for your tutor role so it must be combined with gaining experience of tutoring in action, using a variety of resources and the support mechanisms that we have referred to in this book.

Robust personal tutor training should cover a variety of topics including (but by no means limited to) core values and skills, institutional systems, policies and procedures, setting boundaries, referral processes, reflective practice and record-keeping. It is important that you engage in personal tutoring training as part of your professional development as a tutor. The training in which you participate must be delivered alongside the role that you are performing as a tutor so that you have the opportunity to apply what you have learned in practice. This will not only help you to contextualise and consolidate your learning but also allow you to bring your own insights to the training session(s) that are offered. This is where reflective practice becomes key to your professional development as a tutor and can help you to make sense of the concrete tutoring experience that you are amassing. Training for personal tutors should not happen in isolation and, once training has taken place, this does not signal the end of your development as a tutor. The university environment has undergone many changes recently, particularly following the Covid-19 pandemic, bringing mental health and well-being concerns to the forefront. It is therefore important that you are able to access regular opportunities to reinforce the training that you have been given and find out the latest information about the support that the institution is providing for its students. It is also important that you have the chance to discuss updates and developments, both within the organisation and across the sector, with other tutoring colleagues. Ideally, tutoring refresher training should take place at least once per year and training should be coordinated across the institution so that a degree of consistency can be achieved. In addition, training should provide you with the opportunity to discuss challenges with other colleagues in a supportive environment and offer you the chance to work through these challenges with those who have significant tutoring experience. Tutor training is particularly powerful when it is considered alongside the broader development of the personal tutor role including mentoring, tutor networks such as UKAT and more senior tutoring responsibilities. It is important to seek out the training offered by your organisation, if you have not already done so, and to contribute to the ongoing development of the personal tutor training agenda. The feedback that you provide as a tutor will be invaluable and informative to the training process.

Identifying your training needs

As you go through the reflective process as outlined in this chapter, you will probably identify areas that you need to work on as a personal tutor. As you work through the reflective activities, begin to make notes on any training needs you might have identified, particularly in those areas where you have thought about what you might do differently if a particular situation arose again.

Some examples you may identify could be:

- supporting students in distress;
- referring students to student support services;
- empathetic listening;
- active listening;
- coaching skills;
- knowledge of university systems and processes;
- setting boundaries;
- working with particular student populations;
- digital literacy;
- effective planning for one-to-ones and group tutorials.

It is advisable to focus on one issue at a time rather than try to achieve too much at once, which you could find overwhelming. When looking back over your reflective journal, make a note of how many times you mention a certain issue, and this could be an indication of where to start regarding training.

Your institution may have training programmes on the above issues, so it is a good idea to explore this first. If this is not the case, you could explore UKAT's provision of personal tutor training, or indeed, many of the above areas are covered within this book. Set yourself SMART targets and reflect on your progress in your reflective log.

Personal tutor networks

Active participation in personal tutor networks is another key aspect of your professional development as a personal tutor. Such networks may exist formally or informally and, indeed, externally as well as internally. In recent years, new national networks for tutors in HE have been established to coincide with the increasing level of importance that tutoring is now being given within institutions. There are many benefits to attending and participating in tutoring networks: they offer you the opportunity to discuss tutoring practice, work through difficulties and challenges and identify improvements to the tutoring process. It is possible to identify mentors through tutoring networks and to also mentor colleagues who are new to the tutoring process. One particular example of a tutoring network is an action learning set. Some institutions have action learning sets for personal tutoring which are run more formally and offer opportunities to work through more challenging issues. On the other hand, action learning sets can also be set up informally. Action learning sets, like other tutoring networks, can be used for a variety of different purposes but usually have the following objectives for tutors in mind.

- Assist tutors to define the purposes, timescale and results associated with tutoring.
- Assist others by testing and clarifying ideas.
- Ask the questions others will not ask of themselves.
- Provide additional motivation for tutors to take action, individually and collectively.
- Share ideas on resolving difficulties encountered by others.
- Offer information derived from their functional and managerial experience.
- Monitor progress.
- Share 'air time' effectively and appropriately.
- Enable tutors to manage themselves and review the effectiveness of that management.
- Take charge of individual and group learning.
- Establish ways of reviewing and improving tutors' learning.

(Adapted from Mumford, 1996)

If you do not have action learning sets in your institution, you may consider instigating them yourself.

Tutoring and advising networks

At a national level there are several organisations currently championing the personal tutoring agenda within UK HE, offering those with responsibility for tutoring in universities an opportunity to participate in discussion sessions, webinars, conferences and other developmental activities, such as research. UKAT, mentioned previously, is a sector-wide organisation which supports the development of personal tutoring in UK HE, offering an annual conference and other professional development opportunities. The Centre for Recording Achievement (CRA) (https://www.recordingachievement.org/) also hosts a number of annual events and seminars on personal tutoring and some of these are delivered in partnership with SEDA, the Staff and Educational Development Association (www.seda.ac.uk). At international level, UKAT is allied with NACADA, the Global Community for Academic Advising (www.nacada.ksu.edu). This partnership is designed to strengthen the breadth and depth of support for advisors and tutors globally and to champion advising at every level in HE including advising research.

Developing your professional identity

In Chapter 1 we explored the role of the personal tutor and looked at the different ways tutors might give support to their students. Given that you have to perform a variety of roles as a personal tutor, it can be challenging to develop a professional identity. You may also have a personal tutor team identity (Yale and Warren, 2022) resulting from your connection with other personal tutors. Therefore, your professional identity as a personal tutor is neither fixed, nor subject to being labelled, but involves a fluidity over time, influenced through participation in shared experiences, the development of relationships with tutees, increasing knowledge and, hopefully, feelings of competence. Your skills, values, beliefs and attitudes will also form part of your professional identity. As a personal tutor, you may also have other professional identity labels, such as lecturer, researcher or professional services staff. These labels may be more important to you, and you may not have considered your professional identity as a personal tutor. In other words, your professional identity will not be fixed, and lack of clarity over boundaries can also result in personal tutors not having a sense of professional identity, as they may become confused about their role.

With this in mind, how can you develop your professional identity as a personal tutor? The skills examined earlier on in the book will be important here, along with the partnership approach. Although you may take the partnership approach, you also need to remember that boundaries are necessary in order to keep a professional distance from your students – you are not their new best friend! It could be useful to think of the kind of tutor you want to be, and this may relate to the approach your institution uses, for example, if your institution emphasises pastoral care you might want to be seen first and foremost as caring. It may be helpful to answer the following questions in order to help you consider the type of professional identity you wish to embody:

- What are my beliefs and values?
- How do I want my tutees to see me?
- What aspects of my character seem most appropriate for a personal tutor and how can I enhance these?
- What aspects of myself do I need to work on to be more effective as a personal tutor?
- Which part of the personal tutoring role seems to fit best with my strengths?
- How can I make sure I am treating students as partners?
- What boundaries do I need to put in place to remain professional?

These questions could also form part of your reflections and action planning.

Supporting personal tutors

With the increase in student mental health issues, it is important that personal tutors are supported in looking after their tutees, otherwise the burden remains with the tutor

(Augustus et al, 2023). Augustus et al (2023) make some suggestions on how to manage this, for example, tutors distancing themselves from tutees when feeling fragile themselves, not isolating themselves, and accessing the university's support systems (this is also mentioned in Chapter 4).

Many universities now operate a model of personal tutoring with a senior tutor role (McIntosh, 2018; Alberts, 2025). Perhaps you are a senior tutor in your institution and responsible for supporting a number of personal tutors. The senior tutor role can be a challenging one (Alberts, 2025) so it is important that you make use of support offered. Often, these universities have a Senior Tutor Forum, in which senior tutors can share experiences, good practice and advice regarding supporting personal tutors. These meetings can help senior tutors to find a shared sense of community and purpose, along with being a centre of expertise for personal tutors and students (Greenway, 2022).

Some ways senior tutors can support personal tutors are outlined below.

1. Set up drop-in sessions or regular meetings with your personal tutors. Give them the chance to share any challenges they are facing, share good practice and help each other to find solutions to issues.

2. Give personal tutors access to regular training. You could run training sessions yourself or direct them to the UKAT webinars or make use of the materials in this book.

3. Make sure personal tutors have access to up-to-date information for students within your institution.

4. Encourage personal tutors to reflect on their tutoring practice and identify their own training needs.

5. Keep in regular contact with your personal tutors, either via email or setting up a workspace area where staff can access information and contact each other.

6. Provide personal tutors with document templates to help them in certain situations, for example, writing a reference or expressing a concern about attendance.

7. Make sure personal tutors are aware of the support available to them in your institution. Most universities have a staff counselling service which can offer you debriefs or work through your own reactions to dealing with difficult student cases. If you are a personal tutor and are not aware of the support available to you, we suggest contacting your senior tutor or another senior leader.

Summary

This chapter has discussed reflection and how you might use it in your practice to help you develop as a personal tutor. It may be beneficial for you to experiment with the suggested models to find something which works for you, or even develop your own. Reflecting on your practice will inevitably lead you to identify development opportunities which may be available to you. We would encourage you to explore what is on offer at your institution and make use of UKAT's community and resources. Part of your reflection may also lead you to consider how to develop your professional identity, and we hope that this chapter has given you issues for consideration around this.

As a personal tutor, it is vital that you receive support in your practice, and this chapter has shown ways that you can both give and receive support. If you are unsure of what your institution offers in terms of support for personal tutors, you should contact your senior tutor or head of department.

To aid your development, we recommend keeping a personal tutor log at the end of each week or after an incident that feels particularly significant with a student (or even a colleague). Furthermore, consider discussing your reflections and potential actions with a trusted colleague and mentor or read up about a particular subject and, as a result, you may try to do something differently or possibly decide that what you were doing was the best way. Writing down and discussing your reflections will also inform your professional development needs as a tutor and help you to decide what opportunities to take advantage of in the future.

Critical reflections

1. From your experience of working as a personal tutor so far:
    a. identify two potential barriers to making reflective practice an ongoing, regular activity;
    b. for each potential barrier, explain one small action you could take to overcome it.
2. Which would you find more effective and why: undertaking reflective practice individually or in dialogue with a trusted person?
3. Identify the key opportunity costs of personal tutors not undertaking reflective practice for the:
    a. individual;
    b. university.
4. Evaluate whether reflective practice is equally important for an experienced practitioner and a newly qualified practitioner.

Personal tutor self-assessment system

See the following table.

PERSONAL TUTOR SELF-ASSESSMENT SYSTEM: Chapter 8 Reflective practice and professional development					
	Minimum standard 1 star	Beginner level 2 star	Intermediate level 3 star	Advanced level 4 Star	Expert level 5 Star
Individual	I regularly think about what is working well and what could be improved within my personal tutoring practice.	I carry out reflective practice, related to my personal tutor role, as an ongoing, regular activity.	In response to what I am learning from the reflective practice process, I am seeing incremental improvements in my personal tutoring practice.	In response to what I am learning from the reflective practice process, I am seeing incremental improvements in my students' experience and their educational outcomes.	The outcomes of my reflective practice inform joint practice development projects with colleagues.
Institutional	My institution values the professional development of its personal tutors and actively encourages this through providing opportunities to discuss practice and attend training events.	My institution displays its commitment to its personal tutors undertaking effective individual or peer reflective practice through providing adequate time, resources and support for the process. Honest and open dialogue about critical incidents or issues is embraced as positive and developmental.	Deans and Heads of School value the benefits reflective practice can bring to personal tutors and they actively encourage its use within meetings, individual discussions and appraisals.	Peer and individual reflective practice is routinely used by all personal tutors within the institution. There is an active mentoring scheme for personal tutors within the university.	Action research projects and joint practice development opportunities are routinely used by personal tutors as two of the ways to further develop and disseminate the learning from the reflective practice process.

9 Measuring impact

Chapter aims

This chapter helps you to:

- understand what is meant by 'impact' and 'measuring impact';
- identify reasons for measuring impact, in particular in the context of policy concerning teaching excellence in HE and frameworks for assessing quality of teaching in HE;
- understand how to use professional standards frameworks to assess your individual practice as a personal tutor;
- understand what is meant by quantitative and qualitative data, and the difference between association and causation;
- understand how to develop a theory of change and how a theory of change can be useful for measuring impact;
- understand how different comparisons can help you isolate the impact of personal tutoring from other, external factors;
- critically analyse aspects of measuring impact.

Introduction

Measuring impact tends to be talked about by managers and leaders, and is a common feature of assessments against quality frameworks for teaching in HE by regulatory bodies, such as the Teaching Excellence Framework (TEF) in England, the Tertiary Quality Enhancement Framework (TQEF) in Scotland, the Annual Provider Review (APR) in Northern Ireland or the Quality Enhancement Review (QER) in Wales. By showing you the value of

DOI: 10.4324/9781041055266-10

measuring impact and how it can be carried out at an individual and institutional level, this chapter aims to provide you with clarity about the impact personal tutors have. Some parts of this chapter are useful for individual tutors who want to develop their personal tutoring skills or evidence of their impact for career progression. Other parts of this chapter are aimed at those who oversee personal tutoring, such as senior tutors or leaders; this is indicated in the text accordingly. Nevertheless, it is useful to have an overview of all these approaches and to understand the rationale behind them. We start with considering some definitions.

What do we mean by impact and measuring impact?

Impact is the effect or influence something or someone has. Impact thus relates to *change*. We tend to associate impact with change for the good. Change can, however, be positive or negative and can indeed be intended or unintended, and direct or indirect (AMOSSHE, 2011). In order to measure *change*, it is necessary to make a comparison over time. It requires a baseline measurement against which a measure can be evaluated to determine whether change has taken place (AMOSSHE, 2011).

What we measure is incredibly important, as is discussed later in this chapter. It is, for example, important not to confuse impact with student satisfaction:

> *Customer satisfaction focuses on measuring whether or not students **like** or are **happy** with the educational experience and services they receive. Impact, however, is aimed at measuring whether or not the educational experience/service is making any **difference** to what they do and how.*
>
> (AMOSSHE, 2011, p 9)

Self-assessment is a closely related but separate process from measuring impact and can take place at various levels. At the individual level, you may be required to self-assess your personal tutoring practice, alongside other teaching and learning activities, by your institution. Commonly these mechanisms and reporting requirements include sections on outcomes for students and factors which may affect their continuation and completion (for example, disability, mental health issues, those who are the first in their family to go to university and those from low socio-economic backgrounds). There should be space for you to discuss interventions that have been put in place to support students (both individually and in groups) and this will include a commentary on your personal tutoring approach. This approach can relate to individual and collective tutoring practice and can capture various dimensions of the personal tutoring culture within academic schools or departments. It can also underpin the academic performance review process which can help to inform professional development needs (as discussed in Chapter 8).

Self-assessment can also refer to processes at school, departmental or institutional level. It often relates to an end-of-year reporting process involving discussion with academics and personal tutors but overseen by Deans and Heads of School. Because of the reviews of teaching quality, such as the TEF, TQEF, APR or QER, and annual review mechanisms, self-assessment is often incorporated into wider institutional reporting and monitoring of student success.

Why measure impact?

Personal tutors can have a significant impact on students, but the extent to which is generally not known (Clarke, 2025). Measuring impact is important to evaluate and provide evidence of personal tutoring practice at individual, departmental and institutional level. As an individual, by measuring and quantifying the effect you have on students you can make sure your personal tutoring practice is achieving what you set out to do, inform your practice, and evaluate any new approaches or activities. For example, you might want to see what the impact is of beginning group tutorials with five minutes of welcoming the students and setting the agenda, or whether tailoring your discussion to the student lifecycle helps to improve student engagement.

Measuring impact is also crucial in providing evidence of the effectiveness of your personal tutoring practice. At an individual level you may want to use such evidence in your annual progress review or in applications for progression or promotion.

Critical thinking activity 1

1. List all the ways in which you measure your individual impact.
2. State why you do this for each.

Discussion

1. It is likely you will have come up with some answers that are informal and are daily student interactions, for example:
    - checking verbally with students how they are getting on;
    - checking verbally with students how they are feeling;
    - observing students' integration with their cohort;
    - observing students' engagement.

More formal and longer-term examples might include:

- carrying out 'intervention analysis': monitoring attendance and completion of work of particular students who have been the subject of specific personal tutoring interventions. This analysis can be carried out during the academic year (termly) or at the end of the academic year and can analyse trends and changes over time;

- comparing the overall engagement of your students, the ways in which they have integrated socially, their involvement in co- and extracurricular activities and their levels of well-being, mental health and how their environment helps to improve resilience and confidence. Reflecting on how this has changed because of regular and positive group and one-to-one tutorial sessions;
- analysing how many of your students did not progress as well as they could have the previous year and focus on supporting them through the current academic year with targeted support on progression.

2. There are three main reasons for measuring your individual impact:
    - to check whether what you are doing helps your students (in terms of their learning, progress, motivation and well-being);
    - to ensure your personal tutoring practice is improving;
    - to evidence excellence in personal tutoring practice for progression and promotion.

Measuring impact is arguably even more important at an institutional level. An impact evaluation at scale can show whether a new initiative in personal tutoring is having the desired effect. For example, what is the impact of introducing personal tutoring early on in the induction process? How does this approach impact on attendance levels? An impact evaluation can also highlight areas of excellence within the institution. For example, do personal tutors in all departments use tutoring to provide accurate information and signpost/refer to other support that could help? If so, how many students act on the advice?

It can also identify areas that need addressing. For example, comparing continuation and completion rates, graduate destination or learning gain across ethnicity, gender, disability or socio-economic background can show whether 'equality gaps' exist and can help to inform personal tutoring policy and practice at institutional level.

A final reason to measure impact at the institutional level is to use it as evidence in a submission for a quality of teaching review. Personal tutors support teaching and learning and therefore measuring the impact of personal tutoring is particularly useful in providing evidence for tailored support for students. Here, we focus on the teaching quality review in England (the TEF) as an example, but you could, of course, translate this to your local context.

The TEF was introduced by the government in England in a bid to raise standards in teaching and learning. Participation in the TEF is a condition of registration for providers in England and the award determines the level of tuition fees a provider can charge. Under the current framework, introduced in 2023, institutions are rated on two aspects: student experience and student outcomes. Together these make up the overall award, and institutions are given an overall rating of gold, silver, bronze or 'requires improvement'. The assessment is based on qualitative statements and quantitative impact metrics such as results from the National Student Survey (NSS) on student experience, data on student continuation and completion, and graduate outcomes. It must be noted that the data the assessment is based on, including the impact metrics and their relative weighting, have changed with each iteration of the TEF, and are likely to be modified further in the future.

The overall aim of the TEF is to 'incentivise the improvement of the quality of teaching, learning and student outcomes across the sector and provide information to students about where excellent teaching and outcomes may be found' (OfS, 2022c, p 17). As such, it is crucial for universities to provide clear evidence of the effectiveness and impact of their approach in their TEF submission and metrics are the main way for them to do this (QAA, 2024). There is no specific mention of personal tutoring in the OfS regulatory framework (OfS, 2022c) or the TEF guidance (OfS, 2022b); however, one of the 'features of excellence' in the student experience aspect relates to the learning environment and academic support: 'The provider ensures a supportive learning environment, and its students have access to a wide and readily available range of outstanding quality academic support tailored to their needs (SE5)' (OfS, 2022b, p 74). It is the tailoring of the support specifically that led to higher ratings in the TEF, and providers often cite their personal tutoring approach as evidence of intentional and impactful tailored support for students in their submissions (QAA, 2024). Therefore, the impact of personal tutoring on teaching and learning, specifically personalised learning, must not be underestimated. As discussed later in this chapter, the impact of activities, strategies and processes are, however, difficult to 'prove' given other factors that can influence outcomes.

With the focus firmly on metrics and institutional measures of teaching quality, it is worth remembering a maxim from William Bruce Cameron, 'Not everything that can be counted counts. Not everything that counts can be counted' (Cameron, 1963). Evaluating and measuring impact should always have a specific purpose. Likewise, it is important to accept that certain things are important but are difficult to measure or, indeed, do not need measuring. By asking 'what was the impact on students?' you ensure that you keep students at the centre of your practice.

How you measure impact

There has been increasing interest in evaluating the impact of personal tutoring (Fitch, 2024), which has meant the evidence for personal tutoring interventions and models is starting to build (Bosch and Jacobi, 2025; Waterval et al, 2025). Despite this growing interest, there are currently no agreed models or metrics for assessing the effectiveness of personal tutoring. In the first chapter, we suggested that effective personal tutoring includes the development of students' intellectual and academic ability, as well as the nurturing of their well-being, through personalised and holistic support. Measuring the impact of personal tutoring can be difficult because it is not straightforward to measure academic ability and well-being, and the pace of change may be too slow to capture in an evaluation. There are also many factors outside of personal tutoring that contribute to academic ability and well-being which make it difficult to know to what extent the observed change is due to personal tutoring. These factors, and the small sample sizes involved, make measuring impact at the individual level particularly difficult. This chapter first outlines how professional standard frameworks can be used to measure individual impact, before looking at how a theory of change can inform impact evaluations on a larger scale.

Using professional standards frameworks

In Chapters 3 and 6, we discussed the UKAT Professional Framework for Advising and Tutoring (UKAT, 2023), the NACADA framework of core competencies (NACADA, 2017), the NOS for Personal Tutoring (FETN, 2013) and the PSF 2023 (Advance HE, 2023). All these frameworks can be used as a starting point to consider how to measure the impact of your practice. Here, we have chosen to focus on the NOS (FETN, 2013) because each standard has explicit associated performance criteria which are useful for deciding on how to measure your impact. The 11 standards are as follows.

1. *Manage self, work relationships and work demands.*
2. *Develop own practice in personal tutoring.*
3. *Create a safe, supportive and positive learning environment.*
4. *Explore and identify learners' needs and address barriers to learning.*
5. *Enable learners to set learning targets and evaluate their progress and achievement.*
6. *Encourage the development of learner autonomy.*
7. *Enable learners to develop personal and social skills and cultural awareness.*
8. *Enable learners to enhance learning and employability skills.*
9. *Support learners' transition and progression.*
10. *Provide learner access to specialist student support services.*
11. *Contribute to improving the quality and impact of personal tutoring and its reputation within own organisation.*

(FETN, 2013)

Impact measures can be linked to specific aspects of personal tutoring performance by using the performance criteria descriptors that go along with these standards, as shown for a selection of standards in Table 9.1.

Table 9.1 Linking impact measures with a selection of the National Occupational Standards for Personal Tutoring

NOS	NOS performance criteria	Relevant impact measure
LSIPT02 Develop own practice in personal tutoring.	P5 Assess the extent to which own practice is inclusive and promotes equality and diversity.	Compare student engagement across gender, ethnicity and disability to check for any 'equality gaps'.
LSIPT03 Create a safe, supportive and positive learning environment.	P1 Provide tutorial support in an environment where learners feel safe, secure, confident and valued.	Measure the extent students say they feel safe, secure, confident or valued in tutorials, using a Likert scale in a student survey.
LSIPT04 Explore and identify learners' needs and address barriers to learning.	P3 Communicate regularly with each learner in order to identify at risk indicators.	Analysis of individual data from dashboards on attendance, and completion of assessments of particular students who have been the subject of specific personal tutoring actions; can be carried out in-year (monthly) or end of year.
LSIPT09 Support learners' transition and progression.	P3 Work with learners to identify, where appropriate, goals relating to their career development and suitable and realistic progression options.	Internal progression rates for your student groups. Analysis of destination data for your student groups.

Critical thinking activity 2

» Read the performance criteria from the whole set of standards (available at https://fetn.org.uk/professional-development/national-occupational-standards-for-personal-tutoring-2/) and choose one criterion from each of the 11 and, as shown in the final column of Table 9.2, give a relevant measure of impact for each criterion.

Using the Student Learning Experience model

Another way for institutions to assess their performance is to use the *Student Learning Experience* (SLE) model. The SLE is used in the TQEF in Scotland as a key sector benchmark (sparqs, 2023). The model is made up of nine building blocks, each a key element of the student learning experience. Each element has a set of reflective questions to help institutions assess their performance in that area. The reflective questions listed under 'Support and Guidance' are an excellent starting point for institutions to assess their personal tutoring systems. We think the following questions are particularly relevant, although we recommend you have a look at all questions (www.sparqs.ac.uk):

- *How are students made aware of the variety of student support services available to them and how do they know how and when they can access them?*

> *Is academic, pastoral and financial support signposted to students during induction and consistently throughout the course of study?*

- *Do all students, at all levels of study, have a key contact within the institution who they can go to for initial support and to ask for advice? Do staff have dedicated time set aside in their schedule to provide academic and/or pastoral support to students?*

- *Are all staff trained to accurately and sensitively signpost students to the right support?*

(sparqs, 2023)

Theory of change

When measuring impact at a departmental or institutional level, data are usually not the problem. Universities already hold a lot of data on engagement, progression and outcomes in their analytic systems. The difficulty more often lies with drawing meaningful links between the available data (McVitty and Maxwell, 2024), such as personal tutoring activities and outcomes. A theory of change can be a useful way to make those links and help with the identification of appropriate ways to measure impact.

A theory of change is a description of the overall outcomes you want to achieve and how you think your activities will lead to these outcomes (Noble, 2019). Developing a theory of change is valuable because it makes explicit the assumptions you make about effecting change. Are these based on empirical research, your experience, or a hunch? Developing a theory of change is also useful for measuring impact because it breaks down your overall aim into smaller, intermediate outcomes. For example, it is difficult to test the impact of increasing the number of tutorials during the transition to university on overall degree outcomes, because the change takes place over a long period and there will be many other contributing factors. Rather than looking at whether your personal tutoring practice contributes to your overall aim (an absolutist impact model, McVitty and Maxwell, 2024), using a theory of change allows you to test parts of the model and whether your practice makes a difference to these smaller intermediate aims. These intermediate outcomes together contribute to the overall aim (a contribution model, McVitty and Maxwell, 2024). You may, for example, test whether increasing the number of tutorials during the transition to university has increased students' sense of belonging, which is known to contribute to attainment and progression (Braine and Parnell, 2011; Karp et al, 2021).

We recommend having a theory of change for personal tutoring at an institutional level because it makes the overall aims and purpose of personal tutoring explicit and clear. This means when individual senior or personal tutors develop their personal tutoring systems or activities they can ensure they contribute to this overall aim. Universities in England are already required to have a theory of change as part of their access and participation plans, with which a theory of change model for personal tutoring could be connected.

If your institution has a theory of change for personal tutoring, you can use it to ensure that your individual practice aligns with it and contributes to its intermediate outcomes.

If your institution does not, you might want to develop your own in order to measure your impact. Sharing your methods and results with colleagues might even result in them being used by others for the wider good of students, peers and the institution.

How to develop a theory of change

The process of developing a theory of change involves thinking about the issue you are addressing and the changes you want to see, and then working backwards to think about how you will make those changes happen. The place to start is to think about what you are trying to achieve in your personal tutoring practice. What is your overall aim or purpose? We have proposed throughout the book that the purpose of personal tutoring is to view students holistically and support the development of students' intellectual and academic ability and nurture their well-being but, depending on your institution and student population, your purpose may differ from this. As such, it is useful to develop a theory of change in collaboration with others in your institution.

Second, you should identify specific intermediate outcomes that are needed for you to achieve your overall aim. These intermediate outcomes are steps towards your overall aim and are smaller in scope and timeframe. Here, it is important to think about feasible, short-term outcomes that are within the influence of personal tutors. Examples of intermediate outcomes include increasing a sense of belonging, establishing a meaningful tutor–tutee relationship or increasing confidence in academic skills. Intermediate outcomes are steps towards your overall aim and are usually smaller in scope and timeframe.

Next, you should outline how personal tutor activities relate to these intermediate outcomes. This will include the key activities discussed in Chapter 6. Examples of such activities are organising a lunch during the welcome period to allow tutors and tutees to get to know each other in an informal setting, or giving personal tutors access to the names and pictures of their tutees before the start of term. The way personal tutor activities, outcomes and purpose relate to each other is shown in Figure 9.1.

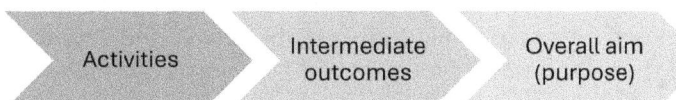

Figure 9.1 Relationship between personal tutoring activities, outcomes and purpose

The final step is drawing causal links between each of the elements you have outlined. Which activities will help achieve which intermediate outcomes? How do intermediate outcomes contribute to the overall aim? It is important to keep in mind that causal links can be interrelated, indirect and overlapping. For example, an activity can contribute to multiple intermediate outcomes, and rather than directly impacting the overall aim, an intermediate outcome can influence the overall outcome via another intermediate outcome. Once you have identified causal links, you should make clear why you think there is that causal link between these two elements. This may be because there is empirical evidence that you've found in the literature, it may be based on your own experience or data you have collected previously. It could also be simply based on common sense or intuition. The strength of using a theory of change is that it makes these assumptions explicit which, in turn, allows you to critically assess whether your practice as personal tutor actually contributes to your overall aim.

Critical thinking activity 3

1. Using the headings set out in Figure 9.1, in three columns write down your overall aim for personal tutoring, your intermediate outcomes and your personal tutor activities.
2. Think about how the elements in the three columns relate to each other and draw causal links. For each link indicate whether this is based on empirical evidence, your own data or experience, or an assumption.

If you want to develop your theory of change further, there are various organisations that have freely available resources to help you with this. Some examples are TASO (taso.org.uk), the Center for Theory of Change (theoryofchange.org) and NCP (thinknpc.org).

Discussion

The process of developing a theory of change can help you think about whether you should make any changes to your personal tutoring practice. For example, in the activity above, do you have any activities that are not linked to your intermediate outcomes or overall aim? If not, you could consider whether to include this activity in future. Likewise, do all your overall aims have associated intermediate outcomes and activities? If not, what activities could you put in place to ensure you reach those intermediate outcomes?

Using a theory of change to measure impact

A theory of change is not only useful for making strategic decisions about personal tutoring practice and to communicate its purpose, it is also useful for measuring impact. A good example of such an approach is the study by Bosch and Jacobi (2025), who used a theory of change to evaluate different personal tutoring interventions for postgraduate students. For measuring your own impact, now you have defined your activities, outcomes and purpose, it is easier to identify what you should measure and how to use data that your institution already collects to assess the impact of personal tutoring.

First, let's consider the activities. It is relatively straightforward to measure your personal tutoring practice, and it is likely that you already collect some of these data. This could be, for example, rates of attendance at tutorials. However, these types of data show *what* you have done rather than the effect that it has had, and therefore this is more akin to monitoring than to impact evaluation.

On the other hand, if we look at your overall aim or purpose, this does highlight the impact of personal tutoring practice. Data on academic performance are routinely collected by universities, who often focus on TEF metrics or Key Performance Indicators (KPIs) such as attendance, continuation, completion and graduate destinations. Yet, it can be difficult to use these metrics to measure the impact of personal tutoring practice because it is not possible to isolate the impact of personal tutoring from other influences. Moreover, overall aims usually take years to have an effect, which make them difficult to report on in, for example, an annual review and less useful for informing your practice in the short term.

Intermediate outcomes or aims are a good place to start identifying how to measure impact because they relate to the impact of practice, are specific and short-term.

Critical thinking activity 4

1. For each of the intermediate outcomes that you listed in the critical thinking activity identify a way you could measure it.

Discussion

Look at the suggested answers in Table 9.2.

Table 9.2 Example of a theory of change and impact measures

Activities	Intermediate outcomes	Overall aim (purpose)	How can impact be measured?
Frequent group tutorials for cohort building.	Create a sense of belonging to aid with the transition to university.	Nurture the well-being of students.	• Ask students to what extent they feel part of a community at university at several points in the year, in e.g. student survey. • Attendance at tutorials • Continuation rates
Discuss time management and relaxation strategies ahead of the assessment period.	Reduce stress around assessment time.	Nurture the well-being of students.	• Measure students' well-being using a validated tool and compare to the score of students in previous years.
Monitor and track students.	Identify students with barriers to learning.	Academic development.	• Compare over time data on attendance, assessment completion.
Discuss feedback on assessments and help students set goals for improvement.	Help students reflect on progress and improve.	Academic development.	• Data on assessment results.

The list is not exhaustive and other ways of measuring could be included.

In the fourth column we have mentioned data from various sources. Some of this information should be available on your student records, personal tutor system or institutional dashboard, if one exists. Usually, individual tutors are responsible for recording data to capture tutoring activity, as discussed in Chapter 8. The benefit of institutional systems is that information should be recorded consistently by all tutors across the institution, along with the monitoring of data such as attendance and assessment marks. It is from here that patterns and trends can be identified for reporting purposes.

Types of measurements

There are many things that you might measure to establish your impact as a personal tutor. What measurements are appropriate depends on what you are trying to achieve with your personal tutoring practice and your evaluation. Measures can be numerical (quantitative), using words (qualitative), or include a combination of both (mixed methods). The type of measurements that you should use depends on whether you want to describe the extent of a phenomenon, see how one thing is influenced by another, or the perceptions and experiences of a group of people. The type of measurement you would use for these different aims are described below.

Quantitative and qualitative data

What did you notice about the different intermediate outcomes in critical thinking activity 4 and how you may measure them? It is noticeable that some of these measures are quantitative while others are qualitative.

Quantitative data include anything that you can count or measure. These kinds of data are useful when you want to measure the extent of something and describe it. It also allows you to see whether different elements are related to each other, and if so, how strongly. For example, quantitative data can tell us whether there is a degree awarding gap across different ethnicities, or whether student engagement with personal tutoring is associated with higher rates of continuation. Quantitative data usually do not show the nuance in those numbers or help us understand *why* we see those results. Quantitative measures allow for looking at very large datasets, such as across the whole institution or even across the whole sector. At an institutional level, the focus is often on such quantitative data. External pressures such as league tables or the reviews of teaching quality such as the TEF mean that universities often focus on KPIs such as attendance, continuation, completion, graduate outcomes, or NSS scores. As such, a lot of quantitative data are already gathered by universities; it is useful if you can access those data, for example within your learning analytics dashboard. You may also want to collect some quantitative data yourself, for example by developing a survey for your tutees, or collecting data on student attendance.

Qualitative data are any data that include language and descriptions. These types of data are useful when you want to get a holistic understanding of people's experiences, perceptions, or beliefs. It is also useful when you are looking at a new area and the data you are collecting are exploratory. Because qualitative data are very rich and can take a long time to analyse, qualitative measures work better with smaller groups of participants. This may be through interviews, focus groups or open-ended questions in surveys.

You can use both types of data (*mixed methods*) to get a holistic, deep understanding of your impact as personal tutor. For example, you could hold a focus group with a small number of your tutees in which you look at some of the results of a larger survey to understand why you got certain survey results (*sequential explanatory design*).

To reiterate, the types of measurement you want to use depends on your theory of change and your intermediate outcomes, what you are trying to measure, and why. Do you, for example, need to have data to show evidence of your impact or are you trying to improve your understanding of your students to improve your practice? The types of measurement also depend on the scale at which you are measuring impact. What works at an institutional level is likely to be disproportionate at the individual level. There will be a greater impact institutionally if individual practice (shown to positively affect a KPI like attendance at an individual level) is consistently applied by the institution through awareness-raising, training and joint development of professional practice. Your individual measuring of impact therefore has a strong link to, and influence on, the institutional measuring of impact and also on institutional performance.

The importance of comparison

When assessing impact it is not just *what* you measure that is important, what you compare it to is just as important. For measuring impact it is crucial to include some comparison. You will notice the mention of timescale and comparison within some of the measures in the last column in Table 9.2 (How can impact be measured?). In order to measure change, it is of course necessary to measure and make comparisons at different points in time. For example, if you collect the same data before and after an activity (*a pre-post comparison*), you can measure the change that has occurred after your students have taken part in your activity. At an institutional level, KPIs tend to have this comparison built in as in-year and end-of-year measures. For these, it is important to look at longer-term trends in addition to shorter-term changes. For example, if there is a slight decrease in some KPI(s) from one year to the next but the overall trend demonstrates a significant increase since a new support strategy was introduced, there is an indicator of positive rather than negative impact. Viewing the end-of-year figure compared to the previous year in isolation would have suggested the opposite.

Comparison is also important to help you narrow down and isolate the effect you have had as a personal tutor and ruling out – to some extent – other influences on student performance. For example, comparing survey results with results from a different group of students in the previous year would help to eliminate some of the effects of the time of year. As we have discussed previously, there are peaks and troughs in the academic year. Every student experiences highs and lows at certain points in the academic year and, broadly speaking, some of these can be anticipated using the student lifecycle approach (see Chapter 6). For example, many students experience heightened anxiety about starting university and worry about assessments in the middle and at the end of the first term or semester. A number of students struggle over the Christmas and New Year period. A lot of these concerns impact directly on retention and progression. If you attempt to measure your impact on students it may therefore be better to make comparisons with data from a different group of students at the same time of the year rather than comparing data over the course of a semester or year. Likewise, you may want to rule out the effects of year group, because we know certain issues are more likely to arise in certain years, such as during transition or final year dissertation. This can be done by comparing results from a year group, with the results from the previous year's cohort.

With making these kinds of comparisons you can test whether there is an association between your personal tutoring practice and a change in your students; however, it is not possible to completely rule out the effect of other factors on student performance, despite careful comparisons.

Acknowledging other factors that influence student outcomes

It can be difficult to measure the impact of personal tutoring and exclude the impact of external factors that shape student outcomes and are outside of a university's control. It is therefore important to acknowledge other factors that affect students' performance. For example, continuation rates are affected by a number of things, as shown in Figure 9.2.

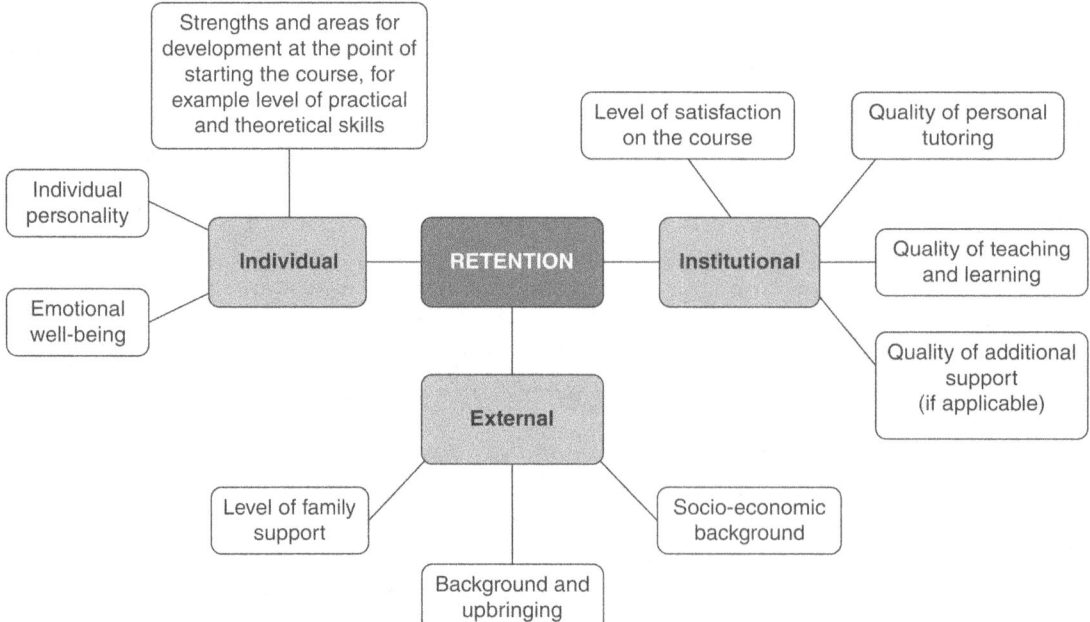

Figure 9.2 *Factors that influence the continuation of students*

The factors shown in Figure 9.2 are by no means exhaustive. As you can see, our example answer has naturally fallen into three types: *institutional*, *external* and *individual* factors. It is important to note that the TEF metrics measure institutional factors, rather than these external or individual factors. Nevertheless, there are some factors, including those highlighted in Figure 9.2, which are outside of our direct control, such as a student's socio-economic background. This is why a TEF institutional statement should focus on discussing institutional interventions in the context of their specific student population, and how they mitigate some of the risks associated with supporting students from different backgrounds and with specific support needs.

Association and causation

When thinking about measuring your impact, it is important to remember that correlation is not the same as causation; in other words, although there may be a correlation (association) between your personal tutor practice and student performance, this does not necessarily mean that your practice has *caused* the change in student performance. For example, there may be a positive association between engagement in tutorials and student outcomes because personal tutors encourage students to do better. Alternatively, the association may exist because students with lower marks tend to avoid having to talk to their personal tutor about this, thus leading to lower engagement. It is therefore important to keep in mind there may be other explanations for any associations you observe.

There are some study designs that can give stronger evidence on causality, such as randomised controlled trials (RCTs). Before looking at RCTs in more detail, it is important to note that while such experimental or quasi-experimental designs are possible at institutional or even departmental level, they are impractical for measuring your individual impact. At individual level, you need to consider measures that are practical, ethical and proportionate. Measuring what you can and acknowledging the importance of external factors and the possibility of a reverse causal link is sufficient. In these cases, it is good practice to triangulate your impact measures (Crawford et al, 2017). Looking at different data sources will allow you to see whether the picture that emerges from different perspectives are similar, thus giving weight to your claims of impact.

Randomised controlled trials

If you are measuring impact across an institution, you may want to consider RCTs. RCTs are often said to be the 'gold standard' in impact evaluation, because they allow you to isolate the impact of your intervention or practice from the impact of other, external factors, thus giving robust evidence. As a result, government bodies often call for the use of RCTs in impact evaluation and to inform educational decision-making (Burnett and Coldwell, 2021).

A RCT is an experimental study design where participants are randomly assigned to two groups. One group receives the new activity or input that you want to measure the impact of ('the treatment group'). The other group does not receive this input and carries on as before ('the control group'). You take your measurements in both groups before the intervention (the baseline) and after the intervention (the outcome). If your groups were randomly selected, the baseline measurement should be the same for both groups (see Figure 9.3). The change that we see in the treatment group that is over and above the change that we see in the control group is due to the activity or intervention. This is the impact your activity has had on student outcomes.

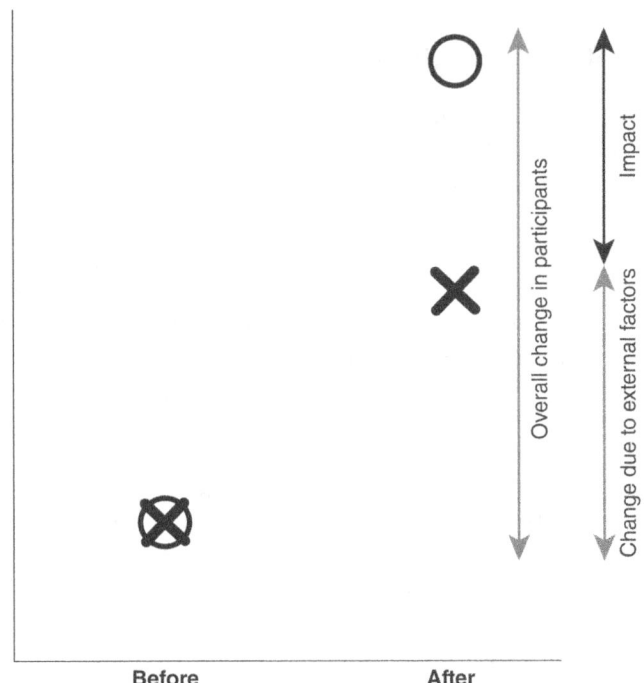

Figure 9.3 Example showing how different comparisons help to isolate your impact from external factors

RCTs help to eliminate the impact of external factors by reducing the systematic differences between the two groups that may have an impact on the outcome. For example, random allocation means both treatment and control groups have a similar allocation of highly engaged students, students who are having to work along their studies, and students who are the first in their family to go to university. These kinds of factors may influence the outcomes, but as this is the same in both groups, you can attribute any additional changes in the treatment group to your activity or intervention.

While RCTs give a robust measure of impact there are several challenges to using RCTs in HE that should be carefully considered. They are notoriously difficult to set up in education because it is often not possible to randomly assign students to different groups (Crawford et al, 2017). Instead, you may want to use a 'quasi-experimental approach', where, rather than randomly assigning students to two groups, you use two groups that already 'naturally' occur. Ideally in RCTs, both participants and experimenters are not aware whether a student is in the control or treatment group (Crawford et al, 2017; Burnett and Coldwell, 2021) to reduce any reaction they may have to being in a particular group. This is evidently not feasible in many instances when evaluating the impact of personal tutoring. Students dropping out is also a challenge, as this can mean that, over time, the control and treatment groups lose their similarity (Parra and Edwards Jr, 2024). Moreover, there are some ethical considerations to using RCTs too. Ideally, they are 'ethically neutral' meaning that we do not know whether the activity being trialled has a positive effect, makes no difference or has a negative effect. In reality, both the students and personal tutors involved in the trial are likely to have a perception that the intervention is 'good' (Hutchison and Styles, 2010). There are concerns about the ethics of giving two groups of students different experiences, and one group will be disadvantaged (Burnett and Coldwell, 2021). There are some ways around this; you may give the two groups a different level of intervention ('dosage') or you can stagger treatment and let the control group have the same activity or invention at a later date.

Overall, there are various challenges with implementing RCTs to measure the impact of personal tutoring. Yet, if you are able to overcome these challenges you will have robust evidence of the impact of personal tutoring in your institution.

Being critical of measuring impact

The adage *you can't fatten a pig by weighing it* came from educator Carolyn Chapman in the world of American primary education, referring to the over-testing of children at the expense of actually educating them. In other words, *we aren't feeding kids' minds when we are assessing them* (Weuntsel, 2011). We can expand this idea to remind us of the dangers of over-measuring. Is too much time and effort spent on measuring so that, ultimately, personal tutoring suffers?

Over the past decades, there has been a rise of managerial practices within academia (Vican et al, 2020), one of which is the use of metrics to measure the performance of staff (Kandiko and Mawer, 2013; Vican et al, 2020). These practices and measures originated in a profit-making commercial context (Gravells and Wallace, 2013). Many academics point, quite rightly, to the fact that quality outcomes of an educational institution are different to those of, for example, a factory (Gravells and Wallace, 2013). When discussing HE institutions, The Association of Commonwealth Universities makes a similar point:

> *For universities it is important too, though, that their work – education and research, and what flows from it – is properly understood, so that institutions are not expected to respond with greater yield in the same way as a production line might if given greater input. Before any measures or judgements of impact can be made, the values and goals which underpin educational investments need to be clarified and made explicit.*
>
> (The Association of Commonwealth Universities, 2012)

In other words, even if more 'input' (for example funding) is given, greater 'yield' (for example positive impact) should not be expected without question. Rather, values and goals need careful thought first. Moreover, education differs from commercial organisations because of the emotional investment that comes with the development and care of others (Lynch, 2014).

> *Managerialist values manifest themselves in education through the promotion of forms of governance (measurement, surveillance, control, regulation) that are often antithetical to the caring that is at the heart of good education. While the nurturing of learners has an outcome dimension, gains are generally not measurable in a narrowly specifiable time frame.*
>
> (Lynch, 2014, pp 6–7)

When it comes to statistics it is important to remember the issues beneath this headline data and that any thorough analysis of impact acknowledges these. With attendance rates for example, several factors, alongside personal tutor actions, play a part in contributing to these, both negatively and positively. Again, it is important to be mindful of, and to acknowledge, that it is impossible to measure student engagement per se, and that any associated measures are just proxies for engagement, as discussed in Chapter 5. This information therefore needs to be contextualised with your own interactions with students and it also needs to be treated with caution or with the necessary caveats. What it does do, however, is indicate a set of trends and actionable insights which provide you with an opportunity for further explanation and discussion with colleagues.

Being pragmatic about measuring impact

Throughout this chapter we have emphasised that however you choose to measure your impact it should be appropriate to the context and proportionate to the scale at which you are measuring. While, at an institutional level, it is possible to develop an annual student survey on personal tutoring or to assess the impact of a new personal tutoring initiative being piloted in a department, at an individual level, measuring impact happens on a smaller scale. You should measure what you can, measure with purpose, and acknowledge external factors that may have an impact. Moreover, measuring impact should be used to improve understanding of personal tutoring provision and needs, and to guide decisions in order to enhance personal tutoring incrementally rather than having a fixed end point in mind (McVitty and Maxwell, 2024).

Summary

This chapter has focused on the impact of personal tutoring practice on students' academic progress and well-being. At an individual level you may want to measure your impact to inform your practice, to monitor your development as a tutor, or to use as evidence in progression or promotion. At an institutional level the impact of personal tutoring can form an important part of a review of teaching quality submission, particularly as evidence of intentional and impactful tailored student support. You should always have a clear rationale and purpose for measuring impact.

This chapter has shown how you can use Professional Standards Frameworks as a starting point for measuring your individual impact and the reflective questions in the SLE model as a starting point for measuring institutional impact. In this chapter, we discussed the value of measuring impact, while at the same time recognising that the complexity of individual students means their progress, both academically and socially/emotionally, can be affected by a number of other factors. We have outlined reasons to be critical of measuring impact; yet, if it is approached in the right way, and has a clear rationale clarifying its purpose, it should be something which is welcomed rather than feared. Throughout the chapter we have emphasised that measuring impact should be proportionate and appropriate, and that measuring impact at an individual level will look different from measuring impact across an institution.

Critical reflections

1. To what extent do you think there is a focus on measuring the impact of personal tutor practice on students' performance:
    a. by you, individually?
    b. by your Dean or Head of School, at a team level?
    c. by senior managers, at an institutional level?
2. To what extent are assumptions about how personal tutoring affects change in student outcomes made explicit:
    a. across your institution?
    b. on any academic training course you have undertaken?
3. To what extent do student-facing staff at your institution perceive measuring impact as having a clear rationale and as meaningful and developmental? What could be done to change this perception?

Personal tutor self-assessment system

See following table.

PERSONAL TUTOR SELF-ASSESSMENT SYSTEM: Chapter 9 Measuring Impact

	Minimum standard 1 star	Beginner level 2 stars	Intermediate level 3 stars	Advanced level 4 stars	Expert level 5 stars
Individual	I know how I can use professional standards frameworks to evaluate my personal tutor practice.	I know the end-of-year figures for the main measures of impact at group level, such as rates of attendance, continuation, completion, learning gain and graduate outcomes. I consider the different influences on student performance relating to these measures.	I review what the main influences on student performance are at the end of the year and this informs changes in my practice the following year.	I measure my own impact on student performance in a variety of ways in-year and at the end of the year. Quantitative and qualitative data are used to inform my future practice.	I engage in joint practice development activities related to measuring the impact of personal tutor practice.
Institutional	Staff in my institution are aware of the main ways through which the impact of personal tutor practice can be measured.	All staff have knowledge of their end-of-year key impact measures related to their personal tutor practice.	Impact measures of personal tutor practice have a clear rationale which the majority of staff support. Staff carry out individual impact measures on this practice and are supported by Deans or Heads of School in this.	My institution has developed a theory of change for personal tutoring, which has been shared with staff. The theory of change has informed how we measure the impact of personal tutor practice. Staff carry out individual impact measures based on this theory of change and are supported by Deans or Heads of School in this.	A culture of meaningful impact measuring of personal tutor practice exists which is based on a theory of change that is underpinned by evidence.

10 What next?

Chapter aims

This chapter helps you to:

- identify your own progress in terms of your personal tutoring professional development, as well as set and prioritise clear improvement actions;
- identify your institution's progress in terms of its approach to personal tutoring and staff development;
- see the 'bigger picture' and think broadly about how you might influence positive organisational change.

Introduction

Following reading this book, it's important to identify the next steps in your development as a personal tutor and take some time to set some goals and priorities for the next six, 12 and 18 months. Consider how many of your personal tutoring goals and priorities you will have progressed six months from now. Contemplate how much knowledge you have gained and what you will be putting into practice, as well as what you will have already embedded into your existing practice. What changes will you make? It is a good idea to work with a mentor or a trusted colleague (see Chapters 8 and 9) to help you do this effectively.

As with most professional development activities, setting goals and priorities should be central to your approach. Nevertheless, there are other factors at play which interface with personal tutor training and development and they can affect how your goals and priorities evolve and change in the medium- to long-term. Some of these things may be outside your sphere of influence but it is important to be aware of them. Effective professional development for personal tutors depends largely on institutional priorities, management buy-in and the relevance of tutoring to your current practice and to students themselves.

Nevertheless, it is important to revisit and follow up on the key elements of training occasionally. This chapter is intended to provide you with guidelines for retaining the knowledge and understanding that you have gained from reading this book and engaging with some of the activities it suggests, alongside your overall development as a personal tutor. It will provide you with some useful tools to ensure that you are able to reach your goals and priorities and embed some of the principles into your daily practice as a personal tutor.

Why retain the information in this book?

All of the activities you undertake outside your day-to-day teaching, particularly the support you provide for your students through personal tutoring, have a significant impact on their academic attainment, motivation, confidence and well-being as well as their ability and desire to remain on the course. This directly supports elements related to their programme of study and intended career pathway, such as engagement and enjoyment.

Displaying your core values and skills alongside your curriculum delivery will help to ensure that you become a highly versatile and adaptable personal tutor who provides effective, holistic support and learning opportunities for students in the many ways in which you work with them. This alone will help to improve your value to students and the institution, as well as develop your wider employability skills for your future career. A proactive approach to personal tutoring will also help to tackle potential issues before they arise rather than working to resolve them after they have been left to become worse. The learning gained is also key to your institution.

Critical thinking activity 1

» *If the institution you work within invested in developing effective personal tutoring practice with students, what possible positive impacts on the following typical key performance indicators would there be?*

- *Continuation*
- *Internal progression*
- *Completion*
- *Success*
- *Attendance*
- *Learning gain*
- *Employability*

How to retain the information in this book

It is difficult to commit to action unless you feel a strong sense of ownership, empowerment and self-efficacy when it comes to your personal tutoring practice. Without this, the knowledge you have developed from this book and other developmental activities may become too abstract and difficult to translate into tangible actions on the ground. Without dedicated time to devote to translating this new knowledge into practice, it will be difficult to make progress with your intended development actions. Professional development is the responsibility of the individual concerned and to approach it objectively you must appreciate your previous accomplishments and strengths as well as consider your goals and developmental priorities, alongside a commitment to progress.

The importance of self-assessment

The individual self-assessment system found at the end of each chapter has been designed to provide you with a tool to help you understand where you are now and what your next developmental level is so that you are able to plan the best way to get there. The following case study provides an example of a personal tutor called Hannah who works within a large university in the South West of England.

CASE STUDY

HANNAH

Hannah is an academic based in a School of Economics. She finished her PhD two years ago and, last year, completed a PG Cert HE. She really enjoys working with students in a teaching capacity, particularly through her personal tutoring role, and she feels passionate about the positive impact that she has on her students' learning. She has a new and supportive Head of School who is open to new ideas and is keen to improve retention and outcomes for students, the quality of provision, as well as the students' experience. Hannah feels valued by her Head of School who recognises her contribution through personal tutoring which, she appreciates, is not always reflected in the efforts of other colleagues in the school.

The university that Hannah works at received 'silver' in their overall TEF award and although the university has good student support in place, retention, attainment and employability are three key priority areas for improvement in the coming years. This is particularly the case for the School of Economics where the attrition rate is 5 per cent higher than in other schools and employability is 3 per cent below the current target set for that area in the institutional plan. Therefore, there is a clear spotlight on the School of Economics for making a sustained improvement. The university in general has a high proportion of students from low socio-economic backgrounds (63 per cent), a large number of whom have entered university with Business and Technology Education Council (BTEC) qualifications rather than A-levels (43 per cent). The School of Economics has a large proportion of international students.

Hannah has recently assessed herself using the individual self-assessment system to understand the level she is working at and to identify actions she can take to improve. The final column of Table 10.1 provides suggested examples of how she could progress to the next level.

The possible actions are only suggestions and the list is not exhaustive. Every person, institution and context is unique and therefore the actions you take to improve need to be appropriate for you and your situation.

Table 10.1 Hannah's individual self-assessment

Chapter	Current level (and stars)	Next level to work towards (and stars)	Text from the next level that Hannah wants to work towards	Possible actions (this is not an exhaustive list)
3 Core values and skills of the personal tutor (values)	2 stars (beginner level)	3 stars (intermediate level)	I often reflect upon the impact that the core values have on the performance of my students. The reflections inform my personal development targets.	I will: • choose a suitable reflection model or create my own; • make reflective practice part of my weekly routine; • consider undertaking reflective practice with a trusted colleague; • keep a personal tutor reflection log; • speak to my students individually or as a group to obtain feedback on what values they think I show in my work and what impact this might have; • ask my students to complete an anonymous online or paper-based questionnaire; • ensure that I make my personal development targets SMART.
3 Core values and skills of the personal tutor (skills)	3 stars (intermediate level)	4 stars (advanced level)	Feedback I receive on my classes, group tutorials and one-to-ones reflect the core skills.	I will: • make a conscious effort to employ the core skills within my lessons, group tutorials and one-to-ones; • use a detailed situational analysis to determine how some of the core skills help my students; • develop a resource for the personal tutor resource bank as a result of my feedback.

	1 star (minimum standard)	2 stars (beginner level)	
4 Setting boundaries		I revisit these boundaries in group tutorials. Through one-to-ones and other support meetings, students have a clear idea of these key boundaries.	I will: • (where appropriate) reaffirm the boundaries I discussed at the beginning of the academic year. I feel this would be useful to build into the general discussions I have with my group about their progress and about my high expectations for the rest of the academic year; • discuss with my colleagues or manager the boundary setting in my personal tutor role. For example, if I feel that there is not an over-reliance of a student on my support then, I take this as a possible sign that my initial boundary setting has been effective.
	3 stars (intermediate level)	4 stars (advanced level)	
5 Key activities: Identifying and supporting student populations		Feedback from my students regarding the key activities is consistently very positive. Feedback from colleagues shows they regard them as having a strong impact on student progress and outcomes.	I will: • ask for feedback from my senior tutor regarding my preparation for, and actions taken following, at risk meetings; • either undertake, or ask someone (for example a trusted colleague) to undertake, an informal quality audit of specific aspects of my tracking and monitoring activities; • ensure that discussion around procedures with colleagues is predominantly focused on the individual needs of the student with awareness of the complex make-up of student populations at my institution; • critically analyse and evaluate on an individual basis, as well as with my department and manager, how these key procedures work to improve my students' attendance, behaviour (in terms of engagement) and completion of work.

Table 10.1 (Cont.)

Chapter	Current level (and stars)	Next level to work towards (and stars)	Text from the next level that Hannah wants to work towards	Possible actions (this is not an exhaustive list)
6 Key activities: Effectively supporting all stages of the student lifecycle	4 stars (advanced level)	5 stars (expert level)	I identify and implement methods to measure the impact of individual and group tutorials on my students' progress and outcomes. I reflect and constructively question key activities with managers and others involved to review and improve them regularly. This is a significant factor in improving some key performance indicators.	I will: • adapt the support I provide according to my tutees' progress at any one point along the stages in the student lifecycle; • have individual, informal discussions with my students at set intervals over a period of time to assess whether there needs to be any changes to how I employ the key activities; • undertake peer observation of my ones-to-ones and group tutorials.
7 Key concepts for effective personal tutoring	1 star (minimum standard)	2 stars (beginner level)	I continually work to improve the engagement of my students in the sessions I provide. I can see that my interactions with students are developing into a positive relationship.	I will: • learn the names of all my tutees; • invite my tutees for a one-to-one every semester. If students do not attend, I will follow up with them; • find out about my tutees' background, interests and aspirations. I will make a note of these and attempt to recall before I meet them; • I will discuss at the start of each year what tutees can expect from me as their tutor and what is expected of them.

	4 stars (advanced level)	5 stars (expert level)	
8 Reflective practice and professional development		The outcomes of my reflective practice inform joint practice development projects with colleagues.	I will: • organise joint practice development sessions with colleagues (within and across departments) to explore the benefits that reflective practice can bring to personal tutoring practice. If I am able to make these sessions a useful and regular event, I will broaden the scope to cover other areas of practice; • facilitate a training session on reflective practice on a staff training day; • enquire if any colleagues are willing to undertake reflective practice sessions together; • explain how reflective practice has helped me to improve my personal practice when discussed in team meetings.
	2 stars (beginner level)	3 stars (intermediate level)	
9 Measuring impact		I review what the main influences on student performance are at the end of the year and this informs changes in my practice the following year.	I will: • undertake a review of what I feel have been the main influences on my students' performance while also comparing this against changes in the key performance indicators for the academic year. My judgements are likely to be drawn from areas such as my general observations and experiences, discussions with colleagues and managers on how they feel the academic year has gone and what progress students have made, student surveys, mentoring (peer and formal) and course reviews, at-risk information and institutional measures; • evaluate and decide what the key changes I would like to make from the review are and ensure these are considered in my planning for the next academic year.

Table 10.1 (Cont.)

Chapter	Current level (and stars)	Next level to work towards (and stars)	Text from the next level that Hannah wants to work towards	Possible actions (this is not an exhaustive list)
10 What next?	2 stars (beginner level)	3 stars (intermediate level)	I use the individual self-assessment system regularly and, for all of the aspects where I am not yet expert level, I have SMART targets to guide my development.	I will: • keep a reflective personal tutor log to inform the SMART target reviews; • always set a review date (for example at the end of each term or semester) for when I will reassess myself against all of the sections of the individual self-assessment system.

Critical thinking activity 2

1. Using Hannah's context as a guide, write your own current context. You may choose to include, but not be limited to, areas such as:

    a. your strengths and areas for development;

    b. your personal tutor values;

    c. your future career goals;

    d. key strengths or 'drivers' of positive change within your department and the institution;

    e. areas for development or aspects that might hold back positive change within the department and the institution;

    f. current feedback from student surveys and Advance HE fellowship assessments;

    g. key performance indicators such as attendance, continuation, completion and graduate destinations;

    h. student experience feedback.

2. Undertake the individual self-assessment system at the end of each chapter to understand:

    a. what level you are currently working at for each chapter theme;

    b. what your cumulative score and overall level is.

3. For each level identified within question 2a, write down one realistic action that you can take to move up one level. You may wish to do this with a trusted colleague or mentor.

4. Using the headings below, list all of the actions you want to take to improve (from question 3) and order them with the highest priority being number one and the lowest priority being the highest number. Ensure you include a date for completion or to review each. Priority should be influenced by factors such as the impact on the students' intellectual and academic progress or well-being, targets from your mentor, appraisal or even departmental or institutional priorities.

Number	Action	Date by when you will have achieved this or when you will review the progress

Regular self-assessment will help you plan your professional development as a personal tutor. Once you are starting to feel confident in your skills as a personal tutor, you could consider applying for recognition for your skills through the UKAT professional recognition scheme discussed in Chapters 3 and 8.

The bigger picture

The most effective personal tutors (and teachers) tend to be not only excellent practitioners, both within teaching/tutorial sessions and other settings, but they are also the ones who ask the most questions and are curious about how what they do at an individual level impacts students and learning more broadly within their institution. This is not to say that the best practitioners aim for academic promotion, but are individuals motivated to excel in their role and who consistently seek out opportunities for new learning and positive impact on learning and students, whether that be at an individual, class, departmental or institutional level.

This section of the book provides you with an opportunity to think more broadly about your personal tutor role and how you might influence other colleagues and effect positive organisational change. Leadership of teaching and learning is a key part of the Professional Standards Framework and, therefore, Advance HE fellowship particularly at Senior and Principal Fellow categories. Think about the phrase 'universities don't change but people do'. Universities are made up of people, you can move them and put structures, job titles, responsibilities, quality checks, reporting and communication lines in place to try to improve performance, but, ultimately, *people* are the most important factor in achieving success.

Developing high-performing people and a high-performance culture in education is not an easy goal to achieve.

Institutional self-assessment

Similar to the individual personal tutor self-assessment system, the institutional template has been designed to provide a forward-thinking personal tutor, existing or aspiring manager or leader (with a remit for personal tutoring development) with a tool to understand where their institution is now and what the next level is so that they are able to plan the best way to get there. The following case study and Table 10.2 provide an example template which can be applied to most institutional contexts.

AN INSTITUTIONAL CASE STUDY

A post-1992 university in the north of England has been given an overall award of silver in the latest TEF exercise. The university was given a bronze rating for student experience, but received silver for student outcomes, largely because the student support system put in place at the university was considered to be of outstanding quality. Over the last academic year, there have been a number of improvements in teaching, learning and assessment, continuation and progression. Nevertheless, student attendance and attainment require additional focus, alongside support for students with disabilities, students from different ethnicities and those from low socio-economic backgrounds. There is a strong senior and middle management team, who are participative in their approach and open to new ideas of working. Staff morale is good and most are agreed that improvements can be made via enhancements to the existing tutorial system. The university is located in an area of economic regeneration with a high number of students from the surrounding locality. The institution is a low-tariff one and many students have additional support needs.

The university has recently assessed itself using the institutional self-assessment system to understand the level it is working at and to identify actions for improvement. The final column in Table 10.2 suggests how it can provide enhancements to its existing approach. The actions have been written from the perspective of a senior manager of, or leader in, the institution.

The possible actions are suggestions for enhancement and the list is not exhaustive. Every person, institution and context is unique and therefore the actions you take to improve need to be appropriate for your institution.

Table 10.2 University institutional self-assessment

Chapter	Current level (and stars)	Next level to work towards (and stars)	Text from the next level that the institution wants to work towards	Possible actions (this is not an exhaustive list)
3 Core values and skills of the personal tutor (values)	3 star (intermediate)	4 star (advanced level)	All staff have a clear understanding of the core values and the importance of embedding them into their day-to-day work.	I will ensure that: • senior managers talk to staff informally and visit team meetings for feedback on how we are meeting the core values and where we still need to do further work; • I will explain the benefit of institutions having shared core values in order to attempt to create an institution that feels it has an identity and that staff, students and stakeholders are happy to be a part of; • the core values form part of the content of all staff recruitment and selection processes; • we visually display the core values in appropriate places within the institution; • curricular and non-curricular operational planning work, such as course reviews, departmental self-assessment reports and quality improvement plans identify which core value is being displayed through actions.

	3 stars (intermediate level)	4 stars (advanced level)	
3 Core values and skills of the personal tutor (values)		The core skills are consistently and routinely improved through varied strategies. Staff are encouraged to implement ways of assessing how effective the core skills are at improving student outcomes.	I will ensure that: · core skills are part of the feedback asked for in student surveys which will directly feed into the strategy for learning; · a clear and consistent skills analysis is carried out with personal tutors, which feeds into departmental and overall institutional analysis. This information will inform professional development priorities and influence budget allocation; · personal tutors are asked about which specific skills they feel they would like to develop further and support is offered where possible; · quality processes are viewed as developmental and that these recognise the effective core skills displayed as well as appropriately challenge staff to improve where required. The institution will provide support where needed. · peer and/or developmental mentoring processes include ways in which feedback on the core skills used with students are discussed; · sufficient resources are allocated to joint practice development and training opportunities with a focus on the value that the core skills bring to students' intellectual and academic progress and well-being.

Table 10.2 (Cont.)

Chapter	Current level (and stars)	Next level to work towards (and stars)	Text from the next level that the institution wants to work towards	Possible actions (this is not an exhaustive list)
4 Setting boundaries	4 stars (advanced level)	5 stars (expert level)	A range of different types of boundaries are set by departments or support functions which are informed by students themselves. As a result of this and other factors, students take responsibility and are independent.	I will ensure that: • information from student surveys is shared clearly with personal tutors in order to inform boundary setting; • boundary setting and recognition for the purpose of student independence and staff welfare form part of the content of all staff recruitment and selection processes; • boundary setting informs mentoring feedback, both in terms of student independence and staff welfare; • a culture of positive boundary setting and recognition exists within the institution, not only in classroom practice but in meetings at all levels. The latter will be ensured by clear 'rules' and purposes to all meetings which all managers responsible for chairing meetings will have as an expectation.
5 Key activities: Identifying and supporting student populations	1 star (minimum standard)	2 stars (beginner level)	The strategy for supporting specific student populations is effectively communicated to all new staff and updates for existing staff are frequent. Where dashboard analytics systems are used there is basic uniformity in their application to record student interactions.	I will ensure that: • dashboard-based analytics are in use across the institution and analysis of the data they produce informs programme and department-level planning; • the institution's student support strategy (including for specific populations) is systematically reviewed against relevant data on key performance indicators; • a rigorous self-assessment system for student support is in place at departmental level leading to quality improvement plans with SMART outcomes; • dashboard and analytics systems are incorporated into staff training and development to promote continuity of practice.

	4 stars (advanced level)	5 stars (expert level)	
6 Key activities: Effectively supporting all stages of the student lifecycle		The key activities are regularly reviewed involving all relevant student-facing staff and a selection of students. As a result, staff feel invested in them. There is a highly consistent approach to the key activities across my institution.	I will ensure that: • there is a clear strategy for managing the progression of all individuals through the student lifecycle and this is reflected in the key activities; • a strong emphasis is placed on the importance of embedding the key activities as a core part of the student academic experience; • there is clear communication to students about the key activities and how they fit in with student support services in a useable and handy format; • students are consulted for their views on the activities and these will be taken into account when shaping how they are developed in future.
	1 star (minimum standard)	2 stars (beginner level)	
7 Key concepts for effective personal tutoring		My institution provides clear guidance to staff on how to improve engagement and positive interactions.	I will ensure that: • tutorials are timetabled wherever possible; • ensure the importance of a meaningful tutor-tutee relationship is emphasised in our personal tutor training; • personal tutors receive guidance on how to set expectations at the start of each academic year.

Table 10.2 (Cont.)

Chapter	Current level (and stars)	Next level to work towards (and stars)	Text from the next level that the institution wants to work towards	Possible actions (this is not an exhaustive list)
8 Reflective practice and professional development	1 star (minimum standard)	2 stars (beginner level)	My institution displays its commitment to its personal tutors undertaking effective individual or peer reflective practice through providing adequate time, resources and support for the process. Honest and open dialogue about critical incidents or issues is embraced as positive and developmental. My institution helps me to identify my training needs and signposts to appropriate resources. My institution displays its commitment to CPD by supporting personal tutors in their training needs.	I will ensure that: - time and support is provided for personal tutors to undertake reflective practice; - training, which explores reflective practice, is offered throughout the year or on staff training days; - Heads of School or Heads of Department, where possible and appropriate, try to encourage reflective practice to take place in pairs either within the school/department; - there is a person within the institution who has considerable knowledge and experience of various aspects of reflective practice and they are encouraged to discuss this with staff proactively or answer questions reactively, if needed; - where appropriate, Heads of School or Department speak to the personal tutors about what progress they feel they are making as a result of their reflective practice. - Learning and teaching leads, or senior tutors help personal tutors identify their training needs and develop their professional identity. They ensure tutors know where to get support.

	3 star (intermediate level)	4 star (advanced level)	
9 Measuring impact		A range of meaningful individual and team-level impact measures of personal tutor practice informs wider institutional practice.	I will ensure that: • I encourage a culture of 'experimenting' ethically and responsibly with different variables in order to positively impact student performance; • measuring impact is regularly discussed within teams along with innovative ways of doing so. • there are small 'action research' teams were willing academics and personal tutors work collaboratively to examine a variable(s) or technique(s) that they feel may influence student performance; • a range of impact measures are included in departmental self-assessment reports and quality improvement plans; • senior managers collate significant departmental impact measures and use this to inform institutional practice.
10 What next?		My institution is making progress against the institutional self-assessment chapter themes. My institution critically analyses the institutional self-assessment system and has adapted it to make it better and, where appropriate, more applicable to its context.	I will ensure that: • the institutional self-assessment system is reviewed and adapted to meet the aims and context of our institution, taking into account the views of as many student-facing staff as possible; • on a yearly basis we review and critically analyse all of the self-assessment tools we use within our institution to ensure that the content and process is still useful and relevant.

Critical thinking activity 3

Depending on your current role and experience, you may need to speak to a manager or someone on the senior leadership team to be able to fully complete questions 1 and 2. This will be valuable experience, particularly to understand these aspects more fully.

1. Using the above Institutional Case Study as a guide, describe your own current context, referring to yourself as an existing or aspiring senior manager or leader for the educational institution you work within. You may choose to include, but not be limited to, areas such as:

    a. key institutional aims;

    b. key strengths or 'drivers' of positive change within departments and the institution;

    c. areas for development or aspects that might hold back positive change within departments and the institution;

    d. the perceived culture from an institution-wide perspective;

    e. typical student profile;

    f. current student feedback.

2. Undertake the institutional self-assessment system to understand:

    a. what level your institution is currently working at for each chapter theme;

    b. what your cumulative score and overall level is.

3. For each level identified within question 2a, write down one realistic action that can be taken to move up one level.

It is important to bear in mind when reading this table that we have written the actions while drawing on leadership and managerial experience. If you have not had this experience, you may find that the actions you come up with are less comprehensive. This is not a concern; the important point is to start thinking more broadly about your personal tutor role and the 'bigger picture', and to start identifying relevant actions.

Institutions can be recognised for their personal tutoring provision and training of personal tutors through the UKAT Institutional Accreditation Scheme (2025).

Summary

Setting yourself small incremental actions to improve your personal tutoring practice will help the learning from the book to become embedded. The self-assessment systems that you have used are intended as a helpful guide for how you and your institution might continually improve. It is, however, important to be constructively critical of them and adapt or improve them to make them relevant and appropriate to you and your institution. You should also keep in mind the bigger picture, because this will help you to recognise why some decisions are made and to understand how you can influence the institution more broadly.

At the beginning of this book, you placed yourself on a scale of one to ten in terms of your knowledge and practice as a personal tutor. On the same scale as before, where are you now and why?

We hope you feel clear and positive about the next steps that you can take to develop effective practice and that this is the beginning or continuation of the increasingly positive impact you will have on your students and the institution you work within.

Critical reflections

1. In relation to all of the learning from the book, identify and explain which aspect you feel:
   a. most proud of in terms of your own personal tutoring practice and why;
   b. you would like to develop first and why;
   c. the institution you work within should be most proud of in terms of its personal tutoring practice and why;
   d. the institution you work within should consider developing first and why.
2. In relation to 'bigger picture' decisions that affect students, staff and the institution more broadly, explain what you feel the three key critical success factors are which will ensure that a new idea, policy or procedure has the greatest chance of being effective.
3. To what extent do you think that, in order for an institution to become most effective, it is all about developing the culture and people?
4. If you skim read this book to identify the key messages from all of the chapters, what would you identify as the top five recommendations in order to make your personal tutoring practice most effective?

Personal tutor self-assessment system

See following table.

PERSONAL TUTOR SELF-ASSESSMENT SYSTEM: Chapter 10 What next?

	Minimum standard 1 star	Beginner level 2 stars	Intermediate level 3 stars	Advanced level 4 stars	Expert level 5 stars
Individual	I feel a strong sense of ownership of my professional development and ultimately view it as my responsibility.	I reflect and think holistically about all aspects of my personal tutoring practice. My ultimate goal is to achieve expert level in all chapter themes.	I use the individual self-assessment system regularly and, for all of the aspects where I am not yet at expert level, I have SMART targets to guide my development.	I am making progress against the individual self-assessment chapter themes. I critically analyse the individual self-assessment system and have adapted it to make it better and, where appropriate, more applicable to my context.	I have achieved expert level for all of the chapter themes within the individual self-assessment system. I am now investigating ways in which I can develop my personal tutoring practice, and that of my colleagues, further.
Institutional	Generally, the personal tutors in my institution feel consulted and supported with regard to their professional development. One of our aims is to help staff take ownership of their professional development.	The majority of our personal tutors are making progress against the individual self-assessment criteria. Our ultimate goal is to achieve expert level in all chapter themes.	My institution uses the institutional self-assessment system regularly, and for all of the aspects where we are not yet at expert level we have SMART targets to guide our development.	My institution is making progress against the institutional self-assessment chapter themes. My institution critically analyses the institutional self-assessment system and has adapted it to make it better and, where appropriate, more applicable to its context.	My institution has achieved expert level for all of the chapter themes within the institutional self-assessment system. We are now investigating ways in which we can sustain this level, as well as continue to develop our staff, systems and processes further.

References

Academic Registrars' Council (2025) *Compassionate Communication*. [online] Available at: https://arc.ac.uk/student-commitment (accessed 10 June 2025).

Adams, R (2025) English Universities' Income Falls for Third Consecutive Year. *The Guardian*.

Advance HE (2021) *Understanding Structural Racism in UK Higher Education: An Introduction*. Advance HE.

Advance HE (2023) *Professional Standards Framework for Teaching and Supporting Learning in Higher Education*. Advance HE.

Advance HE (2024) *Inclusive Learning and Teaching Framework*. Advance HE.

Advance HE (2025) *A Competency Framework for Responding to Students in Distress*. Advance HE.

Alberts, N (2021) *Someone Who Knows You: First-Year Students' Expectations and Experiences of Personal Tutoring at the University of Bristol*. University of Bristol, Bristol. Available at: https://research-information.bris.ac.uk/en/publications/someone-who-knows-you-first-year-students-expectations-and-experi (accessed 10 November 2025).

Alberts, N (2022a) Forced Fun: Questioning the Role of the Personal Tutor in Community Building. *UKAT Annual Conference 2022: Reimagining Personal Tutoring*, 4–6 April 2022. Online.

Alberts, N (2022b) Proactivity as a Route to Care in Personal Tutoring. *The Compassionate Conference*, 21/03/2022. Online.

Alberts, N (2023) *Personal Tutoring: Best Practise and Models*. University of Bristol, Bristol. Available at: https://bit.ly/PT_casestudies (accessed 10 November 2025).

Alberts, N (2024a) Broad Shoulders: The Burden of Being a Senior Tutor. *UKAT Annual Conference 2024: Personal Tutoring in the Spotlight*, 8–9 April 2024. University of Greenwich, London.

Alberts, N (2024b) *High Stakes: UOB Staff Perceptions of Personal Tutoring*. University of Bristol, Bristol. Available at: https://prezi.com/v/view/navjR67dhmUFlDnkA2kM/ (accessed 10 November 2025).

Alberts, N (2025) The Challenges Faced by Senior Tutors in UK Higher Education. *Waypoint – A Reflective Journal of Student Advising and Development in Tertiary Education*, 1: 11–34.

Alves, R (2019) Could Personal Tutoring Help Improve the Attainment Gap of Black, Asian and Minority Ethnic Students? *Blended Learning in Practice*, 50(4): 66–76.

AMOSSHE (2011) *Value and Impact Toolkit. Assessing the Value and Impact of Services That Support Students*. London: AMOSSHE.

AMOSSHE (2023) *AMOSSHE's Position on a Proposed Additional Statutory Duty of Care.* Available at: https://www.amosshe.org.uk/resource/amosshe-s-position-on-a-proposed-additional-statutory-duty-of-care.html?_gl=1@@@@1jn5pu7@@@@_up@@@@MQ.@@@@_ga@@@@MTE2Mzg0OTg0NS4xNzMwODg4NTkx@@@@_ga_YK8ZGL9FK6@@@@MTczMDg4ODU5MC4xLjEuMTczMDg4ODY3Mi4wLjAuMA (accessed 6 November 2024).

Anderson, V, Rabello, R, Wass, R, Golding, C, Rangi, A, Eteuati, E, Bristowe, Z & Waller, A (2020) Good Teaching as Care in Higher Education. *Higher Education*, 79: 1–19.

Andreanoff, J, Chilvers, L, Chin, P, Garratt, C, Lefever, R, Lochtie, D, Perry, C & Rodriguez Falcon, O (2024) *Part 2 – Mapping Sector Wide Practices: Literature Review*. York: Advance HE.

Ashencaen Crabtree, S & Shiel, C (2019) "Playing Mother": Channeled Careers and the Construction of Gender in Academia. *Sage Open*, 9: 2158244019876285.

Assender, J & Leadbeater, W (2022) Supporting Student Employability through Integrated Research Exposure and a Curriculum-Embedded Skills Module, in Lochtie, D, Stork, A & Walker, B W (eds) *The Higher Education Personal Tutors and Advisors Companion*. St Albans: Routledge.

Atkins, S & Murphy, K (1994) Reflective Practice. *Nursing Standard*, 8: 49–54.

Atkinson, S P (2014) *Rethinking Personal Tutoring Systems: The Need to Build on a Foundation of Epistemological Beliefs*. London: BPP University.

Augustus, J, Goodall, D & Williams, B (2023) Does the Role of Personal Academic Tutor Have an Impact on Staff Wellbeing? *Research in Post-Compulsory Education*, 28: 693–719.

Aultman, L, Williams-Johnson, M & Schutz, P (2009) Boundary Dilemmas in Teacher–Student Relationships: Struggling with 'the Line'. *Teaching and Teacher Education*, 25: 636–646.

Ayton, R & Walling, M (2022) The Power of Future Planning: Empowering Personal Tutors to Have Effective Careers and Employability Conversations, in Lochtie, D, Stork, A and Walker, B W (eds) *The Higher Education Personal Tutors and Advisors Companion*. St Albans: Routledge.

Banahene, L (2024) *Diverse Students Need Bespoke Personal Tutoring*. Available at: https://wonkhe.com/blogs/diverse-students-need-bespoke-personal-tutoring/ (accessed 20 November 2025).

Bangs, N & Gallacher, D (2023) Tutoring Matters: Adapting to the Needs of Higher Education Students: Academic Advising, Transformative Education and Closing Attainment Gaps. *UKAT Tutoring Matters webinar series*, 19th January.

Barefoot, B O (2000) The First-Year Experience: Are We Making It Any Better? *About Campus*, 4: 12–18.

Barnes-Powell, T & Letherby, G (1998) 'All in a Day's Work': Gendered Care Work in Higher Education, in Malina, D & Maslin-Prothero, S (eds) *Surviving the Academy: Feminist Perspectives*. St Albans: Routledge. 69–77.

Barrie, S C (2007) A Conceptual Framework for the Teaching and Learning of Generic Graduate Attributes. *Studies in Higher Education*, 32: 439–458.

Bates, E A & Kaye, L K (2014) 'I'd Be Expecting Caviar in Lectures': The Impact of the New Fee Regime on Undergraduate Students' Expectations of Higher Education. *Higher Education*, 67: 655–673.

Battin, J R (2014) Improving Academic Advising through Student Seminars: A Case Study. *Journal of Criminal Justice Education*, 25: 354–367.

Bauer, C & Figl, K (2008) "Active Listening" in Written Online Communication – A Case Study in a Course on "Soft Skills for Computer Scientists". *2008 38th Annual Frontiers in Education Conference*, Saratoga Springs, NY, USA, 2008, p F2C-1-F2C-6.

Bell, K (2022) Increasing Undergraduate Student Satisfaction in Higher Education: The Importance of Relational Pedagogy. *Journal of Further and Higher Education*, 46: 490–503.

Birbeck, D, McKellar, L & Kenyon, K (2021) Moving Beyond First Year: An Exploration of Staff and Student Experience. *Student Success*, 12: 82–92.

Blake, S, Capper, G & Jackson, A (2022) *Building Belonging in Higher Education: Recommendations for Developing an Integrated Institutional Approach*. Pearson and WonkHE: London.

Blau, P M (1964) Justice in Social Exchange. *Sociological Inquiry*, 34(2): 193–206.

Boddy, C (2020) Lonely, Homesick and Struggling: Undergraduate Students and Intention to Quit University. *Quality Assurance in Education*, 28: 239–253.

Bolton, P (2024) *Higher Education Student Numbers*. House of Commons Library, London.

Bolton, P & Lewis, J (2023) *Equality of Access and Outcomes in Higher Education in England*. House of Commons Library, London.

Bordia, S, Hobman, E V, Restubog, S L D & Bordia, P (2010) Advisor-Student Relationship in Business Education Project Collaborations: A Psychological Contract Perspective. *Journal of Applied Social Psychology*, 40: 2360–2386.

Bosch, S & Jacobi, M (2025) Evaluation of Implementation of Models of Academic Advising in Postgraduate Taught Courses. *Waypoint – A Reflective Journal of Student Advising and Development in Tertiary Education*, 1: 84–101.

Bovill, C (2020a) *Co-Creating Learning and Teaching: Towards Relational Pedagogy in Higher Education*. St Albans: Routledge.

Bovill, C (2020b) Co-Creation in Learning and Teaching: The Case for a Whole-Class Approach in Higher Education. *Higher Education*, 79: 1023–1037.

Bowden, J (2008) Why Do Nursing Students Who Consider Leaving Stay on Their Courses? *Nurse Researcher*, 15: 45–58.

Braine, M E & Parnell, J (2011) Exploring Student's Perceptions and Experience of Personal Tutors. *Nurse Education Today*, 31: 904–910.

Brennan, J (2021) *Flexible Learning Pathways in British Higher Education: A Decentralized and Market-Based System*. UNESCO. International Institute for Educational Planning, Paris

Brewster, L, Jones, E, Priestley, M, Wilbraham, S J, Spanner, L and Hughes, G (2022) 'Look after the Staff and They Would Look after the Students' Cultures of Wellbeing and Mental Health in the University Setting. *Journal of Further and Higher Education*, 46: 548–560.

Broad, J (2006) Interpretations of Independent Learning in Further Education. *Journal of Further and Higher Education*, 30: 119–143.

Brookfield, S (1995) *Becoming a Critically Reflective Teacher*. San Francisco: Jossey-Bass.

Brown, E (2022) Making Belonging Explicit by Design, in Lochtie, D, Stork, A and Walker, B W (eds) *The Higher Education Personal Tutor's and Advisor's Companion: Translating Theory into Practice to Improve Student Success*. St Albans: Routledge.

Brown, E & Thomas, L (2022) Dissonant Discourses: Constructing a Consistent Personal Tutoring Experience across the Whole University, in Lochtie, D, Stork, A and Walker, B W (eds) *The Higher Education Personal Tutor's and Advisor's Companion: Translating Theory into Practice to Improve Student Success*. St Albans: Routledge.

Burnett, C & Coldwell, M (2021) Randomised Controlled Trials and the Interventionisation of Education. *Oxford Review of Education*, 47: 423–438.

Cage, E, Jones, E, Ryan, G, Hughes, G & Spanner, L (2021) Student Mental Health and Transitions into, through and out of University: Student and Staff Perspectives. *Journal of Further and Higher Education*, 45: 1076–1089.

Cai, X & Gellai, D (2024) Contexts of the Third Space: Learnings from Two Professional Personal Tutoring Models at King's College London. *UKAT Annual Conference 2024: Personal Tutoring in the Spotlight*, 8–9 April 2024. Greenwich, London.

Calabrese, G, Leadbitter, D-L M, Trindade, N D S M D, Jeyabalan, A, Dolton, D & ElShaer, A (2022) Personal Tutoring Scheme: Expectations, Perceptions and Factors Affecting Students' Engagement. *Frontiers in Education*, 6: 1–11.

Calcagno, L, Walker, D & Grey, D J (2017) Building Relationships: A Personal Tutoring Framework to Enhance Student Transition and Attainment. *Student Engagement in Higher Education Journal*, 1: 88–99.

Cameron, D A, Binnie, V I, Sherriff, A & Bissell, V (2015) Peer Assisted Learning: Teaching Dental Skills and Enhancing Graduate Attributes. *British Dental Journal*, 219: 267–272.

Cameron, W B (1963) *Informal Sociology: A Casual Introduction to Sociological Thinking*. New York: Random House.

Campbell, S M & Nutt, C L (2008) Academic Advising in the New Global Century. *Peer Review*, 10: 4–7.

Chan, K & Rose, J (2023) Conceptualizing Success: A Holistic View of a Successful First-Year Undergraduate Experience, in Willison, D and Henderson, E (eds) *Perspectives on Enhancing Student Transition into Higher Education and Beyond*. Hershey, PA, USA: IGI Global.

Clarke, N (2025) Empowering Excellence in Learning and Teaching – Unscripted Critical Moments and Their Ripple Effect. *Waypoint – A Reflective Journal of Student Advising and Development in Tertiary Education*, 1: 6–10.

The Concise Oxford English Dictionary (1995) Oxford: Clarendon Press.

Conley, C S, Shapiro, J B, Huguenel, B M & Kirsch, A C (2020) Navigating the College Years: Developmental Trajectories and Gender Differences in Psychological Functioning, Cognitive-Affective Strategies, and Social Well-Being. *Emerging Adulthood*, 8: 103–117.

Cook, B (2017) Paulo Freire and the De-commodification of Higher Education in the 21st Century. *Education and Transformative Practice – International Paulo Freire Conference*, 5–7 September 2017. Cyprus.

Crawford, C, Dytham, S & Naylor, R (2017) *The Evaluation of the Impact of Outreach: Proposed Standards of Evaluation Practice and Associated Guidance*. Bristol, UK: Office for Fair Access.

Crookston, B B (1972) A Developmental View of Academic Advising as Teaching. *Journal of College Student Personnel*, 14(2): 5–9.

Dabrowski, V, Atas, N, Ramsey, T & Howarth, N (2025) 'Money Anxiety': Understanding HE Students' Experiences of the Cost-of-Living Crisis. *Social Policy and Administration*, 59: 280–292.

Davis, A (2011) *The Correlation between Attendance [Sic] and Achievement*. Dublin: Dublin Institute of Technology.

Dearing (1997) *The Dearing Report*. London: Her Majesty's Stationery Office.

Department for Business, Innovation and Skills (2011) *Higher Education: Students at the Heart of the System*. London: Department of Business, Innovation and Skills.

Department for Education (2017) *Securing Student Success: Risk-Based Regulation for Teaching Excellence, Social Mobility and Informed Choice in Higher Education*. London: Department for Education.

Department for Education (2023) Higher Education: Standards. Question for Department for Education, Uin 174398, Tabled on 27 March 2023. Available at: https://questions-statements.parliament.uk/written-questions/detail/2023-03-27/174398 (accessed 7 November 2024).

Department for Education (2024) Policy Paper: Lifelong Learning Entitlement Overview.

Dewey, J (1933) *How We Think: A Restatement of the Relation of Reflective Thinking to the Educative Process*. Boston, MA: D.C. Heath.

de Witt, J (2022) The 'Anatomy' of a Solutions-Focused Coaching Conversation in Personal Academic Tutoring, in Lochtie, D, Stork, A and Walker, B W (eds) *The Higher Education Personal Tutor's and Advisor's Companion: Translating Theory into Practice to Improve Student Success*. St Albans: Routledge.

Dickinson, J (2023) What Does Duty of Care Mean When It Comes to Universities and Students? *WonkHE comment* [Online]. Available at: https://wonkhe.com/blogs/what-does-duty-of-care-mean-when-it-comes-to-universities-and-students/ (accessed 6 November 2024).

Dobinson-Harrington, A (2006) Personal Tutor Encounters: Understanding the Experience. *Nursing Standard*, 20: 35–42.

Donnelly, M & Gamsu, S (2018) *Home and Away: Social, Ethnic and Spatial Inequalities in Student Mobility*. The Sutton Trust, London.

Drake, J K (2011) The Role of Academic Advising in Student Retention and Persistence. *About Campus*, 16: 8–12.

Drew, K (2023) Tutoring during Transition: Students' Experiences and Preferences Towards Personal Tutoring in UK Higher Education. *Innovative Practice in Higher Education*, 5: 1–37.

Dunbar-Morris, H (2021) Co-Creating a Student Charter. *Student Engagement in Higher Education Journal*, 3: 26–34.

Dunbar-Morris, H (2022) Personal Tutoring and Development Framework, in Lochtie, D, Stork, A & Walker, B W (eds) *The Higher Education Personal Tutors and Advisors Companion*. St Albans: Routledge.

Earwaker, J (1992) *Helping and Supporting Students. Rethinking the Issues*. Buckingham: Open University Press.

Egan, G & Reese, R (2018) *The Skilled Helper: A Problem-Management and Opportunity-Development Approach to Helping*. Boston: CENGAGE Learning Custom Publishing.

Emsley-Jones, C, Garrett, C & McConnell, C (2024) *Part 3 – Mapping Peer Learning and Support Practices: Findings from a Sector-Wide Survey*. York: Advance HE.

Essien, A, Smith, S & Bukoye, O (2024) The Future of Personal Tutoring: Integrating Analytics and Generative Ai. *UKAT Annual Conference 2024: Personal Tutoring in the Spotlight*. University of Greenwich, London.

European Mentoring and Coaching Council n.d. [online] Available at: www.emccuk.org (accessed 20 November 2025).

Felten, P & Lambert, L M (2020) *Relationship-Rich Education: How Human Connections Drive Success in College.* Baltimore: John Hopkins University Press.

Fergy, S, Marks-Maran, D, Ooms, A, Shapcott, J and Burke, L (2011) Promoting Social and Academic Integration into Higher Education by First Year Student Nurses: The Appl Project. *Journal of Further and Higher Education*, 35: 107–130.

Fitch, P (2024) Evaluation Special Interest Group Inaugural Meeting. *UKAT Annual Conference 2024 Personal Tutoring in the Spotlight.* Greenwich, London.

Flett, G, Khan, A & Su, C (2019) Mattering and Psychological Well-Being in College and University Students: Review and Recommendations for Campus-Based Initiatives. *International Journal of Mental Health and Addiction*, 17: 667–680.

Foy, C & Keane, A (2018) Introduction of a Peer Mentoring Scheme within Biomedical Sciences Education – Easing the Transition to University Life. *Journal of Further and Higher Education*, 42: 733–741.

Foy, K (2020) Contracting in Coaching, in *The Coaches' Handbook.* New York: Routledge.

Freire, P (1998) *Pedagogy of Freedom: Ethics, Democracy, and Civic Courage.* Lanham, Boulder, New York, Oxford: Rowman & Littlefield.

Gabi, J, Braddock, A, Brown, C, Miller, D, Mynott, G, Jacobi, M, Banerjee, P, Kenny, K & Rawson, A (2024) Can the Role of a Personal Tutor Contribute to Reducing the Undergraduate Degree Awarding Gap for Racially Minoritised Students? *British Educational Research Journal*, 50: 1784–1803.

Gabi, J, Hidalgo, A, Leydon, J & Johnson, G (2025) Culturally Affirming, Validating and Relationally Just Personal Tutoring and Advising in Higher Education. *UKAT Annual Conference 2025: Learning Well.* UCL, London.

Gannon, L (2025) Using the 3 C's to Unlock Student Success: A Closer Look at a Coaching Approach to Personal Tutoring. *Waypoint – A Reflective Journal of Student Advising and Development in Tertiary Education*, 1: 53–62.

George, R & Rapley, E (2022) 'Talking the Talk and Walking the Walk' of Personal Tutoring: Using Structured Continuing Professional Development Opportunities to Inform, Develop and Empower Personal Tutors, in Lochtie, D, Stork, A and Walker, B W (eds) *The Higher Education Personal Tutors and Advisors Companion.* St Albans: Routledge.

Ghenghesh, P (2017) Personal Tutoring from the Perspectives of Tutors and Tutees. *Journal of Further and Higher Education*, 42: 570–584.

Gibbs, G (1998) *Learning by Doing: A Guide to Teaching and Learning Methods.* Further Education Unit, Oxford Polytechnic, Oxford.

Gidman, J, Humphreys, A & Andrews, M (2000) The Role of the Personal Tutor in the Academic Context. *Nurse Education Today*, 20: 401–407.

Gilani, D (2024) Challenging Simplistic and Deficit Perceptions of Belonging Amongst Historically Underrepresented Students: Four Self-Reflective Questions for Policy Makers and Practitioners. *Student Engagement in Higher Education Journal*, 5: 17–24.

Goh, E & Richardson, S (2024) Developing Effective Mentoring Programs in Hospitality Higher Education: A Practical Perspective Using the Mentoring Framework. *Journal of Teaching in Travel and Tourism*, 24: 179–188.

Gopalan, M, Linden-Carmichael, A & Lanza, S (2022) College Students' Sense of Belonging and Mental Health Amidst the Covid-19 Pandemic. *Journal of Adolescent Health*, 70: 228–233.

Grant, A (2006) Personal Tutoring: A System in Crisis? in Thomas, L and Hixenbaugh, P (eds) *Personal Tutoring in Higher Education*. Stoke-on-Trent: Trentham Books.

Gravells, J & Wallace, S (2007) *Mentoring in the Lifelong Learning Sector* (2nd Ed). Exeter: Learning Matters.

Gravells, J & Wallace, S (2013) *The A-Z Guide to Working in Further Education*. Northwich: Routledge.

Gravett, K, Kinchin, I M & Winstone, N E (2020) 'More Than Customers': Conceptions of Students as Partners Held by Students, Staff, and Institutional Leaders. *Studies in Higher Education*, 45: 2574–2587.

Gravett, K, Taylor, C A & Fairchild, N (2021) Pedagogies of Mattering: Re-Conceptualising Relational Pedagogies in Higher Education. *Teaching in Higher Education*, 29(2): 1–16.

Gravett, K & Winstone, N E (2021) Storying Students' Becomings into and through Higher Education. *Studies in Higher Education*, 46: 1578–1589.

Gravett, K & Winstone, N E (2022) Making Connections: Authenticity and Alienation within Students' Relationships in Higher Education. *Higher Education Research and Development*, 41: 360–374.

Gray, H & Shanmugam, S (2022) Refreshing the Academic Advising System through Co-Creation and Consensus Development, in Lochtie, D, Stork, A and Walker, B W (eds) *The Higher Education Personal Tutors and Advisors Companion*. St Albans: Routledge.

Greenway, C (2022) Ask Pat: How the Introduction and Implementation of an E-Portfolio Approach Transformed the Nature of Student Support and Development, in Lochtie, D, Stork, A & Walker, B (eds) *The Higher Education Personal Tutors and Advisors Companion*. St Albans: Routledge.

Grey, D, Jones, G, Pedlingham, G & Briggs, S (2024) Developing a Community of Practice around Leadership Challenges in Personal Tutoring. Available at: https://wonkhe.com/blogs/developing-a-community-of-practice-around-leadership-challenges-in-personal-tutoring/ (accessed 11 October 2024).

Grey, D & Lochtie, D (2016) Comparing Personal Tutoring in the UK and Academic Advising in the US. *Academic Advising Today* [Online]. Available at: https://nacada.ksu.edu/Resources/Academic-Advising-Today/View-Articles/Comparing-Personal-Tutoring-in-the-UK-and-Academic-Advising-in-the-US.aspx (accessed 1 July 2022).

Grey, D & McIntosh, E (2017) Student Dashboards: The Case for Building Communities of Practice. *UK Advising and Tutoring Conference*, 12 April 2017. Leeds.

Grey, D & Osborne, C (2020) Perceptions and Principles of Personal Tutoring. *Journal of Further and Higher Education*, 44: 285–299.

Gubby, L & McNab, N (2013) Personal Tutoring from the Perspective of the Tutor. *Capture*, 4: 7–18.

Guiso, L, Sapienza, P & Zingales, L (2013) *The Value of Corporate Culture*. The University of Chicago, Booth School of Business, Chicago.

Gupta, A, Brooks, R & Abrahams, J (2023) Higher Education Students as Consumers: A Cross-Country Comparative Analysis of Students' Views. *Compare: A Journal of Comparative and International Education*, 55(2): 1–18.

Gurbutt, D & Gurbutt, R (2015) Empowering Students to Promote Independent Learning: A Project Utilising Coaching Approaches to Support Learning and Personal Development. *Journal of Learning Development in Higher Education*, 8: 1–17.

Gutiérrez, F, Seipp, K, Ochoa, X, Chiluiza, K, De Laet, T & Verbert, K (2020) Lada: A Learning Analytics Dashboard for Academic Advising. *Computers in Human Behavior*, 107: 105826.

Hallam, I (2023) College Higher Education Commuter Students' Experiences of Belonging, Mattering and Persisting with Their Studies. *Research in Post-Compulsory Education*, 28: 373–389.

Hamer, A (2025) *The Importance of Reasonable Adjustments*. [online] Available at: https://www.hepi.ac.uk/2025/03/18/the-importance-of-reasonable-adjustments/ (accessed 10 June 2025).

Harrison, N (2017) *Moving on Up: Pathways of Care Leavers and Care-Experienced Students into and through Higher Education*. Bristol: University of the West of England.

Hartwell, H & Farbrother, C (2006) Enhancing the First Year Experience through Personal Tutoring, in Thomas, L & Hixenbaugh, P (eds) *Personal Tutoring in Higher Education*. Stoke-on-Trent: Trentham Books.

Harvey, L, Drew, S & Smith, M (2006) *The First Year Experience: A Review of Literature for the Higher Education Academy*. York: Higher Education Academy.

Havergal, C (2015) Is 'Academic Citizenship' under Strain? *Times Higher Education*, 29. https://www.timeshighereducation.com/features/is-academic-citizenship-under-strain/2018134.article

Hayman, R, Coyles, A, Wharton, K & Mellor, A (2020) The Role of Personal Tutoring in Supporting the Transition to University: Experiences and Views of Widening Participation Sport Students. *Journal of Learning Development in Higher Education*, 18: 1–29.

HESA (2025) *Who's Studying in HE?* [online] Available at: https://www.hesa.ac.uk/data-and-analysis/students/whos-in-he (accessed 10 June 2025).

Hicks, T & Heastie, S (2008) High School to College Transition: A Profile of the Stressors, Physical and Psychological Health Issues That Affect First-Year on-Campus College Students. *Journal of Cultural Diversity*, 15: 143–147.

Higgins, E M, Peabody, M A & Gorgas Goulding, H (2021) Faculty and Primary Role Advisors: Building a Relational Partnership. *Academic Advising Today*, 44(3). https://nacada.ksu.edu/Resources/Academic-Advising-Today/View-Articles/Faculty-and-Primary-Role-Advisors-Building-a-Relational-Partnership.aspx (accessed 28 Aug 25).

Hillman, J, Lochtie, D & Purcell, O (2024) Black Students' Experiences of Coaching and Mentoring in Higher Education: A Case Study. *International Journal of Mentoring and Coaching in Education*, 13: 246–257.

Hillman, N (2024). *'Dropouts or Stopouts or Comebackers or Potential Completers?': Non-Continuation of Students in the UK*. Oxford: Higher Education Policy Institute.

Holland, C, Westwood, C & Hanif, N (2020) Underestimating the Relationship between Academic Advising and Attainment: A Case Study in Practice. *Frontiers in Education*, 5: 1–11.

Hughes, G & Bowers-Brown, T (2021) Student Services, Personal Tutors, and Student Mental Health: A Case Study, in Huijser H, Kek MYCA and Padró FF (eds) *Student Support Services. University Development and Administration.* Singapore: Springer, 1–15.

Hughes, G, Panjwani, M, Tulcidas, P & Byrom, N C (2018) *Student Mental Health: The Role and Experiences of Academics*. Oxford: Student Minds.

Hughes, G & Spanner, L (2024) *The University Mental Health Charter* (2nd Ed). Leeds: Student Minds.

Hughes, S J (2004) The Mentoring Role of the Personal Tutor in the 'Fitness for Practice' Curriculum: An All Wales Approach. *Nurse Education in Practice*, 4: 271–278.

Hunt, L & Peach, N (2009) *Planning for a Sustainable Academic Future*. In *Academic Futures: Inquiries into Higher Education and Pedagogy*. Newcastle-upon-Tyne: Cambridge Scholars.

Huppert, F A (2009) Psychological Well-Being: Evidence Regarding Its Causes and Consequences. *Applied Psychology: Health and Well-Being*, 1: 137–164.

Hutchison, D & Styles, B (2010) *A Guide to Running Randomised Controlled Trials for Educational Researchers*. Slough: NFER.

Jackson, P Z & McKergow, M (2007) *Solutions Focus*. London: Nicholas Brealey Publishing.

Jaud, J, Görig, T, Konkel, T & Diehl, K (2023) Loneliness in University Students during Two Transitions: A Mixed Methods Approach Including Biographical Mapping. *International Journal of Environmental Research and Public Health*, 20: 3334.

Jevons, C & Lindsay, S (2018) The Middle Years Slump: Addressing Student-Reported Barriers to Academic Progress. *Higher Education Research & Development*, 37: 1156–1170.

Johns, C (1995) Framing Learning through Reflection within Carper's Fundamental Ways of Knowing in Nursing. *Journal of Advanced Nursing*, 22: 226–234.

Jones, D J & Watson, B C (1990) High-Risk Students and Higher Education: Future Trends. *Ashe-Eric Higher Education Report*, 19: 83–90.

Jones, J, Cureton, D, Hughes, J, Jennings, J, Pearce, M & Virdi, H (2025) Professionalising the Contribution of HE Third Space Professionals – Developing Themselves to Support Others. *Journal of Learning Development in Higher Education*. 33: 1–15.

Kandiko, C B & Mawer, M (2013) *Student Expectations and Perceptions of Higher Education*. King's Learning Institute, London.

Karp, M, Ackerson, S, Cheng, I, Cocatre-Zilgien, E, Costelloe, S, Freeman, B, Lemire, S, Linderman, D, McFarlane, B & Moulton, S (2021). *Effective Advising for Postsecondary Students: Practice Guide Summary*. U.S. Department of Education, What Works Clearinghouse.

Kastelic, M (2024) University Finances Are in a Perilous State – It's the Result of Market Competition and Debt-Based Expansion. *The Conversation* [Online]. Available at: https://theconversation.com/university-finances-are-in-a-perilous-state-its-the-result-of-market-competition-and-debt-based-expansion-234862#:~:text=Marketisation%20began%20with%20the%20introduction,a%20result%20of%20the%20pandemic (accessed 14 November 2024).

Katz, S (2021) Co-Creating with Students: Practical Considerations and Approaches. Available at: https://www.timeshighereducation.com/campus/cocreating-students-practical-considerations-and-approaches (accessed 15 December 2024).

Kendall, L (2017) Supporting Students with Disabilities within a UK University: Lecturer Perspectives. *Innovations in Education and Teaching International*, 55(6): 694–703.

Kift, S & Nelson, K (2005) Beyond Curriculum Reform: Embedding the Transition Experience in Higher Education in a Changing World. Proceedings of the 28th Higher Education Research and Development Society of Australia (HERDSA) Annual Conference, 3–6 July 2005 Sydney.

Kift, S (2009) *Articulating a Transition Pedagogy to Scaffold and to Enhance the First Year Student Learning Experience in Australian Higher Education*.

Kift, S (2015a) A Decade of Transition Pedagogy: A Quantum Leap in Conceptualising the First Year Experience. *HERDSA Review of Higher Education*, 2: 51–86.

Kift, S (2015b) Transition Pedagogy: A Whole Student, Whole-of-Institution Framework for Successful Student Transitions. *International Conference on Enhancement and Innovation in Higher Education*.

Kolb, D (1984) *Experiential Learning: Experience as the Source of Learning and Development*. Englewood Cliffs, NJ: Prentice Hall.

Koskina, A (2013) What Does the Student Psychological Contract Mean? Evidence from a UK Business School. *Studies in Higher Education*, 38: 1020–1036.

Kroshus, E, Hawrilenko, M & Browning, A (2021) Stress, Self-Compassion, and Well-Being during the Transition to College. *Social Science and Medicine*, 269: 113514.

Lamont, B J (2005) *East Meets West – Bridging the Academic Advising Divide* [online]. Available at: http://www.nacada.ksu.edu/Resources/Clearinghouse/View-Articles/East-meets-West–Bridging-the-advising-divide.aspx (accessed 20 November 2025).

Lancer, N & Eatough, V (2018) One-to-One Coaching as a Catalyst for Personal Development: An Interpretative Phenomenological Analysis of Coaching Undergraduates at a UK University. *International Coaching Psychology Review*, 13: 72–88.

Lave, J & Wenger, E (1991) *Situated Learning: Legitimate Peripheral Participation*. Cambridge: Cambridge university press.

Laycock, M (2017) Personal Tutoring in HE: Where Now and Where Next? *Personal Tutoring and Academic Advising: Contemporary Narratives and Developing Practice. The Fourth National Seminar*, 11 October 2017, Sheffield.

Lee, B & Robinson, A (2006) Creating a Network of Student Support, in Thomas, L and Hixenbaugh, P (eds) *Personal Tutoring in Higher Education*. Stoke-on-Trent: Trentham Books.

Lees, D & Woods, K (2022) Supporting Arts and Humanities Student Development and Progression through Integrating Reflection into Personal Tutoring, in Lochtie, D, Stork, A and Walker, B W (eds) *The Higher Education Personal Tutors and Advisors Companion*. St Albans: Routledge.

Levy, J, Tryfona, C, Koukouravas, T, Hughes, N & Worrall, M (2009) Cardiff School of Management Personal Tutors: Building Student Confidence. *Widening Participation and Lifelong Learning*, 11: 36–39.

Little, B, Locke, W, Scesa, A & Williams, R (2009) *Report to HEFCE on Student Engagement*.

Lochtie, D (2015) A 'Special Relationship' in Higher Education? What Influence Might the Us Higher Education Sector Have in Terms of Support for International Students in the UK? *Perspectives: Policy and Practice in Higher Education*, 20: 67–74.

Lochtie, D & McConnell, C (2024) *Student-Led Peer Learning and Support. Part 1 – Executive Summary*. Advance HE, York.

Lochtie, D, Stork, A & Walker, B W (eds) (2022) *The Higher Education Personal Tutors and Advisors Companion*. St Albans: Routledge.

Lowenstein, M (2005) If Advising Is Teaching, What Do Advisors Teach? *NACADA Journal*, 25: 65–73.

Lowes, R (2020) Knowing You: Personal Tutoring, Learning Analytics and the Johari Window. *Frontiers in Education*, 5: 1–11.

Luck, C (2010) Challenges Faced by Tutors in Higher Education. *Psychodynamic Practice*, 16: 273–287.

Lyle, E (ed) (2019) *Fostering a Relational Pedagogy: Self-Study as Transformative Praxis*. Leiden: Brill.

Lynch, K (2014) New Managerialism: The Impact on Education. *Concept*, 5: 11–11.

Malcolm, D (2013) *I Have to Leave My Course before the End – What Do I Do About My Higher Education Funding?* [online] Available at: www.nus.org.uk/en/advice/money-and-funding/i-have-to-leave-my-course-before-the-end–what-do-i-do-about-my-higher-education-funding (accessed 30 June 2018).

Malik, S (2000) Students, Tutors and Relationships: The Ingredients of a Successful Student Support Scheme. *Medical Education*, 34: 635–641.

Markham, F (1967) *Oxford*. London: Weidenfeld and Nicolson.

Matthews, K E & Dollinger, M (2023) Student Voice in Higher Education: The Importance of Distinguishing Student Representation and Student Partnership. *Higher Education*, 85: 555–570.

Maxwell, R & Briggs, S (2024) An Effective Personal Academic Tutor System May Require Specialist Academic Support. *WonkHE comment* [Online]. Available at: https://wonkhe.com/blogs/what-an-effective-personal-academic-tutor-system-could-look-like/ (accessed 11 November 2024).

May, H & Bridger, K (2010) *Developing and Embedding Inclusive Policy and Practice in Higher Education*. York: Higher Education Academy.

Mayhew, M J, Vanderlinden, K & Kim, E K (2010) A Multi-Level Assessment of the Impact of Orientation Programs on Student Learning. *Research in Higher Education*, 51: 320–345.

McCabe, L L & McCabe, E R B (2010) *How to Succeed in Academics* (2nd Ed). Berkeley, CA: University of California Press.

McCluckie, B (2014) Identifying Students 'at Risk' of Withdrawal Using Roc Analysis of Attendance Data. *Journal of Further and Higher Education*, 38: 523–535.

McFarlane, K J (2016) Tutoring the Tutors: Supporting Effective Personal Tutoring. *Active Learning in Higher Education*, 17: 77–88.

McGill, C M, Ali, M & Barton, D (2020) Skills and Competencies for Effective Academic Advising and Personal Tutoring. *Frontiers in Education*, 5.

McIntosh, E (in prep) Early Intervention and Transitional Support – an Integrated Model of Academic Advising and Framework of Advising Principles to Support Student Success.

McIntosh, E (2017) Working in Partnership: The Role of Peer Assisted Study Sessions in Engaging the Citizen Scholar. *Active Learning in Higher Education*, 20(3): 1–16.

McIntosh, E (2018) The 4 Step Tutorial Pathway – A Model of Early Intervention and Transitional Support (Ei) to Facilitate Resilience and Partnership Working in Personal Tutoring. *UK Advising and Tutoring (UKAT) Conference*, 27 March 2018. Derby.

McIntosh, E (2024) Academic Tutoring, Coaching and Student Success – Four Provocations. Keynote Address. *University of Derby Learning and Teaching Conference*, 3 July 2024. Derby.

McIntosh, E & Barden, M (2019) The Leap (Learning Excellence Achievement Pathway) Framework: A Model for Student Learning Development in Higher Education. *Journal of Learning Development in Higher Education*, 14: 1–21.

McIntosh, E & Cross, D (2017) Who Sets the Agenda on Student Engagement? Opinions. *Journal of Educational Innovation, Partnership and Change*, 3: 1–3.

McIntosh, E, Gallacher, D & Chapman, A (2022) A 'Whole of Institution' Approach: What Does a Culture of Advising and Tutoring Really Involve? in Lochtie, D, Stork, A & Walker, B W (eds) *The Higher Education Personal Tutors and Advisors Companion*. St Albans: Routledge.

McIntosh, E & Grey, D (2017) Career Advice: How to Be an Effective Personal Tutor. *Times Higher Education* [online]. Available at: https://www.timeshighereducation.com/news/career-advice-how-to-be-an-effective-personal-tutor [accessed 6 September 2024].

McIntosh, E & May, H (2025) The 3 C's – A Model for Co-Creation of Student Success in Higher Education, in Jamil, M G, O'connor, C and Shelton, F (eds) *Co-Creation for Change in Higher Education: Research-Informed Case Studies from the Field*. London: Palgrave.

McIntosh, E & Shaw, J (2017) *Student Resilience: Exploring the Positive Case for Resilience*. Unite Students Publications, Bristol.

McIntosh, E & Thomas, L (2022) Foreword, in Lochtie, D, Stork, A and Walker, B W (eds) *The Higher Education Personal Tutors and Advisors Companion*. St Albans: Routledge.

McLetchie-Holder, S, Showunmi, V & Bragg, S (2025) Personal Tutoring Black Nursing Students: A Qualitative Study of the Experiences of Students and Tutors. *Nurse Education Today*, 146: 106552.

McVitty, D & Maxwell, R (2024) Once You Can Describe an Academic Support System, You Can Begin to Evaluate It. Available at: https://wonkhe.com/blogs/once-you-can-describe-an-academic-support-system-you-can-begin-to-evaluate-it/ (accessed 10 July 2024).

Meehan, C & Howells, K (2019) In Search of the Feeling of 'Belonging' in Higher Education: Undergraduate Students Transition into Higher Education. *Journal of Further and Higher Education*, 43: 1376–1390.

Millmore, A, Cordy, J, Johnson, J, Isherwood, C, White, E, Firmin, L-M, Bangham, F & Kennedy, O (2022) Levelling Up: From Reactive to Proactive – Shifting the Narrative of Academic Tutoring from Problems to Solutions, in Lochtie, D, Stork, A & Walker, B W (eds) *The Higher Education Personal Tutors and Advisors Companion*. St Albans: Routledge.

Moon, J (2004) *A Handbook of Reflective and Experiential Learning. Theory and Practice*. London: Routledge.

Moore, W G (1968) *The Tutorial System and Its Future*. Oxford: Pergamon Press.

Moores, E, Birdi, G K & Higson, H E (2019) Determinants of University Students' Attendance. *Educational Research*, 61: 371–387.

Morgan, J & O'Hara, M (2023) Belonging, Mattering and Becoming: Empowering Education through Connection. *News + Views* [Online]. Available at: https://www.advance-he.ac.uk/news-and-views/belonging-mattering-and-becoming-empowering-education-through-connection (accessed 20 November 2025).

Morgan, M (2012a) The Evolution of Student Services in the UK. *Perspectives: Policy and Practice in Higher Education*, 16: 77–84.

Morgan, M (2012b) *Improving the Student Experience: The Practical Guide for Universities and Colleges*. Routledge, Abingdon and New York.

Morgan, M (2022) The Student Experience Transitions Model: Integrated Practice to Inspire Staff to Support Students, in Mcintosh, E and Nutt, D (eds) *The Impact of the Integrated Practitioner in Higher Education*. London: Routledge.

Morris, D (2015) Teaching and Research: A Zero-Sum Game? Available at: http://wonkhe.com/blogs/teaching-research (accessed 30 June 2018).

Mullen, C A & Klimaitis, C C (2021) Defining Mentoring: A Literature Review of Issues, Types, and Applications. *Annals of the New York Academy of Sciences*, 1483: 19–35.

Mumford, A (1996) Effective Learners in Action Learning Sets. *Employee Counselling Today*, 8: 3–10.

Mutton, J (2013) Student Engagement Traffic Lighting Project Case Study. [online] Available at: https://studylib.net/doc/5417617/student-experience (accessed 26 August 2025).

Myers, J (2008) Is Personal Tutoring Sustainable? Comparing the Trajectory of the Personal Tutor with That of the Residential Warden. *Teaching in Higher Education*, 13: 607–611.

Mynott, G (2016) Personal Tutoring: Positioning Practice in Relation to Policy. *Innovations in Practice*, 10: 103–112.

NACADA (2006) *NACADA Concept of Academic Advising*. [online] Available at: https://www.nacada.ksu.edu/Resources/Pillars/Concept.aspx (accessed 12 December 2024).

NACADA (2017) *NACADA Academic Advising Core Competencies Model*.

Naidoo, R & Jamieson, I (2005) Empowering Participants or Corroding Learning? Towards a Research Agenda on the Impact of Student Consumerism in Higher Education. *Journal of Education Policy*, 20: 267–281.

National Union of Students (2015) *Academic Support Benchmarking Tool*. [online] Available at: www.nusconnect.org.uk/resources/academic-support-benchmarking-tool/download_attachment (accessed 30 June 2018).

Neenan, M (2009) *Developing Resilience: A Cognitive-Behavioural Approach*. London and New York: Routledge.

Neves, J & Brown, A (2022) *Student Academic Experience Survey 2022*. York and Oxford: Advance HE and HEPI.

Neville, L (2007) *The Personal Tutor's Handbook*. London: Palgarve Macmillan.

Newman, J H (2014) *The Idea of a University*. London: Assumption Press.

NHS (2023) *Safeguarding*. [online] Available at: https://www.england.nhs.uk/long-read/safeguarding/ (accessed 16 September 2024).

Nimmons, D, Giny, S & Rosenthal, J (2019) Medical Student Mentoring Programs: Current Insights. *Advances in Medical Education and Practice*, 10: 113–123.

Noble, J (2019) *Theory of Change in Ten Steps*. London: NPC.

O'Toole, P & Prince, N (2015) The Psychological Contract of Science Students: Social Exchange with Universities and University Staff from the Students' Perspective. *Higher Education Research & Development*, 34: 160–172.

Office for Students (OfS) (2018) *Access and Participation Plans*. [online] Available at: https://www.officeforstudents.org.uk/advice-and-guidance/promoting-equal-opportunities/access-and-participation-plans/ (accessed 22/04/2024).

Office for Students (OfS) (2022a) *Equality, Diversity and Student Characteristics Data Students at English Higher Education Providers between 2010-11 and 2020-21*.

Office for Students (OfS) (2022b) *Regulatory Advice 22: Guidance on the Teaching Excellence Framework (Tef) 2023*.

Office for Students (OfS) (2022c) *Securing Student Success: Regulatory Framework for Higher Education in England*.

Office for Students (OfS) (2023a) *Access and Participation Plans*. [online] Available at: https://www.officeforstudents.org.uk/for-providers/equality-of-opportunity/access-and-participation-plans/ (accessed 10 June 2025).

Office for Students (OfS) (2023b) *Equality of Opportunity Risk Register*. [online] Available at: https://www.officeforstudents.org.uk/advice-and-guidance/promoting-equal-opportunities/equality-of-opportunity-risk-register/ (accessed 22 April 2024).

Office for Students (OfS) (2024a) *'Bold and Transformative Action' Needed to Address Financial Sustainability*.

Office for Students (OfS) (2024b) *Financial Sustainability of Higher Education Providers in England: November 2024 Update*.

Online Etymology Dictionary (n.d.) *Terms Searched For: Personal, Tutor, Coach*. [online] Available at: www.etymonline.com (accessed 30 June 2018).

Owen, M (2002) 'Sometimes You Feel You're in Niche Time': The Personal Tutor System, a Case Study. *Active Learning in Higher Education*, 3: 7–23.

Oxford Dictionaries (n.d.) *Terms Searched For: To Safeguard*. [online] Available at: https://en.oxforddictionaries.com (accessed 30 June 2018).

Palfreyman, D (ed) (2008) *The Oxford Tutorial*. Oxford: OxCHEPS.

Palmer, M, O'Kane, P & Owens, M (2009) Betwixt Spaces: Student Accounts of Turning Point Experiences in the First-Year Transition. *Studies in Higher Education*, 34: 37–54.

Palmer, S & Szymanska, K (2018) *Cognitive Behavioural Coaching: An Integrative Approach*. London: Routledge.

Parkin, H, Heron, E & Jacobi, M (2022) What Do the Students Think? Evaluating Academic Advising across an Institution Using the Listening Rooms Method, in Lochtie, D, Stork, A & Walker, B W (eds) *The Higher Education Personal Tutors and Advisors Companion*. St Albans: Routledge.

Parra, J D & Edwards, D B Jr (2024) Challenging the Gold Standard Consensus: Randomised Controlled Trials (RCTs) and Their Pitfalls in Evidence-Based Education. *Critical Studies in Education*, 65(5): 1–18.

Passmore, J & Fillery-Travis, A (2011) A Critical Review of Executive Coaching Research: A Decade of Progress and What's to Come. *Coaching: An International Journal of Theory, Research and Practice*, 4: 70–88.

Pinnell, J & Hamilton, S (2023) Digital Tools for Personal Tutoring for First-Year Undergraduate Students: Harnessing Digital Potential and Fast-Tracking Relationships. *International Journal of Social Sciences and Educational Studies*, 10: 62–79.

Pownall, I & Raby, A (2022) Using Social Identify Mapping in Personal Tutorials to Aid Students in Their Transition and Social Integration into and Throughout Higher Education, in Lochtie, D, Stork, A & Walker, B W (eds) *The Higher Education Personal Tutors and Advisors Companion*. St Albans: Routledge.

Priest, R & McPhee, S A (2000) Advising Multicultural Students: The Reality of Diversity, in Gordon, V N & Habley, W R (eds) *Academic Advising: A Comprehensive Handbook*. San Francisco: Jossey-Brass.

QAA (2023) *The UK Quality Code for Higher Education*. The Quality Assurance Agency for Higher Education. Available at: https://www.qaa.ac.uk/the-quality-code. Accessed 28 August 2025.

QAA (2024) *Evaluating Excellence: TEF 2023 Submission and Panel Statement Analysis*. The Quality Assurance Agency for Higher Education.

Raby, A (2020) Student Voice in Personal Tutoring. *Frontiers in Education*, 5: 1–9.

Raby, A (2023) *An Exploration of the Relationships between Chinese Students and Their Personal Tutors: An IPA Study*. PhD thesis, University of Lincoln.

Race, P (2010) *Making Personal Tutoring Work*. Leeds: Leeds Met Press.

Ralston, N C & Hoffshire, M (2017) An Individualized Approach to Student Transition: Developing a Success Coaching Model, in Cintron, R, Samuel, J and Hinson, J (eds) *Accelerated Opportunity Education Models and Practices*. Hershey, PA: IGI Global.

Reay, D, Crozier, G & Clayton, J (2010) 'Fitting in' or 'Standing Out': Working-Class Students in UK Higher Education. *British Educational Research Journal*, 36: 107–124.

Rhodes, S & Jinks, A (2005) Personal Tutors' Views of Their Role with Pre-Registration Nursing Students: An Exploratory Study. *Nurse Education Today*, 25: 390–397.

Richardson, A, King, S, Garrett, R & Wrench, A (2012) Thriving or Just Surviving? Exploring Student Strategies for a Smoother Transition to University. A Practice Report. *The International Journal of the First Year in Higher Education*, 3: 87–93.

Riddell, S & Weedon, E (2014) Disabled Students in Higher Education: Discourses of Disability and the Negotiation of Identity. *International Journal of Educational Research*, 63: 38–46.

Ridley, P (2006) Who's Looking after Me?' – Supporting New Personal Tutors, in Thomas, L & Hixenbaugh, P (eds) *Personal Tutoring in Higher Education*. Stoke-on-Trent: Trentham Books.

Robinson, J (2022) Personal Tutoring as a USP: What Happens When Personal Tutoring Is Made a Priority?, in Lochtie, D, Stork, A & Walker, B W (eds) *The Higher Education Personal Tutors and Advisors Companion*. St Albans: Routledge.

Roessger, K M, Eisentrout, K & Hevel, M S (2019) Age and Academic Advising in Community Colleges: Examining the Assumption of Self-Directed Learning. *Community College Journal of Research and Practice*, 43: 441–454.

Rogaten, J & Rienties, B (2021) A Critical Review of Learning Gains Methods and Approaches, in Hughes, C & Tight, M (eds) *Learning Gain in Higher Education*. Leeds: Emerald Publishing Limited.

Roldán-Merino, J, Miguel-Ruiz, D, Roca-Capara, N & Rodrigo-Pedrosa, O (2019) Personal Tutoring in Nursing Studies: A Supportive Relationship Experience Aimed at Integrating, Curricular Theory and Professional Practice. *Nurse Education in Practice*, 37: 81–87.

Rolfe, G, Freshwater, D & Jasper, M (2001) *Critical Reflection for Nursing and the Helping Professions*. Basingstoke: Palgrave.

Ross, J, Head, K, King, L, Perry, P M & Smith, S (2014) The Personal Development Tutor Role: An Exploration of Student and Lecturer Experiences and Perceptions of That Relationship. *Nurse Education Today*, 34: 1207–1213.

Rubie-Davies, C, Meissel, K, Alansari, M, Watson, P, Flint, A & McDonald, L (2020) Achievement and Beliefs Outcomes of Students with High and Low Expectation Teachers. *Social Psychology of Education*, 23: 1173–1201.

Sallai, D (2022) Professional Large Group Mentoring as an Alternative to the 'Traditional' Personal Tutoring System, in Lochtie, D, Stork, A & Walker, B W (eds) *The Higher Education Personal Tutor's and Advisor's Companion: Translating Theory into Practice to Improve Student Success*. St Albans: Routledge.

Sánchez-Elvira Paniagua, A & Simpson, O (2018) Developing Student Support for Open and Distance Learning: The Empower Project. *Journal of Interactive Media in Education*, 1: 1–10.

Sanders, M (2023) *Student Mental Health in 2023: Who Is Struggling and How the Situation Is Changing*. London: The Policy Institute at King's College London and TASO.

Scerri, M, Presbury, R & Goh, E (2020) An Application of the Mentoring Framework to Investigate the Effectiveness of Mentoring Programs between Industry Mentors and Student Mentees in Hospitality. *Journal of Hospitality and Tourism Management*, 45: 143–151.

Schlossberg, N K (1981) A Model for Analyzing Human Adaptation to Transition. *Counseling Psychologist*, 9: 2–18.

Schlossberg, N K (2011) The Challenge of Change: The Transition Model and Its Applications. *Journal of Employment Counseling*, 48: 159–162.

Schön, D (1983) *The Reflective Practitioner. How Professionals Think in Action*. New York: Basic Books.

Seraj, S & Leggett, R (2023) The Challenges of Personal Tutoring in Higher Education: Applying a Coaching Approach at a UK Higher Education Institution. *International Journal of Evidence Based Coaching & Mentoring*, 21(1): 85–98.

Shaheed, J & Kiang, L (2021) A Need to Belong: The Impact of Institutional Diversity Ideologies on University Students' Belonging and Interracial Interactions. *Social Psychology of Education*, 24: 1025–1042.

Shaw, C (2014) How Academics Can Help Ensure Students' Wellbeing. Available at: https://www.theguardian.com/higher-education-network/blog/2014/oct/01/university-academic-support-student-welfare-wellbeing (accessed 20 November 2018).

Sheldon, E, Simmonds-Buckley, M, Bone, C, Mascarenhas, T, Chan, N, Wincott, M, Gleeson, H, Sow, K, Hind, D & Barkham, M (2021) Prevalence and Risk Factors for Mental Health Problems in University Undergraduate Students: A Systematic Review with Meta-Analysis. *Journal of Affective Disorders*, 287: 282–292.

Simpson, O (2006) Rescuing the Personal Tutor: Lessons in Costs and Benefits, in Thomas, L & Hixenbaugh, P (eds) *Personal Tutoring in Higher Education*. Stroke-on-rent: Trentham Books.

Simpson, O (2013) Overcoming the 'Distance Education Deficit' through Proactive Motivational Support. *Distance Education in China*, 7: 1–15.

Small, F (2013) Enhancing the Role of Personal Tutor in Professional Undergraduate Education. *Inspiring Academic Practice*, 1(1): 1–11.

Smith, E M (2008) *Personal Tutoring*. York: Higher Education Academy.

Smith, S (2022) Moving from Distributed to Centralised Academic Advising: Making the Case for Change, in Lochtie, D, Stork, A & Walker, B W (eds) *The Higher Education Personal Tutors and Advisors Companion*. St Albans: Routledge.

Soilemetzidis, I, Bennet, P, Buckley, A, Hillman, N & Stoakes, G (2014) *The HEPI-HEA Student Academic Experience Survey 2014*. York: Higher Education Academy.

sparqs (2023) *Student Learning Experience Model*. [online] Available at: https://www.sparqs.ac.uk/sector.php?page=1116 (accessed 11 October 2024).

Spencer, D (2021) Understanding the Coaching Experiences of Non-Traditional Students in Higher Education in the UK. *International Journal of Evidence Based Coaching and Mentoring*, S15: 84–95.

Spiridon, E, Kaye, L K, Nicolson, R I, Ransom, H J, Tan, A J and Tang, B W (2020) Integrated Learning Communities as a Peer Support Initiative for First Year University Students. *Journal of Applied Social Psychology*, 50: 394–405.

Sprague, J & Massoni, K (2005) Student Evaluations and Gendered Expectations: What We Can't Count Can Hurt Us. *Sex Roles*, 53: 779–793.

Starcher, K (2011) Intentionally Building Rapport with Students. *College Teaching*, 59: 162.

Steele, G (2016) Creating a Flipped Advising Approach. *NACADA Academic Advising Resources* [Online]. Available at: https://nacada.ksu.edu/Resources/Clearinghouse/View-Articles/Creating-a-Flipped-Advising-Approach (accessed 20 November 2025).

Stenton, A (2017) Why Personal Tutoring Is Essential for Student Success. Available at: https://www.scribd.com/document/494932759/Why-personal-tutoring-is-essential-for-student-success (accessed 29 August 2025).

Stenton, A (2018) Reconceptualising Personal Tutoring, Bringing Pedagogy to Principles and Practice. *RaRa Tutor Conference*.

Stephen, D E, O'Connell, P & Hall, M (2008) 'Going the Extra Mile', 'Fire-Fighting', Orlaissez-Faire? Re-Evaluating Personal Tutoring Relationships within Mass Higher Education1. *Teaching in Higher Education*, 13: 449–460.

Stevenson, N (2006) Integrating Personal Tutoring with Personal Development Planning, in Barfield, S, Hixenbaugh, P & Thomas, L (eds) *HEA Casebook: Critical Reflections and Positive Interventions: Critical Reflections and Positive Interventions: An Electronic Casebook on Good Practice in Personal Tutoring*. York: The Higher Education Academy. Retrieved January 12, 2009.

Stevenson, N (2009) Enhancing the Student Experience by Embedding Personal Tutoring in the Curriculum. *Journal of Hospitality, Leisure, Sport and Tourism Education*, 8: 117–122.

Stork, A & Walker, B (2015) *Becoming an Outstanding Personal Tutor: Supporting Learners through Personal Tutoring and Coaching*. Northwich: Routledge.

Stuart, K, Willocks, K & Browning, R (2021) Questioning Personal Tutoring in Higher Education: An Activity Theoretical Action Research Study. *Educational Action Research*, 29: 79–98.

Swain, H (2008) The Personal Tutor. Available at: www.timeshighereducation.co.uk/news/thepersonal-tutor/210049.article (accessed 20 November 2025).

Symonds, E (2020) Reframing Power Relationships between Undergraduates and Academics in the Current University Climate. *British Journal of Sociology of Education*, 42: 127–142.

The Association of Commonwealth Universities (2012) Defining, Understanding and Measuring Impact. Available at: www.acu.ac.uk/membership/acu-insights/acu-insights-2/defining-understanding-and-measuring-impact.

The Further Education Tutorial Network (FETN) (2013) *National Occupational Standards for Personal Tutoring*. Available at: https://fetn.org.uk/professional-development/national-occupational-standards-for-personal-tutoring-2/ (accessed 20 October 2025).

The Great Place to Work Institute (2014) *Organisational Values. Are They Worth the Bother? How Values Can Transform Your Business from Good to Great*. London: Great Place to Work Institute.

The Sutton Trust (2023) New Polling on the Impact of the Cost of Living Crisis on Students. Available at: https://www.suttontrust.com/news-opinion/all-news-opinion/new-polling-on-the-impact-of-the-cost-of-living-crisis-on-students/?gad_source=1&gad_campaignid=20276568153&gbraid=0AAAAApnz-Ut7zDGL9zOo5kqaDJlyBAZN6&gclid=CjwKCAjwxfjGBhAUEiwAKWPwDvsU_6r_I4DcK7BeCvLIGpmupQ53hMu5T_Tl3QwFi9DpsJ69d9qsXBoCC3sQAvD_BwE (accessed 20 November 2025).

Thijm, J (2023) Mattering Vs Belonging and the Impact of Academic Advisors: Online Professional Part-Time Students – A Case Study. *Journal of Learning Development in Higher Education*. 29: 1–6

Thomas, L (2006) Widening Participation and the Increased Need for Personal Tutoring, in *Personal Tutoring in Higher Education*. Stroke-on-Trent: Trentham Books.

Thomas, L (2012) Building Student Engagement and Belonging in Higher Education at a Time of Change: Final Report from the What Works Student Retention and Success Programme. *Paul Hamlyn Foundation*, 100: 1–99.

Thomas, L, Hill, M, O'Mahony, J & Yorke, M (2017) *Supporting Student Success: Strategies for Institutional Change*. London: Paul Hamlyn Foundation.

Thomas, L, Hockings, C, Ottaway, J & Jones, R (2015) *Independent Learning: Student Perceptions and Experiences*. York: Higher Education Academy.

Thomas, L & Jones, R (2017) *Student Engagement in the Context of Commuter Students*. London: The Student Engagement Partnership (TSEP). Available at: http://www.lizthomasassociates.co.uk/projects/2018/Commuter student engagement.pdf (accessed 20 November 2025).

Thomas, L, Orme, E & Kerrigan, F (2020) Student Loneliness: The Role of Social Media through Life Transitions. *Computers and Education*, 146: 103754.

Thompson, M, Pawson, C & Evans, B (2021) Navigating Entry into Higher Education: The Transition to Independent Learning and Living. *Journal of Further and Higher Education*, 45: 1398–1410.

Trowler, V (2010) *Student Engagement Literature Review*. York: Higher Education Academy.

Troxel, W G, Bridgen, S, Hutt, C & Sullivan-Vance, K A (2021) Transformations in Academic Advising as a Profession. *New Directions for Higher Education*, 2021: 23–33.

UCU (2022) *Workload Survey 2021 Data Report*. University and College Union.

UK Advising and Tutoring association (UKAT) (n.d.) *Professional Recognition*. [online] Available at: https://www.ukat.ac.uk/standards/professional-recognition (accessed 4 March 2024).

UK Advising and Tutoring association (UKAT) (2020) *UKAT Core Values of Personal Tutoring and Academic Advising*.

UK Advising and Tutoring association (UKAT) (2023) *The UKAT Professional Framework for Academic Advising & Personal Tutoring*.

UK Advising and Tutoring association (UKAT) (2025) *Introducing the UKAT Institutional Accreditation Scheme: Shaping the Future of Personal Tutoring*. [online] Available at: https://www.ukat.ac.uk/standards/institutional-accreditation-scheme (accessed 10 June 2025).

University of Bristol (2022) *Academic Personal Tutoring Policy*.

UUK (2017) *#Stepchange: Mental Health in Higher Education*. [online] Available at: https://www.universitiesuk.ac.uk/stepchange (accessed 27 March 2024).

Van Nieuwerburgh, C (2017) *An Introduction to Coaching Skills: A Practical Guide* (2nd Ed). London: Sage.

Varghese, A M & Zijlstra-Shaw, S (2021) Teaching to Learn: Using Peer-Assisted Learning to Complement the Undergraduate Dental Curriculum. *European Journal of Dental Education*, 25: 762–767.

Vican, S, Friedman, A & Andreasen, R (2020) Metrics, Money, and Managerialism: Faculty Experiences of Competing Logics in Higher Education. *The Journal of Higher Education*, 91: 139–164.

Vygotsky, L S (1978) *Mind in Society: The Development of Higher Psychological Processes*. Cambridge, Massachusetts: Harvard University Press.

Vytniorgu, R (2022) *Student Belonging and the Wider Context*. Oxford: Higher Education Policy Institute.

Wakelin, E (2023) Personal Tutoring in Higher Education: An Action Research Project on How Improve Personal Tutoring for Both Staff and Students. *Educational Action Research*, 31(5): 1–16.

Walker, B W (2018) A Defining Moment for Personal Tutoring: Reflections on Personal Tutor Definitions and Their Implications. *IMPact: The University of Lincoln Journal of Higher Education Research*, 1(1): 1–16.

Walker, B W (2020) Professional Standards and Recognition for UK Personal Tutoring and Advising. *Frontiers in Education*, 5: 1–14.

Walker, B W (2022) Tackling the Personal Tutoring Conundrum: A Qualitative Study on the Impact of Developmental Support for Tutors. *Active Learning in Higher Education*, 23: 65–77.

Walker, B W (2025) *How Can Approaches to Personal Tutoring in Higher Education Be Enhanced by Action Research? Developing and Disseminating a Framework of Professional Development*. PhD, Oxford Brookes University.

Walker, L (2010) Longitudinal Study of Drop-out and Continuing Students Who Attended the Pre-University Summer School at the University of Glasgow. *International Journal of Lifelong Education*, 13: 217–233.

Wallace, S (2013) When You're Smiling: Exploring How Teachers Motivate and Engage Learners in the Further Education Sector. *Journal of Further and Higher Education*, 38: 346–360.

Wardle, K, Lewiston, K & Shepherd, S (2025) Reflections on the Strategic Use of Artificial Intelligence in Tutor-Tutee Communication. *UKAT Annual Conference 2025: Learning Well*. UCL, London.

Waterval, D, Burks, I & Maussen, I (2025) Uncovering Strategies to Empower Students: A Scoping Review of One-on-One Advising Interventions. *Waypoint – A Reflective Journal of Student Advising and Development in Tertiary Education*, 1: 63–83.

Watts, A G (1999) *The Role of the Personal Adviser: Concepts and Issues*. Derby: Centre for Guidance Studies.

Watts, T (2011) Supporting Undergraduate Nursing Students through Structured Personal Tutoring: Some Reflections. *Nursing Education Today*, 31: 214–218.

Webb, O, Wyness, L & Cotton, D (2017) *Enhancing Access, Retention, Attainment and Progression in Higher Education*. York: Higher Education Academy.

Webb, O J & Cotton, D R E (2019) Deciphering the Sophomore Slump: Changes to Student Perceptions during the Undergraduate Journey. *Higher Education*, 77: 173–190.

Wenger, E (1998) *Communities of Practice: Learning, Meaning and Identity*. Cambridge: Cambridge University Press.

Weuntsel, P (2011) Can't Fatten a Pig by Weighing It: Assessment and the Future of Teacher Education. *The Marquette Educator* [Online]. Available at: www.marquetteeducator.wordpress.com/2011/11/12/you-cant-fatten-a-pig-by-weighing-it-assessment-and-the-future-of-teacher-education (accessed 15 December 2024).

Whannell, R & Whannell, P (2015) Identity Theory as a Theoretical Framework to Understand Attrition for University Students in Transition. *Student Success*, 6: 43–52.

Whitmore, J (2017) *Coaching for Performance: Growing People, Performance and Purpose* (25th Anniversary, 5th Ed). London: BPP University: John Murray Business.

Whittaker, R (2008) *Quality Enhancement Themes: The First Year Experience – Transition to and during the First Year*. Glasgow: Quality Assurance Agency Scotland.

Wilcox, P, Winn, S & Fyvie-Gauld, M (2005) 'It Was Nothing to Do with the University, It Was Just the People': The Role of Social Support in the First-Year Experience of Higher Education. *Studies in Higher Education*, 30: 707–722.

Wisker, G, Exley, K, Antoniou, M & Ridley, P (2007) *Working One-to-One with Students: Supervising, Coaching, Mentoring, and Personal Tutoring*. London: Routledge.

Witt, N, McDermott, A, Kneale, P & Coslett, D (2016) *Effective Learner Analytics: A Senior Leadership–Staff–Student Informed Approach*. Plymouth: Plymouth University.

Wong, B T-m & Li, K C (2020) A Review of Learning Analytics Intervention in Higher Education (2011–2018). *Journal of Computers in Education*, 7: 7–28.

WonkHE (2024a) *From Support to Success: Building Academic Support Systems around Students*. London: WonkHE

WonkHE (2024b) How Universities Are Thinking About Academic Support. Available at: https://wonkhe.com/blogs/how-universities-are-thinking-about-academic-support/ (accessed 10 July 2024).

Woods, A & Lefever, R (2022) Student Success Coaching: Developing a Model That Works to Enhance Personal Tutoring and Student Success, in Lochtie, D, Stork, A and Walker, B W (eds) *The Higher Education Personal Tutor's and Advisor's Companion: Translating Theory into Practice to Improve Student Success*. St Albans: Routledge.

Woods, K (2023) Chapter 18: Academic Advising and Personal Tutoring for Student Success, in Baik, C & Kahu, E R (eds) *Research Handbook on the Student Experience in Higher Education*. Cheltenham: Edward Elgar Publishing.

Wootton, S (2006) Changing Practice in Tutorial Provision within Post-Compulsory Education, in Thomas, L & Hixenbaugh, P (eds) *Personal Tutoring in Higher Education*. Stoke on Trent: Trentham Books.

Wootton, S (2007) *An Inductive Enquiry into Managing Tutorial Provision in Post-Compulsory Education*. PhD, Sheffield Hallam University.

Wright, J (2022) Introducing Group Personal Tutoring to Improve Student Engagement, in Lochtie, D, Stork, A & Walker, B W (eds) *The Higher Education Personal Tutors and Advisors Companion*. St Albans: Routledge.

Yale, A (2020a) Developing Positive Personal Tutor Relationships, in Woolhouse, C and Nicholson, L J (eds) *Mentoring in Higher Education*. Cham: Springer International Publishing.

Yale, A (2020b) Quality Matters: An in-Depth Exploration of the Student–Personal Tutor Relationship in Higher Education from the Student Perspective. *Journal of Further and Higher Education*, 44: 739–752.

Yale, A (2020c) What's the Deal? The Making, Shaping and Negotiating of First-Year Students' Psychological Contract with Their Personal Tutor in Higher Education. *Frontiers in Education*, 5: 170–175.

Yale, A & Warren, D (2022) The 'Hero', the 'Professional' and the 'Nurturer': The Challenge for Personal Tutoring to Negotiate Identities within Systems of Practice in Higher Education, in Lochtie, D, Stork, A and Walker, B W (eds) *The Higher Education Personal Tutor's and Advisor's Companion: Translating Theory into Practice to Improve Student Success*. St Albans: Routledge.

Yale, A T (2019) The Personal Tutor–Student Relationship: Student Expectations and Experiences of Personal Tutoring in Higher Education. *Journal of Further and Higher Education*, 43: 533–544.

Yorke, M & Longden, B (2008) *The First Year Experience of Higher Education in the UK (Final Ed)*. York: Higher Education Academy.

Zawada, C (2022) Exploring the Links between 'Belonging' and 'Mattering' and the Impact on Student Achievement. UKAT Annual Conference, 2022 Online.

Zepke, N & Leach, L (2010) Improving Student Engagement: Ten Proposals for Action. *Active Learning in Higher Education*, 11: 167–177.

Index

Note: Page numbers in **bold** and *italics* refer to tables and figures, respectively.

abstract conceptualisation 161
academic advising 31–33, *32*
academic feedback and development 12
academic peers, boundaries with 70
Academic Support Benchmarking Tool 105
academic tutoring 25; *see also* personal tutor/tutoring
active experimentation 161
active listening **53**
additional support needs (ASN) 100–103; actions, roles and explanations **102–103**
advising networks 172
advising theory and learner-centred advising 33–35
affirmation and action 164
Anderson, V 65
approachability **48**
at risk documentation **92**
at risk meetings **96**
at risk students 82, 91, 133; categories and criteria **92**, **94**; characteristics of 7, **85**; definition of 82; monitoring document (example) **97**
attrition 115
authenticity **49**

Barden, M 38
Berg, Insoo Kim 39
body language 77
boundaries: with academic peers 70; case study 74–76; clear and effective referral 68; definition of 64; expertise boundaries **66**, 68–69; independence boundaries 67, 70–72; letting go and handing over 73–74; overview 63–64; referral boundaries **66**; student engagement **66**, 70–72; student peer boundaries 72–73; temporal boundaries **67**, 69–70; tutor expertise and referral boundaries 65–66; types of **65–67**
Bovill, C 35
Brookfield, Stephen, critically reflective lenses 164–166
building genuine rapport 53, 55–57

causation 191
challenging, core skills **49**
Chan, K 143
Clutterbuck's mentoring model *18*, 18–19

coach, definition and history **14**
coaching **15**; definition 38; focus of 15; and mentoring approaches 38–40; models 17–20; and personal tutoring (*see* personal tutor/tutoring); skills 15; solution-focused approach 38–40, **40**; *see also* solution-focused coaching
cognitive behavioural coaching (CBC) 39
cognitive behavioural therapy (CBT) 39
common sense reflection 160
commuter students 89
compassion 48
confidence 198
consistency **54**
core skills 50; building genuine rapport 55–56; categories 51–52; decision-making and problem-solving 56–57; decision-making skills 56–57; definition of 51; development of 52–56; domain-general skills 51; domain-specific skills 52; of effective personal tutor 50–51; hard skills **52**; personal tutor **53–55**; problem-solving skills 56–57; professional standards 58; recognition 58; soft skills **52**
core values 44–45, **48**, 59; case study 46–47; definition and identification of 45–46; development methods 46–47; individual values 50; shared values 50
correlation 191
cost-of-living crisis 10
course progress feedback **92**
course suspension or change 127–131; case study 128–131; external progression 132; internal progression 139
Covid-19 pandemic, impact of 1–2, 10, 89; cost-of-living crisis 10, 70, **86**, **88**; mental health and well-being concern 170; remote or hybrid learning 89
creativity **54**
critically reflective lenses (Brookfield) 164–166
critical thinking **54**, 74
curriculum-based student support model **21**
curriculum for tutorials 132–138

dashboard systems 11, 16, 24, 106–107; and engagement analytics *105*, 105–108, **106**; features of **106**; practical tips 106–107

data-driven advice 11
data-driven decision-making, future of *105*
Dearing Report 89
decision-making: data-driven *106*; skills 53, **55–56**
De Shazer, Steve 39
differentiation 126–127
digital literacy **54**
diplomacy 49
Disabled Students' Allowance (DSA) 89
disadvantaged student, definition of 83
distress 64
Drake, J K 35

Earwaker, J 20
Earwaker's student support models 20, **21–23**; application 24–25
Eatough, V 39
effective academic teacher 29–30
effective personal tutor/tutoring 142; expectations, managing 145–147; fundamentals of becoming 31; principles, and effective teaching 29–30; relationship building 147–150; student engagement and motivation 151–152; student expectations 145–146, **146**; student success 143–144
effective practice, features of 26
effective referral 68–69
effective teaching 29–30
Egan's Skilled Helper Model 71, *71*
Eisentrout, K 90
embodiment and representative of university 12
emotional circumstances 64
emotional labour 3, 65
emotional well-being 15, 17, 38
encouragement 17, 105; analytics diagram *105*
equality gaps 180
Experiential Learning Cycle theory (Kolb): abstract conceptualisation 161; active experimentation 161; concrete experience 160; reflective observation 160–161
expertise boundaries **66**, 68

feedback **92**, 93
Felten, P 36, 147
First Year Experience (FYE) 37
Freire, P 28

Gibbs, Graham, Reflective Cycle model 161
goal/target setting 12
group tutorial: contextualisation 126; and curriculum lesson, differences between 125–126; planning and teaching 124–125; reflective practice 154
guided reflection 162

hard skills 52; examples **52**
helping styles *19*
Hevel, M S 90
Higher Education and Research Act (2017) 1

Higher Education Mental Health Implementation Taskforce 148
high expectations **48**
Hillman, N 39
Holland, C 143
Huppert, Felicia 42

impact: definition of 178; measurement (*see* measuring impact)
inclusive personal tutoring 89–90
independence boundaries **67**, 70–72
independency, development of **53**
individuality, valuing **49**
individual reflection 126
informal discussions 96, 202
information: regarding transition 12; sharing 54
innovation **54**
institutional self-assessment 206–214; case study 207–214
integrated model of tutoring 25
intervention analysis 179

Jackson, Paul 40
Johns, Chris, Model of Structured Reflection 162–164
Jowett, Benjamin 4

Katz, S 36
key activities, purpose of 83; *see also specific activities*
key performance indicators (KPIs) 198, 203
Kift, S 10, 37
Kift's principles of transition pedagogy 10
Klasen and Clutterbuck's mentoring model 18–19
know-how and resources 40
Kolb, David, Experiential Learning Cycle theory 159

Lambert, L M 36, 147
Lancer, N 39
Leach, L 52
learner analytics 24, 148
learner-centred advising models 33, **34**
learning and engagement analytics *105*, 105–106; features **106**; practical tips 107–108
learning difficulties and disabilities (LDD) 103
learning talk 28
Lowenstein, M 29, 33
Lowenstein's learner-centred model of advising, 38

May, H 35
McIntosh and May's 3 C's model of co-creation 36–37; cohesion 36; collaboration 36; community 36
McIntosh, E 31, 35, 38
McKergow, Mark 40
measuring impact: being constructively critical of 215; comparison and timescale, importance of 189–193; core skills and key activities 50; correlation and causation 191; definition of 178–179; elements 185; National Occupational Standards 58; personal tutor impact measures

182; purpose of 179; qualitative and quantitative methods 180–181
mentoring 18; models 18, *18*, 20; and reflective practice 157–159
Model of Structured Reflection (Johns) 162–166
modern academic profession, personal tutoring role within 9–10
monitoring of achievements 12
Morgan, M 38
Morgan's student experience practitioner model 38

NACADA concept of academic advising 31–33, *32*, 42–43, 58
National Occupational Standards (NOS) 58; for Personal Tutoring 58, **183**
national tutoring 172
National Union of Students (NUS) 105
negative emotions 42
Newman, Henry 4
non-judgemental attitude 45
non-traditional student, definition of 84

observing skills **53**
Office for Students (OfS) 1, 84; higher education objectives 1–2
one-to-ones with students **92**, 98, 118; case studies 119–120; dos and don'ts 122–123
open questions 131
organisational student support models *see* student support models
outstanding personal tutoring principles 11

Passmore, J 38
pastoral student support model **21–22**
pedagogy of personal tutoring 28, 31; academic advising 31–33, *32*; advising theory and learner-centred advising 33–35; coaching and mentoring approaches 38–40; effective teaching 29–30; features 31, 31–42; relational pedagogy 35–37; solution-focused coaching with students 40–42; teaching and personal tutoring, relationship 28–29; transition pedagogy 37–38; *see also* personal tutor/tutoring
Peer Assisted Study Sessions (PASS) 117
peer interaction 73
peer observation 169
peer reflection 126; *see also* reflective practice
personal, definition and history **13**
personalised learning 83
personal tutor logs 164–165
personal tutor–student relationships 145
personal tutor/tutoring **15**, 29, 37; activities and responsibilities 12–13; boundaries setting 65, 80; and coaching 13–17; core pedagogical dimensions *31*; core values and skills 46–47, 58–59; curriculum **133**; definitions of 11–13; focus of 15; future, thinking bigger 215; help and support you get 17–19, *18*; history of 4–5; holistic

and supportive model 30; impact measures (*see* measuring impact); importance of 6–7; inclusive 89–90; integrated model *25*; key activities 109–110; measuring impact 195–196; and modern academic profession 9–10; networks 171; overview 1; reflective practice 175–176; roles and responsibilities 9–11, 17–20, 24; self-assessment system 59–62, 109, **110–111**; solution-focused coaching 12; thinking bigger 206; training 170–171; well-being support 12; *see also individual entries*
positive learning conversation (PLC) **97–98**; review **97–98**
proactivity **54**
problem-focus approach 40
problem-focused approach 40
problem-solving skills 50–51
professional development, reflective practice 169; national tutoring and advising networks 172; peer observation 169; personal tutor networks 171–172; personal tutor training 170–171
professional standards 58
professional student support model 103
progress report or review **99**
psychological contract theory 145

QR codes 107
questioning skills **53**

Raby, A 145
rapport, between tutor and student 55–56
receptive mood 42
re-engagement of students, tools to **98–99**, 100
referrals: active referrals 69; effective referral 24, 68, 80; to further information and support 12; referral boundaries **66**, 68–69
reflecting back and summarising **53**
reflection 155–157; benefits of 158; challenges of 158–159
reflection-in-action 160
reflection-on-action 161
Reflective Cycle (Gibbs) 161–164
reflective practice 172–173; critically reflective lenses (Brookfield) 164–165; description of 155–156; Experiential Learning Cycle theory (Kolb) 159–160; Model of Structured Reflection (Johns) 162–163; models 159–165; national tutoring and advising networks 172; peer observation 169; personal tutor networks 171–2; for personal tutor role 157–159; personal tutor training 170; professional development 169–172; Reflective Cycle (Gibbs) 161; reflective scenarios 166–169
reframing students' perspectives 41–42
relational pedagogy 35–37
remote or hybrid learning 89
resilience 51, 53; development of **53**
retaining information: methods 198–199; reasons for 198
review 146
risk monitoring document **97**

Roessger, K M 90
role modelling 53
Rose, J 143

safeguarding 104
scaling 131
Schlossberg's Transition Theory 114–115
Scholarship of Student Success (SoSS) 29
Scholarship of Teaching and Learning (SoTL) 29
self-assessment 178–179; case study 199, **200**; importance of 199–205; institutional 206–215; and measuring impact *178*; personal tutor/tutoring 59–62, 109, **110–111**
sense of belonging, engendering 12
signposting 68
skilled helper model *71*
SMART targets 19, 91, 93, 98, 107
soft skills 52; examples **52**
solution-focused coaching 12, 38–40, **40**; case study 40–42; characteristics **41**, *81*; definition of 40; helping students to notice 40, 42; reframing 41–42; reframing student's perspective 41–42
solution-focused coaching with students 40–42
Spencer, D 39
Staff and Educational Development Association (SEDA) 172
staff comments **91**
Stenton, A 28–29
Stork, A 11
structural student support models *see* student support models
student attrition 114–115
student engagement 30, 35, 70–72, 83, 151
student engagement and motivation 151–152
Student Experience Transitions model (Morgan) 38, *114*
student lifecycle, stages *113*
student peer boundaries 72–73
student representation 117
student success: concept *144*; definition 143; retention and progression 143
student support models 21; application of 24; established models 20; establishment of **21**; evolution of 20; importance of knowing about models 20
students' well-being tutors 70
student-teacher relationship 35
support actions documentation 85; *see also* student support models
support models *see* student support models

teaching and personal tutoring, relationship 28–29
Teaching Excellence Framework (TEF) 177
teamwork 53
temporal boundaries **67**, 69–70
Thomas, L. 11
tracking and monitoring of students 83; cause for concern **92**; course progress feedback **92**; disadvantaged student, definition of 83; feedback 93; keeping students on track to succeed, tools to 91–92; non-traditional student, definition of 84; one-to-ones with students **92**; positive approach to re-engagement 100; re-engagement of students, tools to 100; risk assignment to student 96; at risk categorisation **91**, **95**; at risk documentation **92**; at risk meetings 84–85, **91**; at risk students 83–85; staff comments about students **92**; student profiling 90–91; tailored support 90–91; vulnerable students 84
transitioning to university 114; effective support 115–116; social dimension 116; tutor's role in 116–118
transition pedagogy 37–38, 113
Troxel, W G 33, 35, 144
tutors: and central services, relationship between 68; clear and effective referral 68–69; definition and history **13**; expertise and referral boundaries 66; role in transitioning to university 116–117; training 170–171; *see also* personal tutor/tutoring
tutor–student relationship 147
tutor–tutee relationship 65

UK Advising and Tutoring (UKAT) 2, 12, 58

virtual learning environment 107
virtual learning environment (VLE) 11
vulnerable students: characteristics of 84, **85**; definition of 84
Vygotsky, L S 36

Walker, B W 11
Wallace, S 100
warm referral 69
well-being 24
working under pressure **54**

Yale, A 90

Zepke, N 52

For Product Safety Concerns and Information please contact our EU representative GPSR@taylorandfrancis.com
Taylor & Francis Verlag GmbH, Kaufingerstraße 24, 80331 München, Germany

www.ingramcontent.com/pod-product-compliance
Lightning Source LLC
Chambersburg PA
CBHW081418230426
43668CB00016B/2278